Library of
Davidson College

EDITED BY
MILTON D. OTTENSOSER
LONG ISLAND UNIVERSITY

& MICHAEL W. SIGALL
FINCH COLLEGE

RANDOM HOUSE / NEW YORK

COPYRIGHT © 1972 BY RANDOM HOUSE, INC.

ALL RIGHTS RESERVED UNDER INTERNATIONAL AND PAN-AMERICAN COPYRIGHT CONVENTIONS. PUBLISHED IN THE UNITED STATES BY RANDOM HOUSE, INC., NEW YORK, AND SIMULTANEOUSLY IN CANADA BY RANDOM HOUSE OF CANADA LIMITED, TORONTO.

ISBN: 0-394-31334-8

LIBRARY OF CONGRESS CATALOG CARD NUMBER: 78-169693

MANUFACTURED IN THE UNITED STATES OF AMERICA

TYPOGRAPHY BY JACK RIBIK

FIRST EDITION
987654321

PREFACE

"'T'WAS THE BEST OF TIMES, T'WAS THE WORST OF TIMES"

In a sense, this statement aptly describes both the state of contemporary American politics and the current conditions of the study of American politics. In order to properly understand American politics, one must have a behavioral overview of the entire system as well as a traditional understanding of its components. It is also necessary to merge a sense of history with a sense of contemporary relevance. Furthermore, to maintain proper perspective, the editors feel that the practitioners' experiences and the journalists' observations give fuller meaning to the scholars' insights.

Consequently the selections in each chapter contain the writings of both scholars and participants. Also, the chapters themselves reflect both the behavioral and traditional biases. We trust that from this synthesis the student of American government will get a meaningful grasp of the American system. It is to this end that this work is dedicated.

The editors wish to express their gratitude to those journals and publishers who granted permission to have their material appear in this collection. A special note of appreciation goes to the people at Random House who made this task an adventure, specifically Mr. Barry L. Rossinoff and Miss Susan Rothstein.

The devotion and understanding displayed throughout by Susan Ottensoser and little Uri Seth merit a separate word of thanks. Also, the more than able research assistance of Miss Ann Holmes is gratefully acknowledged.

Any worth found in these pages reflects the probing insight of the editors' former instructors at the City University of New York and of their students at Long Island University and Finch College, while any shortcomings are their own responsibility.

ZICKA-SOUTH, INC.

911 Northridge Street   Greensboro, N.C. 27420   (919) 299-7534

Instructions by:	Phone No.	Date Sent to Binder
Davidson College		May 1985

ALL INSTRUCTIONS ON BINDING TICKET WILL BE FOLLOWED EXPLICITLY

LETTER SPINE EXACTLY AS FOLLOWS	INSTRUCTIONS TO BINDER
Title: THE AMERICAN POLITICAL REALITY Ottensoser	___ Bind as is (with covers & ads) ___ Remove front covers ___ Remove back covers ___ Remove ads (front & back) ___ Remove all ads (extra charge) ___ Bind title page/contents in front ___ Bind index in front ___ Bind index in back ___ Hand sew if necessary (extra charge) _____ Cover Color Letter in: ___ gold; ___ black; ___ white
Vol.:	
Year: 38271 217	**LIBRARY BOOKS:** ___ Decorated covers; ___ plain covers; ___ picture covers (extra charge)
Call No.:	SUPER-FLEX (economy binding) Uniform height, white lettering. Covers & ads bound in. Cover color for **periodicals only**_____. Books & Paperbacks — cloth colors random selected by binder; binder's choice of black or white lettering. Paperbacks: ___ Mount front cover; ___ Bind in covers; _X_ Discard covers.

Special Instructions:

Send two copies of binding slip with volume; retain one copy for your files. If item returned for correction because of binder's error, original binding slip **must be** returned with volume. **Binders error/missing volumes must be reported within 60 days from date order returned.**

BINDERY COPY

TABLE OF CONTENTS

Preface   v

Introduction   3

CHAPTER ONE   CONSTITUTIONAL FRAMEWORK   11
Clinton Rossiter   *The Grand Convention*   13
James Madison   *Federalist Paper Number 10*   20

CHAPTER TWO   DEMOCRACY IN THEORY AND PRACTICE   29
Alexis de Tocqueville   *Influence of Democracy on the Feelings of the Americans*   31
William L. Riordan   *Bosses Preserve the Nation*   39

CHAPTER THREE   GOVERNMENT AS A SYSTEM   43
David Easton   *A Convenient Guide for Political Inquiry*   45
Henry A. Kissinger   *The Impact of the Administrative Structure*   49

CHAPTER FOUR   POLITICAL PARTIES   59
Frank J. Sorauf   *The Political Party*   61
Michael Harrington   *Don't Form a Fourth Party: Form a New First Party*   70

CHAPTER FIVE ELECTIONS AND VOTING 85
Angus Campbell, Philip E. Converse, Warren E. Miller, and Donald E. Stokes *The Dynamics of Mass Percepts* 87
Lewis Chester, Godfrey Hodgson, and Bruce Page *And Then There Was the One* 93

CHAPTER SIX PUBLIC OPINION AND SOCIALIZATION 99
V. O. Key, Jr. *The Family and the Political System* 100
Leon Festinger, Henry W. Riecken, and Stanley Schachter *Unfulfilled Prophecies and Disappointed Messiahs* 103

CHAPTER SEVEN INTEREST GROUPS 109
H. R. Mahood *Pressure Groups: A Threat to Democracy?* 110
Congressional Quarterly Weekly Report *Oil-Gas Industry Is Powerful Lobby Force* 120

CHAPTER EIGHT CONGRESS 131
  Robert A. Dahl *The Congressman and His Beliefs* 133
  Richard Bolling *The Road to Reform* 143

CHAPTER NINE DOMESTIC POLITICS AND ECONOMICS 149
  John Kenneth Galbraith *Change and the Industrial System* 151
  Berkley Rice *Down and Out Along Route 128* 155

CHAPTER TEN THE PRESIDENCY 163
  Louis W. Koenig *Perspectives on Presidential Power* 165
  Tom Wicker *Alone at the Top and Master of Nothing* 180

CHAPTER ELEVEN FOREIGN POLICY 187
  Arnold A. Rogow *James Forrestal* 189
  Elie Abel *Postscript* 195

CHAPTER TWELVE THE JUDICIARY 203
  Leo Pfeffer *A Most Ingenious Paradox* 205
  Anthony Lewis *Gideon's Trumpet* 215

CHAPTER THIRTEEN CIVIL LIBERTIES AND CIVIL RIGHTS 223
  William Ebenstein *Individual Freedom* 225
  Abe Fortas *The Right and the Limitations* 234

CHAPTER FOURTEEN BUREAUCRACY 245
  Herbert A. Simon, Donald W. Smithburg, Victor A. Thompson *What Is Public Administration?* 247
  Edward F. Cox, Robert Fellmeth, and John Schulz The Nader Report *on the Federal Trade Commission* 251

CHAPTER FIFTEEN THE URBAN ENVIRONMENT 265
  Wallace S. Sayre and Herbert Kaufman *The Stakes and Prizes of the City's Politics* 267
  Robert C. Weaver *Future Development of the Urban Complex* 274

INTRODUCTION

Among the most popular of today's college courses is the one usually titled "Introduction to American Government." Perhaps because of the increasing national concern over issues such as the war in Vietnam, the decay of the environment, the urban crisis, and so forth, a greater number of students than ever before are registering for one or more courses in political science in order to comprehend more fully the problems that beset the American system.

Yet, all too often, students are bored or disillusioned by what is being taught; consequently they turn their energies elsewhere. The root causes of this unhappy situation are numerous and varied. Some may lack the intellectual capabilities to follow college level discussions. Others may have preconceived ideas on the nature of the American system and its component parts, which cause them to reject much of what the professor may be attempting to convey. A third group may be dissuaded by the few instructors who lack the ability to make the course intellectually stimulating.

At times, however, the blame for this situation is not found in the student, his ideas, his professor. Rather, the culprit in such cases can rather be simply identified as the book that is being utilized either as the basic text or as its supplement. Usually the emphasis in these volumes centers on one of several approaches to the study of American government. Often the approach is a detailed description of the various governmental institutions. In other cases, however, the literature is overly theoretical, often employing what is termed the behavioral approach to political science. Thus the student is confronted with a book that is filled with graphs, tables, and equations, and that is often written in a highly jargonistic style that is partially, if not totally, unintelligible to a student who is not versed in the intricacies of contemporary social science research. Beyond this, once a student determines the gist of the book, he is often disappointed because the conclusion either confirms some bit of common knowledge of which he was already aware or is so limited in its applicability that it is almost useless.

On the other extreme, much of the literature that is somehow labeled political science is in essence merely journalism at its worst: the impressionistic reporting of a particular event with little if any effort to discern its significance, or attach to it any meaning. The phenomenon that is selected for investigation is one that has momentarily caught the public's eye such as ecology or women's liberation. In an attempt to be relevant, it is briefly described, and its immediate importance is somehow explained. Often the attempts at interpretation are thinly disguised polemics that seek to persuade the reader of the validity of the author's particular orientation.

In a sense then, much of the contemporary literature in the field is either beyond the intellectual capacity of the student or is merely a downgraded version of a high school current events discussion. Neither of these approaches is satisfactory to the student of the seventies who is seeking at least some of the answers to the dilemmas that confront the political system.

This reader is an attempt to circumvent the negative aspects of both previously described approaches. While recognizing the need for both theory and realistic insights into how the political system actually operates, it is only in a book in which both are properly utilized and then synthesized can any benefits be derived. Thus we have avoided both selections that are highly theoretical and those that can best be described as highly subjective personal accounts of a particular phenomenon. Instead a balance is sought in which the theorist's insight as well as the experience gleaned by a practitioner of politics (or in a few cases, by a first rate journalist) are merged in order to present a dual approach to the study of politics. In no instance is the material so esoteric or so biased as to restrain the intellectual curiosity of the student.

What has emerged is a collection of readings that, for example, combines the insight of Herbert Simon and his associates on bureaucracy with the revelations of Nader's Raiders on the Federal Trade Commission; a theoretical examination on whether or not pressure groups are compatible with democracy with an analysis of the methods of operation of the oil lobby in Washington; a discussion on the role of the Supreme Court in American life along with a brief account on the origins of one of the Court's most significant civil liberties decisions; the systems approach to political science and a piece by Henry Kissinger that demonstrates the relevance of this approach in the policy formulation process.

What should be noted is that no one particular point of view is presented. The theorists represent both the traditional and behavioral approaches, while those who are involved in the actual battles in the political arena are divided among the liberal and conservative perspectives. Hopefully what has been developed is a framework to enable the student to view various problems of government, and the variety of methods and ideas that may be utilized to more fully comprehend them.

It would be unjust if not presumptuous on the part of anyone to require study of any area without first addressing himself to the question of why that area merits the student's attention. Therefore, a fair inquiry by the contemporary college student would be, "Why study American government?" On one level, it might be argued easily that the mere fact that a person resides in a given political society would behoove that person to come to grips with the workings, the strengths, and the weaknesses of that polity, especially as it relates to his own life. This point is reinforced in modern times as that behemoth called government touches, directly or indirectly, on virtually every aspect of one's day-to-day existence.

Added to this, we are living today in times of rapid change. In order to attempt to respond to such change in a meaningful way, we must first understand the dynamics of the total system and then the specifics of any given aspect of that system as it relates to the particulars of public policy.

There is another reason, however, that would make it valuable if not imperative for the contemporary college student to study and analyze the American political system with all its ramifications. Even the most superficial reader of current events can see that young people are playing and will continue to play a greater and more active role in society. The occurrences of the 1960s, whatever one's opinion of the seeming upheavals of that decade, bear witness to this. Certainly, the expansion of the franchise to include eighteen-year-old voters gives formal testimony to the recognition that young people will play an increased role in the political affairs of the United States.

Out of the turbulence of the 1960s another somewhat less pleasant lesson emerged. It became apparent that a great lack of understanding pervaded every strata of the society. Part of this ignorance was a result of misperception, the so-called generation gap being merely one obvious manifestation of this. Different groups within the body politic began talking at, instead of with, their counterparts. An abyss was thus created, somewhat akin to the Tower of Babel of old, making it difficult for meaningful communications, so necessary for the maintenance of any system, to take place. Added to this was a genuine lack of comprehension concerning the actual, day-to-day operations of the government. Whatever one's attitudes or interests, it became clear that it was well nigh impossible to affect policy, as the proper procedures for the redress of grievances were fuzzy and amorphous, at best, in the eyes of many.

The unfortunate result of this sad state of affairs was that slogans and rhetoric replaced dialogue, while vast amounts of energy became misdirected. This then served to create a vicious cycle, merely widening the gap, increasing the tension and frustration and, all in all, creating a destructive atmosphere out of the best of intentions.

Still, one might argue, what is the value of studying traditional or theoretical aspects of the American political structure? Why not, this hypothetical critic might further posit, focus instead on the burning issues of the day? It is beyond a doubt of the highest priority to grapple with and resolve these problems of our contemporary society. Yet it is too easy to merely zero in on them and come up with instant analysis and instant answers. It is probably a lot harder, and yet more fruitful in the long run, to first properly understand the questions. Once articulated clearly, not only can they be answered more thoroughly, but future crises, often only variations on the historical themes of the society, can thus hopefully be prevented or at least anticipated.

Today's timely issue is tomorrow's history, as today's history was yesterday's timely issue. Therefore what is clearly needed, more than instant resolutions, is deeper understanding. To understand the current state of the American political system we have to first place today in historical perspective. To interpret today's pain we have to first understand the hopes and fears of decades, and even centuries, past. To properly evaluate the potential breakdown of a system, especially one as intricate as the one operating in American society, we must first come to grips with the conceptual framework within which the system was meant to operate. It is almost begging the question to ask "how" without first understanding "why."

This is not to say, necessarily, that history repeats itself. Rather, what is being argued here is that no phenomenon exists in a vacuum. A political system, not unlike a biological one, exists in a tense state of homeostasis—the tightrope-like balance being easily upset by improper tampering. In a sense, for every gain a price must be paid. Some societal changes may be worth it, others not. Some are worth it but not at the obvious price, necessitating the arduous and often tedious task of working out alternatives and functional equivalents. Once again the simplistic must give way to the complex. Once understood, however, the potential benefit for society makes the effort worthwhile.

Whether one likes it or not, it is difficult to conceive of a modern society without some form of government. As members of the society, it becomes imperative that we make it our painstaking business to learn the ins and outs of the governmental and political system as a prerequisite to making meaningful choices. And again, whether we like it or not, we all make personal choices of a political nature, and political choices with personal consequences. What is being argued here, to put it in a slightly different manner, is that it is somewhat intellectually dishonest to debate the question of the environment without first fully coming to terms with the way in which domestic policy is made; that it is dodging the issue to discuss the role of the women's liberation movement without first seeing how pressure groups can and do function within the total political society; that it is a disservice to evaluate American involvement in the Vietnamese conflict without first analyzing the process of making foreign policy from its various perspectives. It is much too easy to rigidly adhere to the label of a political party, as it is to totally denounce a given political leader, without first comprehending the dynamics of political socialization or the electoral process. When one takes this easy road, besides the obvious detriments mentioned, one is abrogating the highest role of the individual in society—the right and obligation to come to an independent decision. Rather, the individual is taking the course of least resistance by hiding behind clichés and letting others do his thinking for him. Admittedly, this can be very tempting, especially when the total picture becomes clouded with doubt and ambiguity. Yet it is precisely at these times of crisis and confusion that we must diligently heed our obligation to study, analyze, assess, evaluate, decide, and act, lest more and more of us drift off in a feeling of false security, almost forcing fewer and fewer of us to make more and more decisions affecting all of us. Not to act is a form of acting and not to decide is in and of itself a form of decision.

The truly competent and dedicated physician does not condemn disease but rather strives to understand its origins and workings so as to be better able to prevent or cure it. So it must be with the political scientist, or with any student of society. Perhaps if we spend less time damning the mistakes of our fathers and more time objectively analyzing and understanding the total picture, our children will have less cause to damn us for our ignorance and failure.

CONSTITUTIONAL FRAMEWORK

The motives of the founding fathers, who wrote the Constitution, have been questioned by various historians. Traditional historical accounts of the Philadelphia Convention conferred political sainthood on Franklin, Madison, and the others. Challenging this view were critics like Charles Beard who ascribed narrow economic reasons to the men who framed the Constitution. Despite these disagreements, it is apparent that the net result of the Constitutional Convention was a government that imposed a semblance of unity on what had been a system of individualistic, disparate states.

The Constitution has endured, and today it is the oldest functioning document of its type in existence. Although the American governmental system with its vast bureaucracy bears little resemblance to its 1790 counterpart, change has come about in an orderly fashion. The Constitution has been adapted to changing situations, yet the basic ideas within it, such as separation of powers, checks and balances, and so on, remain fundamentally intact.

Some have proposed that the Constitution is inadequate to meet contemporary political and social challenges. Thus, in 1970 the Center for the Study of Democratic Institutions, a California-based "think tank," offered a new "relevant" constitution. What these arguments ignore is the fact that constitutions themselves do not solve problems. Instead they establish a framework within which men can discuss rationally the directions in which society is to head. Quite clearly, this forum has been provided by the founding fathers of 1787.

In the following selections, the late Clinton Rossiter discusses the Convention and its results, while James Madison, a participant in the Philadelphia convention, discusses the nature of society in a selection from *The Federalist Papers*.

THE
GRAND CONVENTION

CLINTON ROSSITER

Three aspects of the Convention of 1787 should have a special appeal to this generation of Americans. Each of these major themes, whether stated separately or joined with the others in an immense orchestration, will be sounded again and again in this book.

The first is the view of the Convention as a case-study in the political process of constitutional democracy. Americans of this generation are much concerned about the state of their famous form of government. Once upon a time we thought that constitutional democracy, by the simple force of good example, was destined to spread its benevolent sway over all the earth, and we went about our business under the comforting assumption that we, with some useful assistance from our British ancestors and cousins, were the bearers of final political truth. Today this assumption comforts us no longer, and every thinking American is sharply aware that many nations, some new and some old, have neither time nor use for the system of political decision that emphasizes discussion and compromise, open choice and institutionalized dissent, fragmentation of power and balance of interests, constitutional limits and personal rights. Constitutional democracy is hated in some parts of the world, derided in others, and branded as irrelevant in still others. Even in its ancestral homes severe

---

Reprinted with permission of The Macmillan Company from *1787—The Grand Convention* by Clinton Rossiter. Copyright © 1966 by Clinton Rossiter.

doubts exist about its capacity for identifying social problems, generating policies for solving these problems, and moving courageously to transform policy into effective action.

In such a time of doubt Americans may well turn back for inspiration and instruction to their own past and go rummaging through it for periods and events in which the process of democracy worked effectively to achieve the purposes of the people. Such a period was the golden age of American politics between 1765 and 1801; such an event was the Convention of 1787, the creative zenith of the age. Whatever else it was— and it has been many things to many men—the Convention was a notable exercise in the arts of democratic (or, to be precise, pre-democratic) politics. Just how much "democracy" was present in the deliberations and decisions before, during, and after Philadelphia is not an easy question to answer: I shall be touching upon it off and on throughout this book. It should be enough at this point to assert that the Convention —if not as thoroughly democratic in origin, composition, procedure, and accountability as such a body would have to be today (or would have had to be as few as five years after the event) —was popular and responsible enough to be acclaimed as a superlative example of goal-setting and decision-making for a proud, ambitious people through the processes of frank, reasoned discussion and alert, disciplined bargaining. If the political process of the liberal West has any successes to its credit, none can be much more memorable than the intense session of give-and-take at Philadelphia in the summer of 1787.

When we say that the Convention was a superlative example of the workings of a famous political process, we are also saying that the men of the Convention were superlative politicians—in the best sense of that word. It often seems that historians of the period have been commissioned to paint the Framers of the Constitution in any guise other than the one in which they appear most naturally. We know them well as everything from selfless instruments of Divine Intent to selfish agents of Economic Interest. We hardly know them at all as what they were first and foremost: skillful operators of the political machinery of constitutional democracy, men whose chief lesson for Americans of this generation has to do with the capacities and limits of this form of government. . . .

The second large aspect of the Convention that invites the attention of our generation of Americans is the results rather than the methods of this archetype of decision-making. The one result of 1787 that has proved most consequential to all men living today was the resolve, which was gradually brought to life in a hundred or more touch-and-go decisions, to become a self-conscious fledgling nation and to set a political course toward becoming a self-sustaining mighty one. We live in an era of nation-building, a stage of history in which nationalism has been recalled by men of good will from the exile of thirty years ago and begged to serve (without arrogance, of course) as the chief spur to the development of the "underdeveloped" or "disadvantaged" or "emerging" peoples of the world. Although the nationalism of what President Sukarno derides as the Old Established Forces—the United States, Britain, France, Germany, Japan, and perhaps even the Soviet Union—is still suspect in many enlightened circles in these countries, the nationalism of what he hails as the New Emerging Forces—Indonesia, India, Cuba, Ghana, Burma, and perhaps even Tunisia—is recognized as a necessary spur to progress. The promotion of nation-building is pursued relentlessly in the seats of power throughout the West; the study of nation-building is all the rage in the groves of contemplation.

Because the United States of the 1790's was the first of the New Emerging Forces, and because the first of the New Emerging Forces became the United States of the 1960's, the nation-building acts of Washington, Franklin, Hamilton, John Adams, Marshall, Jefferson, Madison, and their successors ought to command far more scholarly and popular interest (if not political imitation) than they have hitherto received, and the largest amount of this interest ought to be focused on the Convention at Philadelphia. Although the full story of how "our fathers brought forth upon this continent a new nation" is one that begins well before 1787 and ends well after, that year was the moment of decision as well as of creation. Although much had been done already to produce the raw materials of nationhood (as witness the raising of a continental army in 1775 and the creation of a national domain in 1784), and much remained to be done to form a nation out of these materials (as witness the tensions of 1798, 1814, and 1832 and the agonies of 1861–1865), the hard bargaining at Philadelphia laid the firm foundation of the American Republic. As a self-conscious act of successful nation-making, the signing of the Constitution on September 17, 1787, stands out starkly in the annals of mankind. The United States of Washington and Jefferson may not be a useful model for the new nations of the twentieth century to imitate—so different indeed from the world today was the world in which we grew to manhood—yet it is an experience from which at least a few hard lessons can still be drawn, and which, in any case, invites attention in its own right as a unique course of events. By far the most remarkable event in the course that ran from, let us say, 1765 to 1815 was the Convention of 1787 in Philadelphia.

The third aspect grows immediately out of the first two: it is the fascinating question, unanswerable yet always demanding to be answered, whether men are the makers or wards of history. Here again we may point to an intense concern of the present age, whose splendid promises and ghastly problems have set us all to wondering whether we may hope to control our destiny, and here again we may find in 1787 an encouraging if not entirely comforting case-study. At several stages I shall attempt to measure the extent to which the Framers were masters or wards principally by calling attention to those of their notable decisions which were truly decisions (because of the existence of genuine alternative choices), those which were not decisions at all (because the Convention was forbidden by circumstances to decide otherwise than it did), and those which turned out within a few years to be decisions that no one had intended (because even the most masterful statesmen may think they are doing one thing and in fact be doing another). Here I will say only that the Convention made enough decisions of the first description to permit us to look upon the delegates as men who made some history for themselves, their descendants, and all the world, and that the one problem about which they were most at liberty to choose among competing alternatives was whether and how to build a nation. The range of choices . . . ran from the edge of disintegration to the edge of total consolidation, and in making their choice for a union both continental and federal the Framers took history by the collar and gave it a rousing shake. Statesmen who dared to seize control of their own destiny, the heroes of Philadelphia deserve study as well as applause.

I call these men heroes in deliberate defiance of the ban placed upon this word by most serious-minded historians. By *hero* I mean a leader of men who engages with clear eye and stout heart in an uncertain enterprise for some purpose larger than the gratification of his own ambition or the rewarding of his own friends, and whose deeds work a benevolent influence on the lives of countless other men. I would contend that an experiment in nationhood as vast and successful as the American Republic could not have been brought through at least a half-dozen of its trials except by men of heroic stature, and that few trials could have demanded more extraordinary talent, virtue, hope, and tenacity than this year of political creation. If not every one of the fifty-five men who gathered in Philadelphia was a hero—then or before or after—the Grand Convention itself was both uncertain enough in prospect and benevolent enough in result to be classed as a heroic event. If not every one of its leading figures was as clear of eye as Madison, as stout in heart as Washington, or as selfless of purpose as Franklin—then or before or after—at least a dozen other delegates rose, in the long struggle to build the political and emotional foundations of nationhood, to join these three giants on the high plateau of heroism. Since men, even at their most heroic, are always men and never gods (nor even demigods), it disturbs me only a little to record that every leader of the Convention, not even excepting Washington, had already had or was later to have brushes with poor judgment, self-indulgence, and one or more of the seven deadly sins.

To assert that some men on some occasions are able to shape the destiny of their society is not at all to deny that even the freest agents of history are, in the end, just that: agents. They are men who are shaped even as they shape, who are given directions by a past they are powerless to alter, who work their apparent miracles within the limits of time and place. Such men manage to turn the flow of history into some new channel only by putting themselves in the middle of the old channel. They are distinguished from other would-be makers of history not by any power to leap over the limits of circumstance—for no man, not even Napoleon or Lenin, has had that godlike power—but by their understanding of what things can and cannot be achieved within those limits.

The men of 1787 were, in short, both dutiful wards of the past and creative makers of the future, and that is why they should have a special appeal to the troubled men of this generation. They were heroes who stayed within the limits of the political, social, economic, and cultural circumstances of their time, heroes who seemed to know instinctively just how far to push their luck in choosing among the alternatives that were to be found within these limits. They were especially alert to the possibilities, and thus also to the restraints, of their position on the continuum of time, and they made, as we shall see, virtually no decision that did not run with the grain of American development. This, in any case, is their claim to greatness as agents of history: on one hand, they knew that 1787 would never have been possible except for 1776 (and 1777, 1778, 1781, and 1783); on the other, they knew that 1776 had not foreclosed 1787, that the agenda for this year left a number of choices open to those who were willing to make them. 1787, to vary the metaphor, was the natural child of 1776, but 1776 was the father of at least three or four possible 1787's. The Framers shaped history as no other group of Americans has ever done exactly because they forced a choice that did not have to be made—certainly not then, perhaps not ever. The Constitution was a possible, but not at all a probable, in the circumstances of the peace that came at last to America with the Treaty of Paris of 1783. While all the happenings in America (and many elsewhere) between 1607 and 1783 prepared the way for Philadelphia, and while Philadelphia prepared the way for all the happenings in America (and many elsewhere) ever since, no one can say that this Great Happening had to unfold in just the way it did.

1787 was, then, a year for political heroes, for men who could distinguish the possible from the impossible and then convert the boldest of possibilities into the most solid of realities. As the one man among the missing who had the best title to be in Philadelphia wrote in December of that year, the Convention was, "if not the greatest exertion of human understanding, the greatest single effort of national deliberation that the world has ever seen." Even after more than 175 years, this judgment of John Adams covers all other deliberate efforts at nation-building. The Framers made a gamble with the destiny of the American people so hazardous and yet so calculated, so contingent and yet so prudent, that they command the highest homage granted to makers of history: an endless retelling of the manner of their ascent to glory.

FEDERALIST PAPER NUMBER 10

JAMES MADISON

To the People of the State of New York:
Among the numerous advantages promised by a well-constructed Union, none deserves to be more accurately developed than its tendency to break and control the violence of faction. The friend of popular governments never finds himself so much alarmed for their character and fate, as when he contemplates their propensity to this dangerous vice. He will not fail, therefore, to set a due value on any plan which, without violating the principles to which he is attached, provides a proper cure for it. The instability, injustice, and confusion introduced into the public councils, have, in truth, been the mortal diseases under which popular governments have everywhere perished; as they continue to be the favorite and fruitful topics from which the adversaries to liberty derive their most specious declamations. The valuable improvements made by the American constitutions on the popular models, both ancient and modern, cannot certainly be too much admired; but it would be an unwarrantable partiality, to contend that they have as effectually obviated the danger on this side, as was wished and expected. Complaints are everywhere heard from our most considerate and virtuous citizens, equally the friends of public and private faith, and of public and personal liberty, that our governments are too unstable, that the public good is disregarded in

From *The Federalist Papers*, by Alexander Hamilton, John Jay, and James Madison, pp. 53–62. New York: Random House.

the conflicts of rival parties, and that measures are too often decided, not according to the rules of justice and the rights of the minor party, but by the superior force of an interested and overbearing majority. However anxiously we may wish that these complaints had no foundation, the evidence of known facts will not permit us to deny that they are in some degree true. It will be found, indeed, on a candid review of our situation, that some of the distresses under which we labor have been erroneously charged on the operation of our governments; but it will be found, at the same time, that other causes will not alone account for many of our heaviest misfortunes; and, particularly, for that prevailing and increasing distrust of public engagements, and alarm for private rights, which are echoed from one end of the continent to the other. These must be chiefly, if not wholly, effects of the unsteadiness and injustice with which a factious spirit has tainted our public administrations.

By a faction, I understand a number of citizens, whether amounting to a majority or minority of the whole, who are united and actuated by some common impulse of passion, or of interest, adverse to the rights of other citizens, or to the permanent and aggregate interests of the community.

There are two methods of curing the mischiefs of faction: the one, by removing its causes; the other, by controlling its effects.

There are again two methods of removing the causes of faction: the one, by destroying the liberty which is essential to its existence; the other, by giving to every citizen the same opinions, the same passions, and the same interests.

It could never be more truly said than of the first remedy, that it was worse than the disease. Liberty is to faction what air is to fire, an aliment without which it instantly expires. But it could not be less folly to abolish liberty, which is essential to political life, because it nourishes faction, than it would be to wish the annihilation of air, which is essential to animal life, because it imparts to fire its destructive agency.

The second expedient is as impracticable as the first would be unwise. As long as the reason of man continues fallible, and he is at liberty to exercise it, different opinions will be formed. As long as the connection subsists between his reason and his self-love, his opinions and his passions will have a reciprocal influence on each other; and the former will be objects to which the latter will attach themselves. The diversity in the faculties of men, from which the rights of property originate, is not less an insuperable obstacle to a uniformity of interests. The protection of these faculties is the first object of government. From the protection of different and unequal faculties of acquiring property, the possession of different degrees and kinds of property immediately results; and from the influence of these on the sentiments and views of the respective proprietors, ensues a division of the society into different interests and parties.

The latent causes of faction are thus sown in the nature of man; and we see them everywhere brought into different degrees of activity, according to the different circumstances of civil society. A zeal for different opinions concerning religion, concerning government, and many other points, as well of speculation as of practice; an attachment to different leaders ambitiously contending for pre-eminence and power; or to persons of other descriptions whose fortunes have been interesting to the human passions, have, in turn, divided mankind into parties, inflamed them with mutual animosity, and rendered them much more disposed to vex and oppress each other than to co-operate for their common good. So strong is this propensity of mankind to fall into mutual animosities, that where no substantial occasion presents itself, the most frivolous and fanciful distinctions have been sufficient to kindle their unfriendly passions and excite their most violent conflicts. But the most common and durable source of factions has been the various and unequal distribution of property. Those who hold and those who are without property have ever formed distinct interests in society. Those who are creditors, and those who are debtors, fall under a like discrimination. A landed interest, a manufacturing interest, a mercantile interest, a moneyed interest, with many lesser interests, grow up of necessity in civilized nations, and divide them into different classes, actuated by different sentiments and views. The regulation of these various and interfering interests forms the principal task of modern legislation, and involves the spirit of party and faction in the necessary and ordinary operations of the government.

No man is allowed to be a judge in his own cause, because his interest would certainly bias his judgment, and, not improbably, corrupt his integrity. With equal, nay with greater reason, a body of men are unfit to be both judges and parties at the same time; yet what are many of the most important acts of legislation, but so many judicial determinations, not indeed concerning the rights of single persons, but concerning the rights of large bodies of citizens? And what are the different classes of legislators but advocates and parties to the causes which they determine? Is a law proposed concerning private debts? It is a question to which the creditors are parties on one side and the debtors on the other. Justice ought to hold the balance between them. Yet the parties are, and must be, themselves the judges; and the most numerous party, or, in other words, the most powerful faction must be expected to prevail. Shall domestic manufactures be encouraged, and in what degree, by restrictions on foreign manufactures? are questions which would be differently decided by the landed and the manufacturing classes, and probably by neither with a sole regard to justice and the public good. The apportionment of taxes on the various descriptions of property is an act which seems to require the most exact impartiality; yet there is, perhaps, no legislative act in which greater opportunity and temptation are given to a predominant party to trample on the rules of justice. Every shilling with which they overburden the inferior number, is a shilling saved to their own pockets.

It is in vain to say that enlightened statesmen will be able to adjust these clashing interests, and render them all subservient to the public good. Enlightened statesmen will not always be at the helm. Nor, in many cases, can such an adjustment be made at all without taking into view indirect and remote considerations, which will rarely prevail over the immediate interest which one party may find in disregarding the rights of another or the good of the whole.

The inference to which we are brought is, that the *causes* of faction cannot be removed, and that relief is only to be sought in the means of controlling its *effects*.

If a faction consists of less than a majority, relief is supplied by the republican principle, which enables the majority to defeat its sinister views by regular vote. It may clog the administration, it may convulse the society; but it will be unable to execute and mask its violence under the forms of the Constitution. When a majority is included in a faction, the form of popular government, on the other hand, enables it to sacrifice to its ruling passion or interest both the public good and the rights of other citizens. To secure the public good and private rights against the danger of such a faction, and at the same time to preserve the spirit and the form of popular government, is then the great object to which our inquiries are directed. Let me add that it is the great desideratum by which this form of government can be rescued from the opprobrium under which it has so long labored, and be recommended to the esteem and adoption of mankind.

By what means is this object attainable? Evidently by one of two only. Either the existence of the same passion or interest in a majority at the same time must be prevented, or the majority, having such coexistent passion or interest, must be rendered, by their number and local situation, unable to concert and carry into effect schemes, of oppression. If the impulse and the opportunity be suffered to coincide, we well know that neither moral nor religious motives can be relied on as an adequate control. They are not found to be such on the injustice and violence of individuals, and lose their efficacy in proportion to the number combined together, that is, in proportion as their efficacy becomes needful.

From this view of the subject it may be concluded that a pure democracy, by which I mean a society consisting of a small number of citizens, who assemble and administer the government in person, can admit of no cure for the mischiefs of faction. A common passion or interest will, in almost every case, be felt by a majority of the whole; a communication and concert result from the form of government itself; and there is nothing to check the inducements to sacrifice the weaker party or an obnoxious individual. Hence it is that such democracies have ever been spectacles of turbulence and contention; have ever been found incompatible with personal security or the rights of property; and have in general been as short in their lives as they have been violent in their deaths. Theoretic politicians, who have patronized this species of government, have erroneously supposed that by reducing mankind to a perfect equality in their political rights, they would, at the same time, be perfectly equalized and assimilated in their possessions, their opinions, and their passions.

A republic, by which I mean a government in which the scheme of representation takes place, opens a different prospect, and promises the cure for which we are seeking. Let us examine the points in which it varies from pure democracy, and we shall comprehend both the nature of the cure and the efficacy which it must derive from the Union.

The two great points of difference between a democracy and a republic are: first, the delegation of the government, in the latter, to a small number of citizens elected by the rest; secondly, the greater number of citizens, and greater sphere of country, over which the latter may be extended.

The effect of the first difference is, on the one hand, to refine and enlarge the public views, by passing them through the medium of a chosen body of citizens, whose wisdom may best discern the true interest of their country, and whose patriotism and love of justice will be least likely to sacrifice it to temporary or partial considerations. Under such a regulation, it may well happen that the public voice, pronounced by the representatives of the people, will be more consonant to the public good than if pronounced by the people themselves, convened for the purpose. On the other hand, the effect may be inverted. Men of factious tempers, of local prejudices, or of sinister designs, may, by intrigue, by corruption, or by other means, first obtain the suffrages, and then betray the interests, of the people. The question resulting is, whether small or extensive republics are more favorable to the election of proper guardians of the public weal; and it is clearly decided in favor of the latter by two obvious considerations:

In the first place, it is to be remarked that, however small the republic may be, the representatives must be raised to a certain number, in order to guard against the cabals of a few; and that, however large it may be, they must be limited to a certain number, in order to guard against the confusion of a multitude. Hence, the number of representatives in the two cases not being in proportion to that of the two constituents, and being proportionally greater in the small republic, it follows that, if the proportion of fit characters be not less in the large than in the small republic, the former will present a greater option, and consequently a greater probability of a fit choice.

In the next place, as each representative will be chosen by a greater number of citizens in the large than in the small republic, it will be more difficult for unworthy candidates to practise with success the vicious arts by which elections are too often carried; and the suffrages of the people being more free, will be more likely to centre in men who possess the most attractive merit and the most diffusive and established characters.

It must be confessed that in this, as in most other cases, there is a mean, or both sides of which inconveniences will be found to lie. By enlarging too much the number of electors, you render the representative too little acquainted with all their local circumstances and lesser interests; as by reducing it too much, you render him unduly attached to these, and too little fit to comprehend and pursue great and national objects. The federal Constitution forms a happy combination in this respect; the great and aggregate interests being referred to the national, the local and particular to the State legislatures.

The other point of difference is, the greater number of citizens and extent of territory which may be brought within the compass of republican than of democratic government; and it is this circumstance principally which renders factious combinations less to be dreaded in the former than in the latter. The smaller the society, the fewer probably will be the distinct parties and interests composing it; the fewer the distinct parties and interests, the more frequently will a majority be found of the same party; and the smaller the number of individuals composing a majority, and the smaller the compass within which they are placed, the more easily will they concert and execute their plans of oppression. Extend the sphere, and you take in a greater variety of parties and interests; you make it less probable that a majority of the whole will have a common motive to invade the rights of other citizens; or if such a common motive exists, it will be more difficult for all who feel it to discover their own strength, and to act in unison with each other. Besides other impediments, it may be remarked that, where there is a consciousness of unjust or dishonorable purposes, communication is always checked by distrust in proportion to the number whose concurrence is necessary.

Hence, it clearly appears, that the same advantage which a republic has over a democracy, in controlling the effects of faction, is enjoyed by a large over a small republic,—is enjoyed by the Union over the States composing it. Does the advantage consist in the substitution of representatives whose enlightened views and virtuous sentiments render them superior to local prejudices and to schemes of injustice? It will not be denied that the representation of the Union will be most likely to possess these requisite endowments. Does it consist in the greater security afforded by a greater variety of parties, against the event of any one party being able to outnumber and oppress the rest? In an equal degree does the increased variety of parties comprised within the Union, increase this security. Does it, in fine, consist in the greater obstacles opposed to the concert and accomplishment of the secret wishes of an unjust and interested majority? Here, again, the extent of the Union gives it the most palpable advantage.

The influence of factious leaders may kindle a flame within their particular States, but will be unable to spread a general conflagration through the other States. A religious sect may degenerate into a political faction in a part of the Confederacy; but the variety of sects dispersed over the entire face of it must secure the national councils against any danger from that source. A rage for paper money, for an abolition of debts, for an equal division of property, or for any other improper or wicked project, will be less apt to pervade the whole body of the Union than a particular member of it; in the same proportion as such a malady is more likely to taint a particular county or district, than an entire State.

In the extent and proper structure of the Union, therefore, we behold a republican remedy for the diseases most incident to republican government. And according to the degree of pleasure and pride we feel in being republicans, ought to be our zeal in cherishing the spirit and supporting the character of Federalists.

PUBLIUS

DEMOCRACY IN THEORY AND PRACTICE

Democracy, like the weather, is something that we all talk about but apparently have little control over. This situation is largely a result of the failure to come to grips with exactly what we mean by the word. Democracy to an American might easily incorporate variables that would be left out of an Englishman's definition, and vice versa. Yet our ability to clearly articulate those factors that we feel are essential to democracy is only half the problem; the other half is the impact of modern times on our various social, economic, and political institutions.

Technology, urbanization, nuclear weaponry, population growth, just to name a few developments, have forced many to reassess what they mean by a working democracy, let alone to evaluate whether or not they still have faith in its operational feasibility.

In a sense, every aspect of the contemporary American political and governmental system, whether it is the growth of the Office of the Presidency or the seeming apathy in public political participation, relates to democratic theory. Therefore, it is incumbent upon us to squarely face the issue of what democracy means and how it operates prior to addressing ourselves to the various specific governmental institutions and political processes.

It is interesting to note that the questions implicit in the observations made by Alexis de Tocqueville when he visited the United States over a century and a quarter ago are still so relevant for us today. Combined with this are the perhaps cynical observations concerning democracy in theory and practice of George Washington Plunkitt as recorded by William L. Riordon. The most that can be asked is that the reader come to terms with these points; his conclusions, however, must be his own.

INFLUENCE OF DEMOCRACY ON THE FEELINGS OF THE AMERICANS

ALEXIS DE TOCQUEVILLE

I think that democratic communities have a natural taste for freedom; left to themselves, they will seek it, cherish it, and view any privation of it with regret. But for equality their passion is ardent, insatiable, incessant, invincible; they call for equality in freedom; and if they cannot obtain that, they still call for equality in slavery. They will endure poverty, servitude, barbarism, but they will not endure aristocracy.

This is true at all times, and especially in our own day. All men and all powers seeking to cope with this irresistible passion will be overthrown and destroyed by it. In our age freedom cannot be established without it, and despotism itself cannot reign without its support.

OF INDIVIDUALISM IN DEMOCRATIC COUNTRIES

I have shown how it is that in ages of equality every man seeks for his opinions within himself; I am now to show how it is that in the same ages all his feelings are turned towards himself alone. *Individualism* is a novel expression, to which a novel idea has given birth. Our fathers were only acquainted with *égoïsme* (selfishness). Selfishness is a pas-

---

From *Democracy in America*, Vol. 2, by Alexis De Tocqueville. Translation by Henry Reeve, Francis Bowen, and Phillips Bradley, pp. 97–99, 102–105. New York: Alfred A. Knopf. Copyright © 1963. Reprinted by permission.

sionate and exaggerated love of self, which leads a man to connect everything with himself and to prefer himself to everything in the world. Individualism is a mature and calm feeling, which disposes each member of the community to sever himself from the mass of his fellows and to draw apart with his family and his friends, so that after he has thus formed a little circle of his own, he willingly leaves society at large to itself. Selfishness originates in blind instinct; individualism proceeds from erroneous judgment more than from depraved feelings; it originates as much in deficiencies of mind as in perversity of heart.

Selfishness blights the germ of all virtue; individualism, at first, only saps the virtues of public life; but in the long run it attacks and destroys all others and is at length absorbed in downright selfishness. Selfishness is a vice as old as the world, which does not belong to one form of society more than to another; individualism is of democratic origin, and it threatens to spread in the same ratio as the equality of condition.

Among aristocratic nations, as families remain for centuries in the same condition, often on the same spot, all generations become, as it were, contemporaneous. A man almost always knows his forefathers and respects them; he thinks he already sees his remote descendants and he loves them. He willingly imposes duties on himself towards the former and the latter, and he will frequently sacrifice his personal gratifications to those who went before and to those who will come after him. Aristocratic institutions, moreover, have the effect of closely binding every man to several of his fellow citizens. As the classes of an aristocratic people are strongly marked and permanent, each of them is regarded by its own members as a sort of lesser country, more tangible and more cherished than the country at large. As in aristocratic communities all the citizens occupy fixed positions, one above another, the result is that each of them always sees a man above himself whose patronage is necessary to him, and below himself another man whose co-operation he may claim. Men living in aristocratic ages are therefore almost always closely attached to something placed out of their own sphere, and they are often disposed to forget themselves. It is true that in these ages the notion of human fellowship is faint and that men seldom think of sacrificing themselves for mankind; but they often sacrifice themselves for other men. In democratic times, on the contrary, when the duties of each individual to the race are much more clear, devoted service to any one man becomes more rare; the bond of human affection is extended, but it is relaxed.

Among democratic nations new families are constantly springing up, others are constantly falling away, and all that remain change their condition; the woof of time is every instant broken and the track of generations effaced. Those who went before are soon forgotten; of those who will come after, no one has any idea: the interest of man is confined to those in close propinquity to himself. As each class gradually approaches others and mingles with them, its members become undifferentiated and lose their class identity for each other. Aristocracy had made a chain of all the members of the community, from the peasant to the king; democracy breaks that chain and severs every link of it.

As social conditions become more equal, the number of persons increases who, although they are neither rich nor powerful enough to exercise any great influence over their fellows, have nevertheless acquired or retained sufficient education and fortune to satisfy their own wants. They owe nothing to any man, they expect nothing from any man; they acquire the habit of always considering themselves as standing alone, and they are apt to imagine that their whole destiny is in their own hands.

Thus not only does democracy make every man forget his ancestors, but it hides his descendants and separates his contemporaries from him; it throws him back forever upon himself alone and threatens in the end to confine him entirely within the solitude of his own heart.

That the Americans Combat the Effects of Individualism by Free Institutions

Despotism, which by its nature is suspicious, sees in the separation among men the surest guarantee of its continuance, and it usually makes every effort to keep them separate. No vice of the human heart is so acceptable to it as selfishness: a despot easily forgives his subjects for not loving him, provided they do not love one another. He does not ask them to assist him in governing the state; it is enough that they do not aspire to govern it themselves. He stigmatizes as turbulent and unruly spirits those who would combine their exertions to promote the prosperity of the community; and, perverting the natural meaning of words, he applauds as good citizens those who have no sympathy for any but themselves.

Thus the vices which despotism produces are precisely those which equality fosters. These two things perniciously complete and assist each other. Equality places men side by side, unconnected by any common tie; despotism raises barriers to keep them asunder; the former predisposes them not to consider their fellow creatures, the latter makes general indifference a sort of public virtue.

Despotism, then, which is at all times dangerous, is more particularly to be feared in democratic ages. It is easy to see that in those same ages men stand most in need of freedom. When the members of a community are forced to attend to public affairs, they are necessarily drawn from the circle of their own interests and snatched at times from self-observation. As soon as a man begins to treat of public affairs in public, he begins to perceive that he is not so independent of his fellow men as he had at first imagined, and that in order to obtain their support he must often lend them his cooperation.

When the public govern, there is no man who does not feel the value of public goodwill or who does not endeavor to court it by drawing to himself the esteem and affection of those among whom he is to live. Many of the passions which congeal and keep asunder human hearts are then obliged to retire and hide below the surface. Pride must be dissembled; disdain dares not break out; selfishness fears its own self. Under a free government, as most public offices are elective, the men whose elevated minds or aspiring hopes are too closely circumscribed in private life constantly feel that they cannot do without the people who surround them. Men learn at such times to think of their fellow men from ambitious motives; and they frequently find it, in a manner, their interest to forget themselves.

I may here be met by an objection derived from electioneering intrigues, the meanness of candidates, and the calumnies of their opponents. These are occasions of enmity which occur the oftener the more frequent elections become. Such evils are doubtless great, but they are transient; whereas the benefits that attend them remain. The desire of being elected may lead some men for a time to violent hostility; but this same desire leads all men in the long run to support each other; and if it happens that an election accidentally severs two friends, the electoral system brings a multitude of citizens permanently together who would otherwise always have remained unknown to one another. Freedom produces private animosities, but despotism gives birth to general indifference.

The Americans have combated by free institutions the tendency of equality to keep men asunder, and they have subdued it. The legislators of America did not suppose that a general representation of the whole nation would suffice to ward off a disorder at once so natural to the frame of democratic society and so fatal; they also thought that it would be well to infuse political life into each portion of the territory in order to multiply to an infinite extent opportunities of acting in concert for all the members of the community and to make them constantly feel their mutual dependence. The plan was a wise one. The general affairs of a country engage the attention only of leading politicians, who assemble from time to time in the same places; and as they often lose sight of each other afterwards, no lasting ties are established between them. But if the object be to have the local affairs of a district conducted by the men who reside there, the same persons are always in contact, and they are, in a manner, forced to be acquainted and to adapt themselves to one another.

It is difficult to draw a man out of his own circle to interest him in the destiny of the state, because he does not clearly understand what influence the destiny of the state can have upon his own lot. But if it is proposed to make a road cross the end of his estate, he will see at a glance that there is a connection between this small public affair and his greatest private affairs; and he will discover, without its being shown to him, the close tie that unites private to general interest. Thus far more may be done by entrusting to the citizens the administration of minor affairs than by surrendering to them in the control of important ones, towards interesting them in the public welfare and convincing them that they constantly stand in need of one another in order to provide for it. A brilliant achievement may win for you the favor of a people at one stroke; but to earn the love and respect of the population that surrounds you, a long succession of little services rendered and of obscure good deeds, a constant habit of kindness, and an established reputation for disinterestedness will be required. Local freedom, then, which leads a great number of citizens to value the affection of their neighbors and of their kindred, perpetually brings men together and forces them to help one another in spite of the propensities that sever them.

In the United States the more opulent citizens take great care not to stand aloof from the people; on the contrary, they constantly keep on easy terms with the lower classes: they listen to them, they speak to them every day. They know that the rich in democracies always stand in need of the poor, and that in democratic times you attach a poor man to you more by your manner than by benefits conferred. The magnitude of such benefits, which sets off the difference of condition, causes a secret irritation to those who reap advantage from them, but the charm of simplicity of manners is almost irresistible; affability carries men away, and even want of polish is not always displeasing. This truth does not take root at once in the minds of the rich. They generally resist it as long as the democratic revolution lasts, and they do not acknowledge it immediately after that revolution is accomplished. They are very ready to do good to the people, but they still choose to keep them at arm's length; they think that is sufficient, but they are mistaken. They might spend fortunes thus without warming the hearts of the population around them; that population does not ask them for the sacrifice of their money, but of their pride.

It would seem as if every imagination in the United States were upon the stretch to invent means of increasing the wealth and satisfying the wants of the public. The best-informed inhabitants of each district constantly use their information to discover new truths that may augment the general prosperity; and if they have made any such discoveries, they eagerly surrender them to the mass of the people.

When the vices and weaknesses frequently exhibited by those who govern in America are closely examined, the prosperity of the people occasions, but improperly occasions, surprise. Elected magistrates do not make the American democracy flourish; it flourishes because the magistrates are elective.

It would be unjust to suppose that the patriotism and the zeal that every American displays for the welfare of his fellow citizens are wholly insincere. Although private interest directs the greater part of human actions in the United States as well as elsewhere, it does not regulate them all. I must say that I have often seen Americans make great and real sacrifices to the public welfare; and I have noticed a hundred instances in which they hardly ever failed to lend faithful support to one another. The free institutions which the inhabitants of the United States possess, and the political rights of which they make so much use, remind every citizen, and in a thousand ways, that he lives in society. They every instant impress upon his mind the notion that it is the duty as well as the interest of men to make themselves useful to their fellow creatures; and as he sees no particular ground of animosity to them, since he is never either their master or their slave, his heart readily leans to the side of kindness. Men attend to the interests of the public, first by necessity, afterwards by choice; what was intentional becomes an instinct, and by dint of working for the good of one's fellow citizens, the habit and the taste for serving them are at length acquired.

Many people in France consider equality of condition as one evil and political freedom as a second. When they are obliged to yield to the former, they strive at least to escape from the latter. But I contend that in order to combat the evils which equality may produce, there is only one effectual remedy: namely, political freedom.

BOSSES PRESERVE THE NATION

WILLIAM L. RIORDAN

When I retired from the Senate, I thought I would take a good, long rest, such a rest as a man needs who has held office for about forty years, and has held four different offices in one year and drawn salaries from three of them at the same time. Drawin' so many salaries is rather fatiguin', you know, and, as I said, I started out for a rest; but when I seen how things were goin' in New York State, and how a great big black shadow hung over us, I said to myself: "No rest for you, George. Your work ain't done. Your country still needs you and you mustn't lay down yet."

What was the great big black shadow? It was the primary election law, amended so as to knock out what are called the party bosses by lettin' in everybody at the primaries and givin' control over them to state officials. Oh, yes, that is a good way to do up the so-called bosses, but have you ever thought what would become of the country if the bosses were put out of business, and their places were taken by a lot of cart-tail orators and college graduates? It would mean chaos. It would be just like takin' a lot of dry-goods clerks and settin' them to run express trains on the New York Central Railroad. It makes my heart bleed to think of it. Ignorant people are always talkin' against party bosses, but just wait till the bosses are gone! Then, and not until then, will they get

---

From the book *Plunkitt of Tammany Hall* by William L. Riordan. Published in 1963 by E. P. Dutton and Co., Inc., in a paperback edition and reprinted with their permission; pp. 81–83.

the right sort of epitaphs, as Patrick Henry or Robert Emmet said.

Look at the bosses of Tammany Hall in the last twenty years. What magnificent men! To them New York City owes pretty much all it is today. John Kelly, Richard Croker, and Charles F. Murphy—what names in American history compares with them, except Washington and Lincoln? They built up the grand Tammany organization, and the organization built up New York. Suppose the city had to depend for the last twenty years on irresponsible concerns like the Citizens' Union, where would it be now? You can make a pretty good guess if you recall the Strong and Low administrations when there was no boss, and the heads of departments were at odds all the time with each other, and the Mayor was at odds with the lot of them. They spent so much time in arguin' and makin' grandstand play, that the interests of the city were forgotten. Another administration of that kind would put New York back a quarter of a century.

Then see how beautiful a Tammany city government runs, with a so-called boss directin' the whole shootin' match! The machinery moves so noiseless that you wouldn't think there was any. If there's any differences of opinion, the Tammany leader settles them quietly, and his orders go every time. How nice it is for the people to feel that they can get up in the mornin' without bein' afraid of seein' in the papers that the Commissioner of Water Supply has sandbagged the Dock Commissioner, and that the Mayor and heads of the departments have been taken to the police court as witnesses! That's no joke. I remember that, under Strong, some commissioners came very near sandbaggin' one another.

Of course, the newspapers like the reform administration. Why? Because these administrations, with their daily rows, furnish as racy news as prizefights or divorce cases. Tammany don't care to get in the papers. It goes right along attendin' to business quietly and only wants to be let alone. That's one reason why the papers are against us.

Some papers complain that the bosses get rich while devotin' their lives to the interests of the city. What of it? If opportunities for turnin' an honest dollar comes their way, why shouldn't they take advantage of them, just as I have done? As I said, in another talk, there is honest graft and dishonest graft. The bosses go in for the former. There is so much of it in this big town that they would be fools to go in for dishonest graft.

Now, the primary election law threatens to do away with the boss and make the city government a menagerie. That's why I can't take the rest I counted on. I'm goin' to propose a bill for the next session of the legislature repealin' this dangerous law, and leavin' the primaries entirely to the organizations themselves, as they used to be. Then will return the good old times, when our district leaders could have nice comfortable primary elections at some place selected by themselves and let in only men that they approved of as good Democrats. Who is a better judge of the Democracy of a man who offers his vote than the leader of the district? Who is better equipped to keep out undesirable voters?

The men who put through the primary law are the same crowd that stand for the civil service blight and they have the same objects in view—the destruction of governments by party, the downfall of the constitution and hell generally.

GOVERNMENT AS A SYSTEM

Systems analysis is a methodological tool that can aid the student of many disciplines, those in the precise sciences as well as those in the social sciences. The concept of a system is meant, on the simplest level, to offer us two major benefits. First, it allows the observer to gain an overview rather than seeing merely one segment at a time, and second, it affords us the opportunity of seeing interaction in the dynamic rather than the static state. That is, a systems approach is like viewing a moving picture taken with a wide-angle lens rather than having our perspective limited to a snapshot taken within a narrow focus.

Applied to politics, systems theory is meant to present to the student a theoretical means of understanding the demands put into the public arena (inputs), the anticipations of the decision-makers (withinputs), the decision-making process (the so-called little black box), the outcome in terms of policies and laws (outputs), the way in which these decisions are reacted to by groups within the society (feedback), and finally, whether or not this leads to a greater acceptance of the legitimacy of the entire process or not (supports).

This technique permits an ongoing analysis and its benefits are clearly explained by one of its greatest exponents, David

Easton. In the other selection, Presidential adviser Henry A. Kissinger, in describing how a policy decision is arrived at, objectively illustrates for us the strengths and weaknesses of the process as it operates, thereby giving graphic meaning to the systems model. Certainly such scientific analysis is necessary to help us clear away the underbrush of contemporary rhetoric about "the political system" and channel it into meaningful communications.

A CONVENIENT GUIDE FOR POLITICAL INQUIRY

DAVID EASTON

The Common Sense Idea of Political Life

The question that over the centuries has inspired the research of those interested in the political side of life, even though they themselves did not always take the trouble to verbalize it, is this: First and foremost, what is the nature of the good life, that is, what kind of goals ought men to seek?;[1] and once they are articulated, what steps ought the society to take to put them into effect as an authoritative statement of policy? From this initial inquiry there flows a series of questions out of which empirical political research has stemmed. To find out how a society can realize its goals, we must immediately seek answers to such questions as these: What are the actual authoritative policies adopted by a society? How are they determined and how are they put into effect? These are the lead or orienting questions around which the study of political life revolves. In a moment we shall refine these questions and explore the meaning of the constituent terms. Here, however, we need first, by an appeal to common sense, to test the validity of thus identifying the central problems of politi-

---

From *The Political System*, by David Easton. Copyright 1953 by Alfred A. Knopf, Inc. Reprinted by permission of the publisher, pp. 126–129.
[1] See L. Strauss, "On Classical Political Philosophy," 12 *Social Research* (1945), 98–117.

cal research. If our orienting concepts do not appeal initially to common sense, there is little likelihood that they could be made more attractive simply by incorporating them in a technical vocabulary.

Let us for a moment retrace our steps as social scientists and return to the outlook of the ordinary person who has not received technical training in either political or social science. If we can recapture for a moment our original and unembellished naïvete about matters political, it will help us to perceive their primary characteristics. In the mind unburdened with professional learning two things immediately associate themselves with the political aspect of life. In the first place, there is an immediate awareness of the pervasiveness of a kind of activity that in our idiom we call politicking. Wherever we find a group of people, whatever their purposes or form of organization, there we usually encounter maneuvering for position and power. We speak in this sense about the politicking within a group, and if we have not had very much experience with social groups we might be inclined to deplore this kind of activity. We might join Emerson in speculating on "what satire on government can equal the severity of censure conveyed in the word *politic,* which now for ages has signified *cunning,* intimating that the State is a trick?"[2] Experience, however, quickly leads us to the conclusion that there is seldom a group, however noble and even sacred its purposes, in which such practices do not occur. When these practices are detected in large social groups such as trade unions, or among nations, we call them the struggle for power.

Upon pressing our inquiry further we find that, if freed of special knowledge, when we speak about a political problem we also use the term "political" in a second typical sense which includes politicking and yet goes beyond it. In this second sense, the word normally refers to an activity related in some vague way to problems of government or the making

---

[2] R. W. Emerson, "Politics" in *Essays and Other Writings* (London: Cassell, 1927), p. 343.

of policy for the whole society in which we live. We have in mind some dispute over the policies accepted as authoritative for the society; what we mean by authoritative can be set aside for the moment. What is certain is that we know quite naturally that not all policies made in a society are of the same scope. Some, adopted by private groups such as a family, an association, or the like, are expected to apply only to the members of these groups or to others who wish to abide by them. But other policies apply to members of the whole society by virtue of their presence in or ties with the society. Such policies are considered to be authoritative for the society. There is politicking or a struggle among various groups to influence the kind of policy adopted as authoritative for the society of which they are part.

In this quite natural and unstrained kind of reasoning we can see that in its most comprehensive aspect and in the sense normally used when referring to public affairs, the central theme of a political problem is as much the kind of policy at stake as the means used to influence that policy. In ordinary conversation when we engage in political dispute, the point at issue is usually the kind of program we approve, the kind of policy we would like to see adopted for our society. We may deplore the kind or amount of politicking that may exist in relation to political issues but we consider ourselves embroiled in a political situation when we differ about the ends to be adopted in the name of the broadest group to which we belong.

Normally, therefore, we may speak of the power struggle in a fraternal organization as politics in a narrow sense; but we do not speak of dispute over the kind of decisions this group ought to make with regard to its internal matters as a political issue. We reserve the term "political" in this sense for public or social matters. Although inescapable, our interest in politicking or the struggle for power is only derivative; it helps us to understand the kind of policy finally adopted for the society and the way in which such a policy has been put into effect. If we were to sum up our common sense conception of politics it might conceivably take the following form: Political life concerns all those varieties of activity that influence significantly the kind of authoritative policy adopted for a society and the way it is put into practice. We are said to be participating in political life when our activity relates in some way to the making and execution of policy for a society.

THE AUTHORITATIVE ALLOCATION
OF VALUES FOR A SOCIETY

Let us examine more closely, within the framework of our discussion to this point, what is implied in these conclusions derived from just ordinary knowledge about politics. In effect, what we have here described in the crude terms of common sense is the empirical or concrete political system. We are in effect saying that all those kinds of activities involved in the formulation and execution of social policy, in what has come to be called elliptically in political science, the policy-making process, constitute the political system. The principle upon which these activities can be said to cohere or provide a minimum of relatedness is the fact that they all bear some relevance to the way in which policy for a society is created and effectuated. It is this, consequently, that must give the political system a quality distinguishing it, for example, from the economic system. And because political science has historically set for itself the task of understanding what social policy ought to be, how it is set and put into effect, its general objective must be to understand the functioning of the political system. We have in the concept of authoritative policy for a society a convenient and rough approximation to a set of orienting concepts for political research. It provides us with the essential property of that complex of activity, called political, that over the years men have sought to understand.

THE IMPACT OF THE ADMINISTRATIVE STRUCTURE

HENRY A. KISSINGER

In the contemporary period, the very nature of the governmental structure introduces an element of rigidity which operates more or less independently of the convictions of statesmen or the ideology which they represent. Issues are too complex and relevant facts too manifold to be dealt with on the basis of personal intuition. An institutionalization of decision-making is an inevitable by-product of the risks of international affairs in the nuclear age. Moreover, almost every modern state is dedicated to some theory of "planning" —the attempt to structure the future by understanding and, if necessary, manipulating the environment. Planning involves a quest for predictability and, above all, for "objectivity." There is a deliberate effort to reduce the relevant elements of a problem to a standard of average performance. The vast bureaucratic mechanisms that emerge develop a momentum and a vested interest of their own. As they grow more complex, their internal standards of operation are not necessarily commensurable with those of other countries or even with other bureaucratic structures in the same country. There is a trend toward autarky. A paradoxical consequence may be that increased control over the domestic environment is purchased at the price of loss of flexibility in international affairs.

Reprinted from *American Foreign Policy*, Three Essays by Henry A. Kissinger. By permission of W. W. Norton & Company, Inc. Copyright © 1969 by Henry A. Kissinger. Pp. 17–26.

The purpose of bureaucracy is to devise a standard operating procedure which can cope effectively with most problems. A bureaucracy is efficient if the matters which it handles routinely are, in fact, the most frequent and if its procedures are relevant to their solution. If those criteria are met, the energies of the top leadership are freed to deal creatively with the unexpected occurrence or with the need for innovation. Bureaucracy becomes an obstacle when what it defines as routine does not address the most significant range of issues or when its prescribed mode of action proves irrelevant to the problem.

When this occurs, the bureaucracy absorbs the energies of top executives in reconciling what is expected with what happens; the analysis of where one is overwhelms the consideration of where one should be going. Serving the machine becomes a more absorbing occupation than defining its purpose. Success consists in moving the administrative machine to the point of decision, leaving relatively little energy for analyzing the merit of this decision. The quest for "objectivity"—while desirable theoretically—involves the danger that means and ends are confused, that an average standard of performance is exalted as the only valid one. Attention tends to be diverted from the act of choice—which is the ultimate test of statesmanship—to the accumulation of facts. Decisions can be avoided until a crisis brooks no further delay, until the events themselves have removed the element of ambiguity. But at that point the scope for constructive action is at a minimum. Certainty is purchased at the cost of creativity.

Something like this seems to be characteristic of modern bureaucratic states whatever their ideology. In societies with a pragmatic tradition, such as the United States, there develops a greater concern with an analysis of where one is than where one is going. What passes for planning is frequently the projection of the familiar into the future. In societies based on ideology, doctrine is institutionalized and exegesis takes the place of innovation. Creativity must make so many concessions to orthodoxy that it may exhaust itself in doctrinal adaptations. In short, the accumulation of knowledge of the bureaucracy and the impersonality of its method of arriving at decisions can be achieved at a high price. Decision-making can grow so complex that the process of producing a bureaucratic consensus may overshadow the purpose of the effort.

While all thoughtful administrators would grant in the abstract that these dangers exist, they find it difficult to act on their knowledge. Lip service is paid to planning; indeed planning staffs proliferate. However, they suffer from two debilities. The "operating" elements may not take the planning effort seriously. Plans become esoteric exercises which are accepted largely because they imply no practical consequence. They are a sop to administrative theory. At the same time, since planning staffs have a high incentive to try to be "useful," there is a bias against novel conceptions which are difficult to adapt to an administrative mold. It is one thing to assign an individual or a group the task of looking ahead; this is a far cry from providing an environment which encourages an understanding for deeper historical, sociological, and economic trends. The need to provide a memorandum may outweigh the imperatives of creative thought. The quest for objectivity creates a temptation to see in the future an updated version of the present. Yet true innovation is bound to run counter to prevailing standards. The dilemma of modern bureaucracy is that while every creative act is lonely, not every lonely act is creative. Formal criteria are little help in solving this problem because the unique cannot be expressed "objectively."

The rigidity in the policies of the technologically advanced societies is in no small part due to the complexity of decision-making. Crucial problems may—and frequently do—go unrecognized for a long time. But once the decision-making apparatus has disgorged a policy, it becomes very difficult to change it. The alternative to the status quo is the prospect of repeating the whole anguishing process of arriving at decisions. This explains to some extent the curious phenomenon that decisions taken with enormous doubt and perhaps with a close division become practically sacrosanct once adopted. The whole administrative machinery swings behind their implementation as if activity could still all doubts.

Moreover, the reputation, indeed the political survival, of most leaders depends on their ability to realize their goals, however these may have been arrived at. Whether these goals are desirable is relatively less crucial. The time span by which administrative success is measured is considerably shorter than that by which historical achievement is determined. In heavily bureaucratized societies all pressures emphasize the first of these accomplishments.

Then, too, the staffs on which modern executives come to depend develop a momentum of their own. What starts out as an aid to decision-makers often turns into a practically autonomous organization whose internal problems structure and sometimes compound the issues which it was originally designed to solve. The decision-maker will always be aware of the morale of his staff. Though he has the authority, he cannot overrule it too frequently without impairing its efficiency; and he may, in any event, lack the knowledge to do so. Placating the staff then becomes a major preoccupation of the executive. A form of administrative democracy results, in which a decision often reflects an attainable consensus rather than substantive conviction (or at least the two imperceptibly merge). The internal requirements of the bureaucracy may come to predominate over the purposes which it was intended to serve. This is probably even more true in highly institutionalized Communist states—such as the U.S.S.R.—than in the United States.

When the administrative machine grows very elaborate, the various levels of the decision-making process are separated by chasms which are obscured from the outside world by the complexity of the apparatus. Research often becomes a means to buy time and to assuage consciences. Studying a problem can turn into an escape from coming to grips with it. In the process, the gap between the technical competence of research staffs and what hard-pressed political leaders are capable of absorbing widens constantly. This heightens the insecurity of the executive and may thus compound either rigidity or arbitrariness or both. In many fields—strategy being a prime example—decision-makers may find it difficult to give as many hours to a problem as the expert has had years to study it. The ultimate decision often depends less on knowledge than on the ability to brief the top administrator—to present the facts in such a way that they can be absorbed rapidly. The effectiveness of briefing, however, puts a premium on theatrical qualities. Not everything that sounds plausible is correct, and many things which are correct may not sound plausible when they are first presented; and a second hearing is rare. The stage aspect of briefing may leave the decision-maker with a gnawing feeling of having been taken—even, and perhaps especially, when he does not know quite how.

Sophistication may thus encourage paralysis or a crude popularization which defeats its own purpose. The excessively theoretical approach of many research staffs overlooks the problem of the strain of decision-making in times of crisis. What is relevant for policy depends not only on academic truth but also on what can be implemented under stress. The technical staffs are frequently operating in a framework of theoretical standards while in fact their usefulness depends on essentially psychological criteria. To be politically meaningful, their proposals must involve answers to the following types of questions: Does the executive understand the proposal? Does he believe in it? Does he accept it as a guide to action or as an excuse for doing nothing? But if these kinds of concerns are given too much weight, the requirements of salesmanship will defeat substance.

The pragmatism of executives thus clashes with the theoretical bent of research or planning staffs. Executives as a rule take cognizance of a problem only when it emerges as an administrative issue. They thus unwittingly encourage bureaucratic contests as the only means of generating decisions. Or the various elements of the bureaucracy make a series of nonaggression pacts with each other and thus reduce the decision-maker to a benevolent constitutional monarch. As the special role of the executive increasingly becomes to choose between proposals generated administratively, decision-makers turn into arbiters rather than leaders. Whether they wait until a problem emerges as an administrative issue or until a crisis has demonstrated the irrelevance of the standard operating procedure, the modern decision-makers often find themselves the prisoners of their advisers.

Faced with an administrative machine which is both elaborate and fragmented, the executive is forced into essentially lateral means of control. Many of his public pronouncements, though ostensibly directed to outsiders, perform a perhaps more important role in laying down guidelines for the bureaucracy. The chief significance of a foreign policy speech by the President may thus be that it settles an internal debate in Washington (a public statement is more useful for this purpose than an administrative memorandum because it is harder to reverse). At the same time, the bureaucracy's awareness of this method of control tempts it to shortcut its debates by using pronouncements by the decision-makers as charters for special purposes. The executive thus finds himself confronted by proposals for public declarations which may be innocuous in themselves—and whose bureaucratic significance may be anything but obvious—but which can be used by some agency or department to launch a study or program which will restrict his freedom of decision later on.

All of this drives the executive in the direction of extra-bureaucratic means of decision. The practice of relying on special emissaries or personal envoys is an example; their status outside the bureaucracy frees them from some of its restraints. International agreements are sometimes possible only by ignoring safeguards against capricious action. It is a paradoxical aspect of modern bureaucracies that their quest for objectivity and calculability often leads to impasses which can be overcome only by essentially arbitrary decisions.

Such a mode of operation would involve a great risk of stagnation even in "normal" times. It becomes especially dangerous in a revolutionary period. For then, the problems which are most obtrusive may be least relevant. The issues which are most significant may not be suitable for administrative formulation and even when formulated may not lend themselves to bureaucratic consensus. When the issue is how to transform the existing framework, routine can become an additional obstacle to both comprehension and action.

This problem, serious enough *within* each society, is magnified in the conduct of international affairs. While the formal machinery of decision-making in developed countries shows many similarities, the criteria which influence decisions vary enormously. With each administrative machine increasingly absorbed in its own internal problems, diplomacy loses its flexibility. Leaders are extremely aware of the problems of placating their own bureaucracy; they cannot depart too far from its prescriptions without raising serious morale problems. Decisions are reached so painfully that the very anguish of decision-making acts as a brake on the give-and-take of traditional diplomacy.

This is true even *within* alliances. Meaningful consultation with other nations becomes very difficult when the internal process of decision-making already has some of the characteristics of compacts between quasi-sovereign entities. There is an increasing reluctance to hazard a hard-won domestic consensus in an international forum.

What is true within alliances—that is, among nations which have at least some common objectives—becomes even more acute in relations between antagonistic states or blocs. The gap created when two large bureaucracies generate goals largely in isolation from each other and on the basis of not necessarily commensurable criteria is magnified considerably by an ideological schism. The degree of ideological fervor is not decisive; the problem would exist even if the original ideological commitment had declined on either or both sides. The criteria for bureaucratic decision-making may continue to be influenced by ideology even after its élan has dissipated. Bureaucratic structures generate their own momentum which may more than counterbalance the loss of earlier fanaticism. In the early stages of a revolutionary movement, ideology is crucial and the accident of personalities can be decisive. The Reign of Terror in France was ended by the elimination of a single man, Robespierre. The Bolshevik revolution could hardly have taken place had Lenin not been on the famous train which crossed Germany into Russia. But once a revolution becomes institutionalized, the administrative structures which it has spawned develop their own vested interests. Ideology may grow less significant in creating commitment; it becomes pervasive in supplying criteria of administrative choice. Ideologies prevail by being taken for granted. Orthodoxy substitutes for conviction and produces its own form of rigidity.

In such circumstances, a meaningful dialogue across ideological dividing lines becomes extraordinarily difficult. The more elaborate the administrative structure, the less relevant an individual's view becomes—indeed one of the purposes of bureaucracy is to liberate decision-making from the accident of personalities. Thus while personal convictions may be modified, it requires a really monumental effort to alter bureaucratic commitments. And if change occurs, the bureaucracy prefers to move at its own pace and not be excessively influenced by statements or pressures of foreigners. For all these reasons, diplomacy tends to become rigid or to turn into an abstract bargaining process based on largely formal criteria such as "splitting the difference." Either course is self-defeating: the former because it negates the very purpose of diplomacy; the latter because it subordinates purpose to technique and because it may encourage intransigence. Indeed, the incentive for intransigence increases if it is known that the difference will generally be split.

Ideological differences are compounded because major parts of the world are only in the first stages of administrative evolution. Where the technologically advanced countries suffer from the inertia of overadministration, the developing areas often lack even the rudiments of effective bureaucracy. Where the advanced countries may drown in "facts," the emerging nations are frequently without the most elementary knowledge needed for forming a meaningful judgment or for implementing it once it has been taken. Where large bureaucracies operate in alternating spurts of rigidity and catastrophic (in relation to the bureaucracy) upheaval, the new states tend to make decisions on the basis of almost random pressures. The excessive institutionalization of one and the inadequate structure of the other inhibit international stability.

4

POLITICAL PARTIES

It is only rarely that one hears a kind word about American political parties. They have been scored by foreign observers, such as the Englishman James Bryce and the Russian M. I. Ostrogorski, as not being compatible with democracy because they are usually headed by elites. Journalists and cynics have called them corrupt and boss ridden. Political scientists have labeled them undisciplined, irresponsible, and irrelevant to the needs of the 1970s. Political parties are not even mentioned in the Constitution.

Yet despite all of these criticisms, one important fact stands out: Our party system, despite its nonprogrammatic, nonideological stance, is a mechanism that offers citizens an opportunity to participate in the policy formulation process. In most areas of the United States the party organization is understaffed, and will welcome nearly anyone who wishes to work for it. Consequently the price for the ticket of admission into the political process is rarely more than a willingness to do some dull but necessary task.

By opening their doors to those who indicate their desire to be active in the political system, the American party system has accomplished much to integrate large numbers of citizens into the political process, and thereby legitimize our form of government.

In the following selections, Professor Frank J. Sorauf analyzes the structure of the party system, while Michael Harrington discusses a solution to what he feels is the major problem facing the Democratic party in the 1970s.

THE
POLITICAL PARTY

FRANK J. SORAUF

As there are many roads to Rome and many ways to skin a cat, there are also many ways to look at a political party. One can see in the party a burning contemporary issue or an ideological way of life, a bustling corps of political militants, a casual alliance of indifferent or even cynical voters, or a compelling and charismatic leader. For political parties as complex and multi-faceted as the major American parties, what they appear to be may depend on the general political context of the moment, on the particular part or activity of the party one views, or on the eye of the beholder. Amid this variety and diversity the greatest problem is that of perceiving the political party in its entirety.

Indeed, the inclination is great to let the political party slip out of focus entirely. It easily gets lost in the colorful and anecdotal milieu of American politics. So intently may we follow the progress of Presidential campaigns in the United States, so fascinated may we be by the clash of great personalities, by campaign charges and counter-charges, that we lose sight of the role the parties play in the nomination and election of Presidential candidates. Even if we do not, we have seen only some parts of the American parties engaged in only one aspect of one of their functions—the contesting of elections.

From Frank J. Sorauf, *Political Parties in the American System*, pp. 1–8. Copyright © 1964 by Little, Brown and Company (Inc.). Reprinted by permission.

A full-length portrait of the political party demands full assessment of the various organizations and personnel within the political party, as well as a complete picture of the functions the party performs in the political system. And so greatly do the political parties differ in structure and function that the generic concept of a "political party" may include the competitive electoral parties of Great Britain and the United States, the class-based parties of Latin American ruling elites, and the mass movements for independence in the new nations of Asia and Africa. Even within the United States "party" embraces the vital, electoral, major parties and esoteric splinter movements devoted to abolishing the income tax or alcoholic beverages.

Party
as Function and Role

Unquestionably the most common function among the parties of the world's democracies—and the one that separates them most efficiently from other political organizations—is the mobilization of voters behind candidates for election. The major American parties, far more than most other parties, are dominated by the electing function. They are, indeed, great and overt conspiracies for the capture of public office. Yet within the entire American party system parties differ in the vigor and seriousness with which they pursue the electing function. For the major parties it is virtually the alpha and the omega. The cycle and seasons of their activity depend almost completely on the calendar of elections. But for the minor parties the election is little more than a convenient occasion for the achievement of some other political purpose. Not in their moments of wildest optimism can the Socialist Workers or Prohibitionists hope to capture the American Presidency or any of the governorships for which they contend. The ballot is for them a priceless, and low-priced, vehicle for publicizing and proselytizing their views.

Second only to the electing function is the party's role as a teacher—its function as a propagandist for political attitudes, ideas, and programs. Generally, the American parties have avoided the burden of promoting the vast world view that ideological parties such as the European Socialists assume. Their ambitions are more modest: a diffuse identification with the interests of labor or business or agriculture, for instance, or a platform with indistinct and often ambiguous policy stands. At a given time the American party may even adopt no more than a broad posture as the party of peace or prosperity.

The American parties—as all others—also perform the even more general educational role of political socialization. For its loyalists the party arranges the confusion of the political world. It teaches them how to view the political universe and its options. Its symbols offer them a point of reference in judging officeholders or in finding the "right" side in an issue or controversy. At the simplest level the parties help their clienteles to divide the political world into the statesmen and the scoundrels. For the more sophisticated follower the party relates a value or set of values—conservatism, racial equality, or national pride—to the policy or candidate alternatives he faces. Even though the American political parties share this function of organizing and directing political perceptions with the mass media and interest groups, they remain nonetheless a potent focus for organizing knowledge about American politics.

The parties of the democracies, third, assume in varying degrees the function of organizing the policy-making machinery of government. In the United States Congress and in state legislatures the basic unit of organization is the party caucus; from it flows the appointment of powerful presiding officers, committee chairmen, floor leaders, and steering committees. Performance of this function, of course, depends on the party's success as an electoral organization. The American party unable to win more than a handful of legislative seats and only an occasional executive post plays little or no part in organizing legislative and executive branches. Even though small bodies of voters may enable parties in multi-party systems to garner a share of parliamentary and cabinet power, policy-making power within the American political system depends on majorities.

The failure of the American parties to seize and use the policy-making power they so frantically pursue in their electing function has occasioned a fifteen-year debate within American political science. The academic advocates of "party responsibility" castigate the parties for failing to elect men who are loyal to an articulated program and who will enact the program into public policy once elected. More of that controversy later. It suffices to point out here that the failure of the American parties to assume this party function has become a subject of prickly controversy. Indeed, the major share of the history of the major American parties has been marked by an inversion of the usual party policy-making roles within government. Within the parliamentary systems of the Western democracies the parties have organized legislative majorities and blocs, at the same time as inviolable traditions of professional administrative services have kept them isolated from much of executive and administrative control. In the United States, though, the major parties have traditionally organized legislative chambers without using the party power for party-originated and party-identified policies. But they have, thanks to a long and largely honorable tradition of patronage, often been able to control the selection and operation of administrative services. Even as they yield the bulk of the patronage to merit-system appointees, they continue to control more top-level administrative appointments than do, say, the British political parties.

Finally, the political parties seem to be involved in a series of "non-political" functions. European parties, more frequently than the American, sponsor boy scout troops, social clubs for senior citizens, adult-education classes, and benevolent societies that offer group health and life insurance programs. In its fabled heyday the urban machine in America offered the new arrivals to the cities a range of services that made it, in contemporary terms, a combination of employment agency, legal aid society, social worker, domestic relations counselor, and community social center. And in the new style, urban "club" parties in the American cities and suburbs, the parties cater to the social and intellectual needs of a mobile, educated, ideological, often isolated upper middle class. The style may have changed from "beer all around" at the local tavern to martinis at the cocktail hour, but the parties continue to concern themselves with more than just campaigns and elections.

To refer to these functions as "non-political" is, of course, somewhat misleading. Although they may not seem to promise an immediate political payoff, the party hopes that in the long run they will create loyalties, obligations, and ties that will facilitate the successful performance of the other, more directly political tasks. The political party, in fact, exists solely for political purposes and performs only political functions. The other forms of political organization—the Church, the ethnic group, the informal community elite, the voluntary interest group such as a trade union or medical association—move freely from the non-political to the political function and quickly back again. Not so the political party. Its exclusively political character sets it apart from the other political organizations.

The emphasis a party places on one or two of these functions, and the style with which it carries them out, distinguishes it from its competitors and from the parties of other political systems. The balance of these functions that any party achieves, however, is not only a matter of making scarce energies and resources go around. Within many political systems the performance of one may be incompatible with the successful performance of another. In this regard American parties have long argued that they would compromise their success as electoral organizations were they to stress the development of programs and ideologies. They devote themselves entirely to the electing function and pay comparatively little attention to the business of promoting ideologies or organizing the powers of government. That electoral preoccupation distinguishes them not only from the minor parties in the United States but from the competitive parties of the other mature democracies as well.

The fact that political parties are exclusively political in function is no assurance that they monopolize the functions of contesting elections, proclaiming political programs and values, and organizing the machinery of government. The American parties, in fact, share the function of selecting and electing candidates with informal community elites in many localities. They also share with interest groups the maintenance of a system of responsibility in the American legislature. And in the function of spelling out political programs and alternatives they operate in uneasy competition with the mass media, educational institutions, and voluntary associations. The classic urban machine in the United States came close to monopolizing these functions, but its palmier days are past. That the parties can no longer monopolize them suggests a changing role for them within the American political system.

THE PARTY AS STRUCTURE

The political party, though, is more than the sum of its fervid electoral campaigns, its advocacy of issues and programs, and its attempts to discipline officeholders. It is a stable organization, and it is a number of individuals and groups of individuals held together in a reasonably stable pattern of relationships by a multitude of purposes, incentives, and traditions.

There is an old and hoary image that pictures the political party as a series of concentric circles, like the ever-widening pattern of waves and ripples created by the pebble thrown into the pond. At the party's center of impact are the most active and most deeply committed partisans—the party cadre, the officialdom that maintains and leads the party organization. Then, in circular waves of decreasing vigor and impulse are arranged the party regulars and workers, the rank and file of party members, and finally the party's voters and identifiers.

The image is a simple and orderly one, although too precise for the reality of any political party, least of all the loosely organized American parties. Its shortcomings, however, suggest the problems in viewing any political party purely as an organization. For one thing, the metaphor of concentric circles suggests a regular, stable pattern of authority and activity within the party. Though some American parties may contain a series of groups differentiated by their activity and degree of involvement, others do not. It is a significant fact for countless local party organizations that their "active cadre" consists of no more than a county chairman and a few spiritless hangers-on. The lines of authority and the degrees of activity also may shift in time. The circles shrink, contract, and even collapse in the slack periods between elections.

Indeed, the image of the concentric circles assumes a party organization with a clear division of labor among its parts, a continuous pattern of activity through the year, and a clearly defined body of members and activists. The American political party matches none of these assumptions. None of the concentric circles within the American parties are clearly marked out. Because in many communities the American precinct committeeman is elected at an open primary, he may be either hostile to party leadership or largely uninterested in party operations. Informal leadership groups, coopted by a powerful party chairman or a party elite, frequently supplant the formal party organization. Nor is it easy to separate the party cadre and party workers from the personal followings of officeholders and candidates. Most local American parties are, especially around election time, an irrational and confusing amalgam of formal party officeholders, informal party leadership groups, and the personal followings of candidates. And since in the United States card-carrying party membership is not widespread—and is, indeed, even faintly suspect—the circle of formal membership does not even exist in many American parties.

The most vexing problem with the analysis of the concentric-circle model concerns the question of whether or not, in searching for the party as an organization, we follow the circles to infinity. The party officials, the party actives, and even the party members, we may call the party "organization." Popular usage in the United States does. Beyond the "organization" are the party's voters, its supporters, and its "identifiers." Their ties of loyalty and activity are often most tenuous. These identifiers, the passive "fellow travellers" of the party, may share the party goals or ally themselves loosely with its prospects and fortunes. In those Western countries systematically furrowed by the opinion pollers, they are the men and women who respond to questions such as: "Do you think it will make a good deal of difference to the country whether the Democrats or the Republicans win the elections this November, or that it won't make much difference which side wins?" or "In politics, do you consider yourself a Democrat or a Republican or a member of some other party?" With the identifiers on the outer peripheries of the party are the partisans who vote (with some regularity) for the candidates of the party. The identifiers and the voters overlap considerably. But even though their support is crucial to the party's success, they hardly share the stable relationships and authority of the party structure. In this sense the "party-in-the-electorate" is less an organization than a reaction to a symbol and a tradition.

The political party as an organization consists, however, of much more than a series of concentric circles or superimposed layers of organization. It is a hierarchy of parties, from local unit to national party, through which the parties achieve a geographical division of effort. In federal systems such as that in the United States the parties' decentralized internal relations parallel and reflect the decentralization of the political system. The multitude of delicate relationships between and among the party units suggest another important aspect of party organization. So do the decision-making processes by which the party selects leaders and candidates, makes and enforces policy decisions, and allocates effort and responsibility within the party. Furthermore, the political party may be approached organizationally as a system of incentives and goals that bind the partisans together and spur them to action.

Viewed as systems of power and authority, the political parties exhibit sharply contrasting organizational features. They run from the centralized, militant, and disciplined structures of the European Socialist and Communist parties to the decentralized, virtually autonomous, cadre organizations of the American major parties. Even within American local party organizations the range extends from the tough, almost hyperactive urban machine to the immobile, chaotic, disorganized parties of many rural areas, from the traditional party of the exclusive circle of workers to the new, membership, club types of parties. Often, indeed, the variations in party organization from time to time and place to place within one party are more interesting and instructive than the differences among a number of parties.

DON'T FORM A FOURTH PARTY: FORM A NEW FIRST PARTY

MICHAEL HARRINGTON

The United States may well come apart at the seams unless there is a new, radical political party, but the worst way to get one at this moment is to start one.

Less than a decade ago everyone except a few of us on the left margin of the society was convinced that the two-party system in general, and the Democrats and Republicans in particular, were an invention of the uniquely American genius. The united front of integrationists and racists in the Democratic party, and of Neanderthals and moderate liberals in the Republican, was supposed to be our inspired way of avoiding the instability of European ideological politics. Precisely because our major parties were so utterly unprincipled, we were told, they had to gravitate toward the center, where all solutions were miraculously to be found.

Now the mood has altered radically. Samuel Lubell talks of "the beginnings, at least, of both a voter revolution and a realignment of our parties unlike any experienced in our history." Senator Eugene McCarthy advances . . . the theory that a new party could be "a real force" in 1972. Alan Otten reports in The Wall Street Journal that Washington is alive with talk of a "fourth party," a relatively liberal party, oriented to better-educated suburbanites and to students and other campus dwellers—led, perhaps, by Eugene McCarthy,

---

From *Don't Form a Fourth Party: Form a New First Party*, by Michael Harrington. *The New York Times Magazine*, September 13, 1970. © 1970 by The New York Times Company. Reprinted by permission.

John Lindsay or John Gardner. And shortly thereafter, Mr. Gardner himself is reported to have "freely acknowledged" to The New York Times that a citizen's lobby he is organizing could turn into a new party to the left of the Democrats and Republicans.

It is certainly true, as all these gentlemen realize, that America cannot much longer afford the obfuscation and geriatric incompetence of its party system. Every Presidential commission in the last five years—on automation, civil disorders, violence and all the rest—has soberly concluded that we must change basic institutions, innovate and spend billions (or tens of billions). These commissions have, at the expense of a capitalist government, been a sort of collective Karl Marx, providing extensive Federal proof of how rotten the society is. And two reasons that their proposals have been so universally ignored are the Democratic and Republican parties. Since our miseries in this regard are familiar to the point of banality, I will refer to them only in summary fashion.

The Democratic party of McGovern, Muskie, Mendel Rivers and Eastland faces a Republican party of Goldwater, Hruska, Javits and Hatfield. These fratricidal coalitions help decide who will be President and which party will organize the houses of Congress. After these trivial questions have been settled, the parties dissolve, and under normal conditions a bipartisan conspiracy of Dixiecrats and conservative Republicans takes over the legislative branch, particularly the House. The system is scientifically designed to stifle serious debate about why society is tearing itself apart and, of course, to subvert any legislation that might deal with basic problems.

Despite the din of speeches demanding a reordering of basic priorities, we have not, will not and cannot do anything about our most desperate problems as long as this situation prevails. That is why we must have a new party capable of winning a democratic majority for a radical program. How do we get it? The most obvious, logical and exciting answer is to start a fourth party to challenge the Democrats, Republicans and

Wallacites. Only it won't work—or, more precisely, it will work only in the interest of Richard Nixon and the Dixiecrat-Republican coalition in Congress. For it is quite literally a strategy for creating a *fourth* party, a party that can never win a majority.

The last majority party built from the ground up was the Republican party of Abraham Lincoln, born more than 100 years ago. It succeeded because there were so many different people from different classes who were willing to break from the old alignments and rally to a new banner. There were abolitionists concerned with the moral issue of slavery, businessmen who wanted high tariffs, Western farmers and Eastern workers who wanted free land and feared that they would be destroyed in a competition with slave labor.

But today such a vast constituency does not exist for a fourth party. To be sure, discontent is epidemic, but it is either moving people to the right or confirming them in their loyalty to the Democrats. And even the most optimistic projection of the number of voters who *might* turn to a fourth party indicates that they do not add up to a majority and never can.

There is no question that mass higher education is creating a large new constituency at least as concerned with the ethical implications of politics as with self-interest. The McCarthy and Kennedy campaigns of 1968 were an obvious example of this trend; so was the angry explosion over the Cambodian invasion and the killings at Kent State. This phenomenon is, of course, essentially young and middle class, which is to say that it lacks cohesion and organization and expresses itself in great bursts of energy at moments of crisis. Moreover, the activists are still isolated from the rest of the society, a point I make with real sadness since I worked with them in the McCarthy and Kennedy campaigns and will do so again this fall in the effort to elect a liberal, antiwar Congress.

Some statistics on 1968 are particularly sobering when one tries to estimate the political depth of the antiwar movement.

They were analyzed by Philip E. Converse, Warren E. Miller, Jerrold G. Rusk and Arthur C. Wolfe last December in American Political Science Review. And even if I find these scholars much too hostile to the McCarthyites and the peace demonstrators, their figures cannot be wished away. A clear majority of the Americans who were against the Vietnam war also said that they were negative toward the protesters, and 23 per cent of them were "extremely hostile." This would suggest that at least some of the peace sentiment in America developed in spite of, rather than because of the activists (particularly, in my opinion, in spite of those who flaunted Vietcong flags). And, according to one report, 70 per cent of the people did *not* think that the Chicago police used too much force during the Democratic convention.

The scholars also have a depressing estimate of the number of "hard-core" McCarthyites, the people who might be immediately available for a fourth-party venture. In the early stages of the 1968 primaries, they say, the data suggest that Senator McCarthy received support from all those who were dissatisfied with President Johnson—from hawks as well as doves.

This explains the extraordinary strength McCarthy showed in the primaries. But when his supporters of the spring were interviewed again in the fall and asked to rate the primary candidates on the basis of their current attitudes, he was the favorite of only 6 per cent of the Democrats with a clear preference and 3 per cent of all Democrats. Even more significant were the new loyalties of the former McCarthyites. In retrospect a small plurality felt that they should have favored Wallace; slightly smaller groups backed Robert Kennedy (whose tragic death may have enhanced his posthumous popularity) and Richard Nixon, and about 15 per cent had switched to Hubert Humphrey. In other words, a majority of McCarthy's supporters in the primaries (those who had moved to Wallace and Nixon) were generally to the right of center by the fall.

The hard-core McCarthy strength turned up exactly where one would expect to find it; it was disproportionately college-educated, Jewish and metropolitan. Because the college-educated and metropolitan populations are increasing and because the strength of their commitment magnifies their numbers, I think they are an important force. But a careful look at the McCarthy phenomenon suggests that only a minority of those who voted for the Senator could be counted as possible recruits to a fourth party of the left. And this lack of numerical strength is not going to be made up by the minorities and liberal Republicans joining in with the McCarthyites, as some argue.

The minorities are a minority; that in many ways is the essence of their problem. All the blacks, Puerto Ricans and Mexican-Americans together are not a fifth of society. And since an outrageously disproportionate percentage of these people is poor, their political effect is even less than their numbers. For poverty is politically debilitating and saps the physical and civic energy required for participation in public life. So the poor register, vote and campaign less than any other group, and are consequently underrepresented at every level of government. Even if the minorities went over to a fourth party en masse, that would not begin to create a national majority.

Moreover—and here I am relying primarily on data about the blacks—there is no sign that the minorities are ready to desert the Democrats for a fourth party. In 1968, for instance, Dick Gregory and Eldridge Cleaver were on the ballot in some states, yet more than 90 per cent of the blacks voted for Humphrey, even though they were more antiwar than any other group. Why?

I suspect that the answer is found in a pattern one could notice in the days of Malcolm X's greatest popularity. Malcolm undoubtedly had a great resonance within the black community because he articulated bitter, strangled emotions that many people felt but could not utter. But he did not succeed organizationally because those same people did not believe that he had found a practical, political way to defend their everyday interests. And today there are probably many blacks who share the racial pride of the Panthers and admire their intransigence (but not, I think, their attitude that Robert Kennedy's murder marked the death of just another pig or their adulation for Stalin, Mao and the North Korean dictator, Kim Il Sung). Again, these people understand that the gains they have made inside the Democratic party are going to be the source of black political power in the foreseeable future.

Similarly, the Mexican-Americans who have joined together in La Raza Unida, which could be one of the most important insurgencies in years, are not nearly numerous enough to change national politics on their own. And they are fighting for such minimal decencies as jobs and housing and union organization; they, like the blacks, cannot afford, as the college sons and daughters of the affluent can, to devote 5 or 10 years to gesture politics.

Finally there are the liberal Republicans, usually symbolized by John V. Lindsay and John Gardner. The Republican party is the party of American business. As a result, its liberal wing tends to seek reforms within the rather narrow limits of the status quo; it represents, if I may try to put a little content into a New Leftist curse, a brand of corporate liberalism. The left wing of this current might well be defined by the Urban Coalition: a sophisticated, sincere, socially conscious organization that seeks to solve our crises by having the Government underwrite and work with the private sector. However, even the most humane and shrewd manipulation of the private market is not going to provide every American with the decent dwelling Congress first solemnly promised him in 1949 or with a well-paid job. Those goals demand a vast increase in planned public investment. When liberal Republicans begin to face up to this fact—as Mayor Lindsay seems to have done—they lose their base in the Republican party.

There is not, in short, a large constituency of nominal Republicans who are cryptoradicals. There are a good many decent people of that party's liberal wing who will join in a campaign against the war, but not many who are recruits for a fourth party of the left.

So even the most optimistic assumptions about a fourth party's ability to win over middle-class activists, minorities and liberal Republicans do not produce a majority. And a more realistic view of the percentages of those groups it is likely to attract suggests that it would be voluntarily condemning itself to a permanent minority status. But if it cannot win the Presidency or Congress in the foreseeable future, it could help re-elect Richard Nixon and strengthen the Dixiecrat-Republican coalition in Congress. At great sacrifice and with great enthusiasm and idealism, it could have the effect of defeating liberal Democrats running for the White House or Congress.

And if the fourth party were able to pick up significant strength in a Presidential election, the only alliance it could make to increase its power would be with the liberal Humphreyites (it could hardly coalesce with the Nixon or Wallace forces). In other words, having split the left and given the right an excellent opportunity to win, it would discover that the only coalition open to it was the one it had disdained in the first place. Since the enormous risks of such an undertaking are not justified, I reject the proposal for a fourth party.

What the nation needs is not just a new party of conscience and ideas, but a new party that can win as well. Programs are easy enough to write, but national majorities are hard to organize. At present, the only possibility of creating one is to reunite the liberal supporters of Hubert Humphrey, the Kennedy and McCarthy antiwarriors and the minorities on the basis of a common domestic program and the immediate task of averting a national shift to the right this November. And

I see that *ad hoc* coalition as having the potential, after the tragedy in Vietnam, of winning and so transforming the Democratic party that it becomes, in fact if not in name, a new party.

Clearly the most controversial element in my analysis—unconscionable, some might say—is the contention that the liberal Humphreyites (primarily the labor movement) must play an important role in a progressive new coalition. There are three major reasons why middle-class liberals and radicals do not understand the necessity of this reconciliation: the war in Vietnam, race and ignorance.

The war is the simplest of these factors to describe and the most difficult to deal with politically. Most, but not all, of the big unions have supported the Vietnam policies of Lyndon Johnson and Richard Nixon. In this I suspect that they have reflected the sentiments of their members, who, for a number of reasons—the knowledge that Communism does not permit genuine trade unionism, the influence of hard-line Catholic anti-Communism, national ties to countries ruled by Communist dictatorships in Eastern Europe, the conditions of working-class life, etc.—are more hawk than dove. They have been wrong, in my opinion, with regard to the horror in Southeast Asia and the profoundly conservative consequences it has had for American politics.

So long as the Vietnam tragedy dominates our national politics, I do not see the possibility of the basic kind of realignment I am proposing. But I do see the opportunity to prepare, even now, for that postwar period in which domestic priorities will be crucial and the agreement on social issues among the labor-movement liberals, the middle-class antiwarriors and the minorities will provide a basis for transforming the party system. In November, 1970, for instance, the A.F.L.-C.I.O., to its credit, will be giving enthusiastic support to the senatorial doves who are also liberal on such questions as health care and housing. And if the peace movement could overcome some of its middle-class prejudices about unions (more on that in a moment) we would have a very good chance to start rebuilding a majority coalition during the next several months.

But then there is the issue of race, which is complicated and more difficult to describe than Vietnam since the labor movement contains elements which are very bad and very good on this question. The unions have their share of conscious racists. And there is a conservative tradition, particularly in the building trades, whereby one ethnic group wins monopoly control over an occupation and defends it against all comers. This strategy, which has been used by the Irish against the Italians and vice versa, has now been turned against the blacks. It is being challenged by reformers in the unions and by angry militants on the outside.

The problem is that most of the middle-class critics of the labor movement do not know that these patterns of intolerable discrimination exist in a declining minority of the unions and almost exclusively in the old-fashioned strongholds of craft organizations. For the dominant type of union in America today, the mass-production union organized on an industrial basis, is the most integrated institution in the entire society and has unquestionably done more to subvert the economic bases of racism than any other force. For a generation now, these unions have been insisting on equal pay for equal work and access to jobs for all. That is why in some basic industries like auto and steel the labor force is around 25 per cent black, and it also explains why the scandalous gap between black and white wages that is so marked for the country as a whole hardly exists in Michigan, where the United Auto Workers play such an important role.

Indeed Brendan Sexton of the U.A.W. has suggested—rightly, I think—that in 10 years industrial unions will be the most important centers of black power. For the increasing percentage of Negroes in these organizations has already been reflected in the election of black officers. Moreover, when the war in Vietnam ends, there will be an even greater convergence of black and trade-union concerns. At that point, labor will be the largest and most decisive movement calling for those full-employment and social-spending policies which alone will put black America to work.

But the ignorance of the middle class could keep these hopeful trends from working themselves out. Most of the issue-oriented activists, passionately concerned with social questions, are not aware of one of the most fundamental facts of American political life: that the largest, most effective force for social change is, and has been for some years, the labor movement. When it is a question of electing a President or of rounding up votes for Medicare, national health insurance, housing, voter rights or Supreme Court nominations, the union lobbyists are the major liberal force. They have more strength than the churches, students and the liberal and radical organizations put together.

This fact became particularly apparent in 1968. At the moment of his nomination, Hubert Humphrey was effectively deserted by some of his major supporters; the machine professionals, like Mayor Daley, and the Johnson Southerners were convinced that they had a loser on their hands and did practically nothing for him. As a result, in a good many states the Humphrey campaign and the trade unions were almost identical, for it was not until late in the battle that a significant number of McCarthy and Kennedy people rallied to the Vice President. Labor, which has been declared moribund by most intellectuals in recent years, came very close to electing a President of the United States single-handedly.

That is why Theodore White, who had all but ignored the unions in his accounts of earlier campaigns, was so struck by their effectiveness in 1968. The A.F.L.-C.I.O., he reported, registered 4.6 million voters, printed 5.5 million leaflets in Washington and 60 million in various locals, and provided 72,225 canvassers and 94,457 volunteers on election day.

But then the middle-class antilaborites have a second line

of defense. The trade unionists, one is told, are hopelessly old-fashioned men whose attitudes can never transcend their nostalgic New Dealism, and the solutions of the thirties hardly apply to the seventies. Here again there is a sophisticated ignorance, abetted in this instance by an American press which devotes little space to the organization of so many millions of workers. In three conventions during the sixties, the A.F.L.-C.I.O. adopted a sweeping program which goes far beyond anything proposed in the days of Franklin Roosevelt and is specific about how to reconstruct this society in a way the intellectuals might emulate.

At the 1963 convention, the A.F.L. endorsed national economic planning; in 1965 there was another proposal for a national planning agency and advocacy of a massive commitment to rebuild the cities and a peacetime G.I. Bill; and in 1967, George Meany told the delegates that "increasingly the problems of our members . . . are not so much problems of the work place itself, but problems of environment and problems of living and raising a family in today's complex, crowded, urbanized and suburbanized society." At this moment the fact that national health insurance is on the political agenda is, in considerable measure, a result of the work of the A.F.L.-C.I.O. and the late Walter Reuther.

Am I then suggesting that the worker, far from being the reactionary slob (or near fascist) of the chic stereotype, is a secret social democrat? Among the best and the most talented of the unionists that is fairly accurate. They do not speak in a socialist idiom, yet the program they adopted in the sixties —and support politically every day with the power Theodore White described—is roughly comparable to the action program of the European social-democratic parties. In the case of the less politically conscious rank-and-file, matters get somewhat more complicated, not the least because there is often a contradiction between the union member's personal opinions and prejudices and his political behavior.

Middle-class liberalism and radicalism are in essence based

upon position-taking and debate. It is assumed that one strives for a one-to-one correspondence between inner conviction and political action; to admit that self-interest intervened would be shameful. This ethical view of politics is extremely valuable, and it should be the privilege of every citizen. But it isn't, and for good economic reasons. It is precisely because the grinding, everyday problems of making a living have been basically solved that the middle-class reformer can pay such attention to his conscience and to the issues. Most Americans can't afford that attitude.

For workers, politics must serve mundane but crucial ends, above all the maintenance of a full-employment economy. So in 1968 workers with considerable Wallace sentiment voted for Humphrey. They placed their economic interest above their prejudices. Indeed there is no question that the most effective anti-Wallace force in 1968 was the labor movement. But this predominance of economics over other interests is not ordained on high and forever. If the middle-class reformers persist in their barely concealed contempt for working people, they may help drive the union men to the right. Meany's angry comment on the New Left last month indicates that exasperation toward the ultra-activists already exists at the highest levels.

And Richard Nixon is preparing to welcome labor defectors who might be thus infuriated by their former liberal and radical allies. He has received a report from Assistant Secretary of Labor Jerome M. Rosow on the economic and social problems that bedevil blue-collar workers: They can't send their children to college without great financial strain; their jobs have lost status; they feel threatened by blacks. And he is clearly going to try to appeal to the most conservative trends among the unionists so as to end their alienation from the Republican party. In "The Real Majority," a new study of American politics, Richard M. Scammon and Ben J. Wattenberg suggest that if the President can cope with the pocketbook issues he has a chance to exploit the rampant fears of the society and win over his traditional enemies among the workers.

The middle-class activists would also aid Mr. Nixon in this historic attempt to build a new, reactionary majority if they pursued a fourth party. But if they would transcend their own college-educated parochialism, they could help create a progressive majority. For if they and the unionists and the minorities would realize their common concerns in domestic politics, the result could be an anti-Nixon, anticonservative coalition in this fall's election. And once the war is over, these groups could rout the Dixiecrats and machine pols in the Democratic party and in that way build a new party.

But a warning is in order. If such a new party does emerge, it must be a genuine coalition or it will fall apart. I am indebted to Kevin Phillips, the theorist of Richard Nixon's Southern strategy, for emphasizing this point in a recent column. Phillips, referring to Eugene McCarthy's article . . . and to reports of a speech of mine making some of the points discussed here, said I was more correct than the Senator because a fourth-party movement would indeed help Nixon. But we are both really wrong, he said, for even if the left were to win the Democratic party, the victorious McCarthyites would not be able to carry the country.

Phillips is quite right. If the peace activists conceive of the struggle within the Democratic party as bringing them alone the victory, the party will inevitably lose. The problem is to unite the liberal-labor Humphreyites, the Kennedy and McCarthy veterans and the minorities. And that will require forbearance on all sides, a search for a genuine equilibrium in the reformed party, not the organization of a faction fight.

If I may conclude on an autobiographical note, as the chairman of the Socialist party of the United States I wish all that I have just written were not true. I would prefer it if Gene

Debs had fulfilled his dream and led the Socialists from the founding convention in 1901, through the great campaign of 1912, onward and upward to become a mass labor party of the democratic left. I wish Norman Thomas could have built on those almost one million votes of 1932 and helped create that broad coalition he sought to the left of the New Deal. But these things did not come to pass for reasons that are deeply embedded in American history (and too complex to bring up here).

And so those of us who see the need of a truly radical restructuring of the society have to have the courage of our convictions. To seek the transformation of the Democratic party, to emphasize the need for coalition and even forbearance, to insist upon the crucial relevance of working people to the future of the country—these things are not as exhilarating and satisfying as writing the perfect program and summoning the convinced to an uncompromising banner. But they might actually change the United States of America, and therefore they are the most radical things we can do.

ELECTIONS AND VOTING

The literature in the field of American voting behavior and electoral processes is vast and fast growing. This is not to say that the specific endeavors undertaken in this area necessarily build on the knowledge gained through other studies or that there has as yet been devised a given theory or methodology for understanding such behavior. The many studies of American voting behavior that have been done in recent years testify, however, to the realization of the importance of this area for the understanding of the American governmental and political process.

The act of voting is perhaps the most useful and easily observable political phenomenon through which we are able to study man, the political animal, as he responds to stimuli, makes decisions, and finally, acts or chooses not to act. Voting behavior serves as a basis for such study in that it is a concrete and regular event involving large numbers of people, whose results may have far-reaching consequences for the entire social context. Naturally the act of voting and the electoral process merit study in and of themselves. In addition to the purposes just mentioned, the implications of such research raise questions that cut deeply into the fiber of classical liberal democratic thinking.

Thus the question of "why" people in fact vote as they do is central to students of political, social, and behavioral science and is the one to which Professors Campbell, Converse, Miller, and Stokes address themselves. The other selection provides an insightful analysis of the 1968 American Presidential election by three British journalists, Lewis Chester, Godfrey Hodgson, and Bruce Page.

THE DYNAMICS OF MASS PERCEPTS

ANGUS CAMPBELL / PHILIP E. CONVERSE /
WARREN E. MILLER / DONALD E. STOKES

The materials we have reviewed disclose the elements of presidential politics, not as they were, but as the public perceived them in the Eisenhower years. Taken together, the cognitive and affective themes recorded in our interviews suggest the "sense" the electorate made of the objects it acted toward in two elections. When they are laid against what we know of the objects themselves, the images found in these interviews suggest, too, some general ideas about the factors that have shaped their content.

Generalization and the Permanence of Objects

The individual voter sees the several elements of national politics as more than a collection of discrete, unrelated objects. After all, they are parts of one political system and are connected in the real world by a variety of relations that are visible in some degree to the electorate. A *candidate* is the nominee of his *party;* party and candidate are oriented to the same *issues* or *groups,* and so forth. Moreover, we may assume that the individual strives to give order and coherence to his image of these objects. As a means of achieving order,

---

Angus Campbell, Philip E. Converse, Warren E. Miller, and Donald E. Stokes, *The American Voter,* © 1964, by permission of John Wiley & Sons Inc., pp. 24, 26–30.

the transfer of cognitive attributes and affective values from one object to another undoubtedly plays an important role. A good deal of psychological research leads us to assume that under certain conditions the properties that one political element is perceived to have will be generalized to another, or that the emotion directed toward one object will be extended to a second. The "conditions" of this transfer may be exceedingly simple—as two elements bearing the same party label—although in the intellective processes of the most sophisticated, politically involved portion of the electorate they are probably very complex.

The fact that one element of politics may color another in both a cognitive and an affective sense is of especial importance because political objects enter public awareness at different times and have greatly different degrees of permanence. The world of politics is full of novelty, yet some of its elements persist for relatively long periods. Moreover, the features of these objects that are most widely known may heighten the sense of their unchanging character. At the simplest level, the elements of politics, like so much else in the external world, are known to the individual by name, and these symbols are of considerable cognitive importance to the electorate. What is more, a good deal else about the objects of politics may be characterized by symbols, such as the terms "New Deal" or "Fair Deal," whose persistence through time may give the objects an unchanging aspect despite wide changes in their "real" properties.

The most enduring objects of the political environment are of course the Republican and Democratic Parties, and the relative permanence of our major parties has two main consequences for the dynamics of popular attitude. First, the novel objects of presidential politics may receive a marked initial coloration by reason of their association with one or the other of the parties. The frequencies of [the] [t]able [below] show that nearly a thousand references to party were among the responses to the two new candidates for President

References to Candidates in Terms of Party

	1952	1956
Favorable to Eisenhower	121	57
Unfavorable to Eisenhower	220	162
Favorable to Stevenson	264	202
Unfavorable to Stevenson	360	64
Totals	965	485

in 1952. Second, perception and feeling that were initially associated with other objects may survive in the image of the parties after the elements from which they arose have left the political environment. To a great extent the image of the Republican and Democratic Parties in 1952 and 1956 *was* the public's response to issues and events of the past generation, whereas popular perceptions of Eisenhower and Stevenson seemed to be fashioned of more current materials.

The Threshold of Awareness

A great deal of change in the electorate's map of politics can be explained in terms of what has and what has not penetrated the public consciousness.[1] In the electorate as a whole the level of attention to politics is so low that what the public is exposed to must be highly visible—even stark—if it is to have an impact on opinion. The evidential basis of this remark must await the discussion of later chapters, but its correctness is strongly implied by some of the frequencies we have examined. For example, despite a concentration on foreign

---

[1] It is here that information is most needed on communication variables. Awareness is partly a matter of motivation and predisposition: the individual is aware of things he wants to attend. But it is also a matter of sheer currency or visibility, as the success of modern advertising suggests. Hence, the decisions of those who control communication are partial determinants of public awareness, and more information is needed about them.

issues by Mr. Stevenson, which must have been at least as great as that of any candidate in this country, the public was largely unaware of his positions. Nor in some respects did Mr. Eisenhower fare better as President. Despite the fact that his action or inaction as Chief Executive had wide impact on the course of our affairs at home, the public connected him with issues of domestic policy only to a slight degree in 1956.

Some implications of the low salience that most of national politics has for the electorate may seem fairly novel. For example, it is not unlikely that most new Presidents take office without their stance towards issues or groups having had much impact on popular attitude. What perceptions the public has are likely to be highly derivative carry-overs from perceptions of the President's party. In this respect the extent in 1952 of public knowledge of Eisenhower's orientation in world affairs, arising as it did out of the impact of his career as a soldier-diplomat, must have been quite unusual. It is largely *after* the President has taken office and has assumed the position of matchless visibility in American politics that his image begins to acquire the large number of issue themes we might expect. The acquisition may be dramatically sudden, as it probably was in the case of Roosevelt; it may be slow and uneven, as it clearly was in the case of Eisenhower.

The Social Bases of Stability

The stability of mass percepts depends importantly on how well they are bound into the social fabric. To make this point clear let us return to the problem of the impact on subsequent attitude of the wars in which America has been involved. We have remarked that the world wars of the twentieth century did surprisingly little to remake the partisan perceptions held by the electorate. Of course these wars had a deep impress on American thinking in a variety of ways. But they left in their wake relatively few issues that would continue to divide the electorate, and, what is most important, except perhaps for the alienation of those of German ethnicity [2] from the administration party, these issues failed to coincide well with stable groupings within the population. The impact of the Civil War was very different, opening as it did issues of intense partisan contest, which coincided very closely with enduring regional and racial fissures in the social order. The stability of percepts arising out of the Civil War experience undoubtedly was greatly reinforced by the fact that they became enmeshed in conflict between enduring social groupings.

Additional weight is lent this view if we consider the group themes associated with the parties and candidates in the Eisenhower years. We have said that these references usually implied a status dimension: the Democratic Party was approved for championing lower status groups, the Republican Party disapproved for failing to do so or for favoring high status groups. The group themes associated with the two parties actually increased in vitality between 1952 and 1956; the vitality of these group-related percepts may be due in part to the fact that they are supported by the mechanisms that conserve social norms. Here the group may serve not only as an element of politics to which parties and candidates adopt some attitude; it may also serve as a reference group whose perceived opinion reinforces the individual's own perception of what is the stance toward the group of other actors in the political environment.

To say this much is to raise the broader question of how perceptions of the political world differ between the groupings that make up the whole electorate. The measurements of this chapter have been of the composite image held by the total population, but the fact of differences between groups

---

[2] For evidence on this point see Samuel Lubell, *The Future of American Politics* (Harper and Brothers, New York, 1951), especially Chapter 7, "The Myth of Isolationism," pp. 129–157.

is clear enough. Although a survey of these differences is beyond the scope of discussion here, we may note that the stability of the partisan perceptions dividing the electorate will depend in part on the extent to which these divisions coincide with enduring social groupings.

AND THEN THERE WAS THE ONE

LEWIS CHESTER / GODFREY HODGSON / BRUCE PAGE

> "You know, Dick, a shift of only fourteen thousand votes, and we would have been the heroes, and they would have been the bums."
>
> —LEONARD HALL,
> *Richard Nixon's campaign manager in 1960,
> after election of that year.*

When Nixon came down to the ballroom of the Waldorf-Astoria hotel in New York, just after eleven-thirty A.M. on November 6 to make his victory statement, it was natural that he should choose the language of national unity. He produced the famous Presidential seal which his daughter had made for him in crewelwork. He said that the object of his Administration would be to build bridges. And he took as his motto the sign which he had seen held up to him during the campaign in Deshler, Ohio, imploring him to "Bring Us Together."

It sounded rather moving at the time, but the symbolism was treacherous, as it is apt to be. Thirteen-year-old Vicki Cole, the Methodist minister's daughter who had waved the sign, had not made it herself. Her own original thought, written on a banner that had been lost in the crush, had been

---

From *An American Melodrama* by Lewis Chester, Godfrey Hodgson, and Bruce Page. Copyright © 1969 by Times Newspapers Ltd. All rights reserved. Reprinted by permission of The Viking Press, Inc., and André Deutsch Limited.

more partisan. "LBJ Taught Us," she had written, "Vote Republican!" Worse, it also turned out that young Vicki had not been for Nixon at all. She thought both Nixon and Humphrey were "good men," but subsequently confessed shyly that her first favorite had been Robert Kennedy. Nixon had chosen to make Vicki Cole a symbol of the American people's aspirations for unity. In so far as one thirteen-year-old girl could fairly be taken as a symbol of anything, she was a far better symbol of something less anodyne: the fact that for a large majority of the American people, the result of the election was a foregone disappointment, because none of the nominated candidates was their first choice. Between them an assassin's bullets and the nominating convention system had seen to that.

The language of Nixon's speech was restrained, and he showed himself graceful toward his defeated opponent. "A great philosophy," he said,

> *is never won without defeat. It is always won without fear. What is important is that a man or a woman engage in battle, be in the arena, participate, and I hope that all of those who supported Mr. Humphrey will continue their interest in politics. They will perhaps be in the other party; we may be contesting again. Who knows?*

He gave no such invitation to the Wallace supporters. But he pledged that

> *this will be an open Administration, open to new ideas, open to men and women of both parties, open to critics as well as to those who support us.*

Proper obeisance was naturally made in the direction of various national figures: to Hubert Humphrey, for example, to ex-President Eisenhower, and to President Johnson. One figure, however, was conspicuously not mentioned: Nixon's own running mate.

That was understandable, too. For this was the moment for high thoughts and talk of national unity; and Governor Agnew had not only shown himself the specialist in below-the-belt politics: he had been specifically chosen to exploit national division, and his choice had been an integral part of Nixon's essential strategy. The election had not been won on promises of unity or reconciliation. It had been won by making a mathematical calculation that, as George Wallace had said, "there's more of us than there is of them." Early in the year, Richard Scammon had reminded Americans in danger of being bemused by the Kennedy and McCarthy campaigns that the majority of the electorate was made up of "the unyoung, the unblack, and the unpoor." Nixon had grasped that point. He had calculated that he could be elected without significant help from the poor, the foreign, the black, the angry, or the troubled, and he had been right. But it had been a desperately close thing.

In the end he had been elected by a smaller proportion of the voters—43.4 per cent—than any President since Woodrow Wilson in 1912. And this was not only because of the unavoidable competition of George Wallace. It was also true that a shockingly high proportion of the electorate remained indifferent to all the issues and all the candidates' attempts to engage their interest, and just plain didn't bother to vote. Voter participation has historically been far less keen in the United States than in Europe, where 75-to-80-per-cent turnouts are normal. Since 1948, however, the percentage of Americans voting had been creeping up, and the average for the five elections between 1948 and 1964 had edged above 60 per cent. Nineteen sixty-eight, in spite of all the excitement and the earnest importance of the issues, marked a pause in that improvement, and the final figure for participation was almost exactly the running post–World War II average: a fraction over 60 per cent. That meant that out of one hundred and twenty million Americans of voting age, roughly forty-eight million did not vote.

What happened to the missing forty-eight million? About four million could not vote because they were technically aliens, or were in prisons or mental hospitals. Another seven million were either sick or disabled. Three million were away from home, and another three million claimed they could not leave their jobs to vote. (These figures are projected from a Gallup survey carried out after the election.) No less than five million were prevented from voting in a *national* election by *state or local* residence requirements—a little-noticed anomaly of American Federalism. That left at least twenty-six million who did not vote essentially because they didn't want to or didn't bother to. ("At least," because there is no way of knowing how many of those who claimed they were unable to vote because they were away from home or at work might have managed to vote in other circumstances or in another country.) Of the twenty-six million, fifteen million were registered voters, but either didn't like any of the candidates or were totally uninterested. Ten million could have registered but didn't. And another one million failed to obtain absentee ballots. In other words, those who either didn't bother or didn't choose to vote amounted to at least 36 per cent of those who did, and perhaps more. For all the tumult and the shouting, the campaigns had failed to get through at all to more than a quarter of those who were not prevented from voting.

Nixon's campaign strategy had been low-key from the start. He knew that a high vote favors the Democrats, and he had aimed to keeping the excitement low. In terms of the proportion who voted, he had been successful. Even so, he came closer to losing than would have seemed possible a month before the election. Up to the eve of polling, John Mitchell continued to make blandly confident noises about a five-million plurality. But he knew better than that. His own polls, by Opinion Research Corporation, were telling him by then that Nixon would be lucky to scrape together enough popular votes to carry the Electoral College, and everything depended on where they were.

Exactly as Walter de Vries had foretold in September, the voters made their minds up later than ever in 1968. Blocks of voters were still swinging turbulently from one candidate to another in the last few days and hours. The big gap between Nixon and Humphrey disappeared startlingly fast. On the Friday before the election, Louis Harris reported Nixon leading 40–37. On the Sunday, Gallup reported 42–40. On election day, Harris reported the election "too close to call," but with Humphrey a nose ahead. Cautiously, after a traumatic year, all the pollsters agreed that opinion was so fluid that prediction was unsafe, and perhaps meaningless.

PUBLIC OPINION AND SOCIALIZATION

If "motivation" has become the key word in research into voting behavior, then "perception" should become its counterpart in studies of public opinion and socialization. It was almost half a century ago in his classic work *Public Opinion* that Walter Lippmann observed that public opinion is based on "pictures in our heads," as the actual political world is beyond our personal reach. As interest in this phenomenon grew, the question arose as to how an individual developed his perceptual framework through which later events are selectively screened. It is out of this avenue of inquiry that the now popular subfield of political socialization arose.

The main thrust of this research led to the discovery that children "learn" their political values—or at least the latent basis from which the manifestations of later political behavior would develop—at extremely early ages from their primary group, especially from their parents. This occurs in much the same way that small children develop other value, belief, and ethical systems. The educational system and peer group identifications at later stages in life tend to modify and/or reinforce aspects of the original political values and beliefs already internalized.

The selection by V. O. Key serves to illustrate this process, while that by Leon Festinger and his colleagues presents their psychological findings concerning beliefs and convictions.

THE FAMILY AND THE POLITICAL SYSTEM

V. O. KEY, JR.

The family is obviously a major agency in the formation of basic political attitude.[1] In addition to whatever qualities he inherits, the child acquires in the family circle social outlooks of varying political content and relevance. Some anthropologists ascribe fundamental characteristics of political systems to individual behavior resulting from specified child-rearing practices: swaddling or not, permissive or not, rigid toilet training or not, families child-centered or not, feeding by the clock or demand. Thus if the little monsters are fed whenever they yell, they are said to become, not apathetic nonvoters, but adults with confidence in their control of their environment and with a sense of efficacy in relation to those in authority.[2] Such interpretations lend themselves to statement with plausibility, but their persuasiveness evaporates once the sparseness of their support in systematic observation is perceived. The object here, though, is not to push the analysis back to the impact of family on personality. Rather,

---

Pages 293-295; 313-314 from *Public Opinion and American Democracy*, by V. O. Key, Jr. Copyright © 1961 by V. O. Key, Jr. Reprinted by permission of Alfred A. Knopf, Inc.

[1] See Herbert Hyman's admirable analysis of existing information about the topic: *Political Socialization* (Glencoe: Free Press; 1959).

[2] It might be as plausible to deduce that demand-feeding would produce adults who would complain loudly when even slightly frustrated and, hence, a political system in continuous and senseless turmoil. One of the troubles about Freudian psychology is that once a person begins to believe it, he can believe anything. For some Freudianism, see E. H. Erikson: *Childhood and Society* (New York: Norton; 1950).

it is to ascertain the relations, if any, between a limited number of family political characteristics and the political outlooks of offspring within the American political culture.

. . .

While the evidence about the bearing of family experience on the subsequent political activities and outlooks of children is scant, it is consistent with the view that the family must be regarded as a conserving factor in the political system. The family is conserving in that it tends to project into the future the prevailing pattern of social and occupational status with the associated political outlooks. It is conserving in that it tends to perpetuate the prevailing system of identifications with political parties and other politically relevant groups. To a degree offspring probably also take on attitudinal orientations in the general direction of those of their parents. Yet to say that the family is a conserving influence is not to say that it is necessarily conservative in the usage of our day. A radical father may also have a radical son, but collectively families tend to project the existent national pattern of party loyalties and to a lesser extent the existent attitudinal pattern on policy into the future where it becomes subject to reinforcement or alteration by new forces.[3] Families may or may not develop in the offspring an interest in and concern about politics. Doubtless the family indoctrinates the child with a variety of social norms and values some of which in the long run have an importance for the nature of the political order.[4]

This broad interpretation of the place of the family in the

---

[3] Alex Inkeles, on the basis of a study of Russian defectors, concludes that parents who have themselves undergone the experience of extreme social change may not, in rearing their own children, simply recapitulate their own experience but may attempt to adjust their child rearing practices "the better to prepare their children for the life" they expect "those children to lead."—"Social Change and Social Character: The Role of Parental Mediation," *Journal of Social Issues*, XI, 2 (1955), 12–23.

[4] See the provocative discussion, based on prolonged interviews with 15 New Haven adults, by Robert E. Lane: "Fathers and Sons: Foundations of Political Belief," *American Sociological Review*, XXIV (1959), 502–11.

political order receives recognition, if not verification, in the practices of revolutionary regimes—and reactionary regimes as well. Those orders—be they communist, fascist, Nazi, or whatnot—that seek to break with their political past establish special youth organizations to separate the young, even the very young, from family influences and to impress the new political orthodoxy upon the youth. And they may go to the contemptible extreme of converting the child into a political spy to ferret out parental deviationism.[5]

One of the most significant political functions of the family is almost completely missed as the few cases concerned slip through the tines of the apparatus for sampling national populations—the function of producing political leaders, political activists, politicians. Evidence on the sources from which political activists come, though thin, indicates that families of politicians, of public officials, of bureaucrats, and of officeholders contribute a disproportionate share of those who run for office and otherwise provide leadership within the community. It would be unexpected if full evidence established that this relationship did not prevail. Conspicuous political families—the Adamses, the Tafts, the Lodges, the Kennedys, the Roosevelts, the Longs, the Talmadges—come to mind, but doubtless sprinkled through the population are many families in which there runs a political activism of a less spectacular sort.

---

[5] The insistence of the Roman Catholic Church that children of mixed marriages be reared in the faith represents another practical recognition of the role of the family as the mold of the adult. The church fathers are skilled applied social scientists.

UNFULFILLED PROPHECIES AND DISAPPOINTED MESSIAHS

LEON FESTINGER / HENRY W. RIECKEN / STANLEY SCHACHTER

A man with a conviction is a hard man to change. Tell him you disagree and he turns away. Show him facts or figures and he questions your sources. Appeal to logic and he fails to see your point.

We have all experienced the futility of trying to change a strong conviction, especially if the convinced person has some investment in his belief. We are familiar with the variety of ingenious defenses with which people protect their convictions, managing to keep them unscathed through the most devastating attacks.

But man's resourcefulness goes beyond simply protecting a belief. Suppose an individual believes something with his whole heart; suppose further that he has a commitment to this belief, that he has taken irrevocable actions because of it; finally, suppose that he is presented with evidence, unequivocal and undeniable evidence, that his belief is wrong: what will happen? The individual will frequently emerge, not only unshaken, but even more convinced of the truth of his beliefs than ever before. Indeed, he may even show a new fervor about convincing and converting other people to his view.

How and why does such a response to contradictory evidence come about? This is the question on which this book

---

Leon Festinger, Henry W. Riecken, and Stanley Schachter, *When Prophecy Fails*. University of Minnesota Press, Minneapolis. © 1956 University of Minnesota. Reprinted by permission, pp. 3–6, 25–26.

focuses. We hope that, by the end of the volume, we will have provided an adequate answer to the question, an answer documented by data.

Let us begin by stating the conditions under which we would expect to observe increased fervor following the disconfirmation of a belief. There are five such conditions.

1. A belief must be held with deep conviction and it must have some relevance to action, that is, to what the believer does or how he behaves.

2. The person holding the belief must have committed himself to it; that is, for the sake of his belief, he must have taken some important action that is difficult to undo. In general, the more important such actions are, and the more difficult they are to undo, the greater is the individual's commitment to the belief.

3. The belief must be sufficiently specific and sufficiently concerned with the real world so that events may unequivocally refute the belief.

4. Such undeniable disconfirmatory evidence must occur and must be recognized by the individual holding the belief.

The first two of these conditions specify the circumstances that will make the belief resistant to change. The third and fourth conditions together, on the other hand, point to factors that would exert powerful pressure on a believer to discard his belief. It is, of course, possible that an individual, even though deeply convinced of a belief, may discard it in the face of unequivocal disconfirmation. We must, therefore, state a fifth condition specifying the circumstances under which the belief will be discarded and those under which it will be maintained with new fervor.

5. The individual believer must have social support. It is unlikely that one isolated believer could withstand the kind of disconfirming evidence we have specified. If, however, the believer is a member of a group of convinced persons who can support one another, we would expect the belief to be maintained and the believers to attempt to proselyte or to persuade nonmembers that the belief is correct.

These five conditions specify the circumstances under which increased proselyting would be expected to follow disconfirmation. Given this set of hypotheses, our immediate concern is to locate data that will allow a test of the prediction of increased proselyting. Fortunately, there have been throughout history recurring instances of social movements which do satisfy the conditions adequately. These are the millennial or messianic movements, a contemporary instance of which we shall be examining in detail in the main part of this volume. Let us see just how such movements do satisfy the five conditions we have specified.

Typically, millennial or messianic movements are organized around the prediction of some future events. Our conditions are satisfied, however, only by those movements that specify a date or an interval of time within which the predicted events will occur as well as detailing exactly what is to happen. Sometimes the predicted event is the second coming of Christ and the beginning of Christ's reign on earth; sometimes it is the destruction of the world through a cataclysm (usually with some select group slated for rescue from the disaster); or sometimes the prediction is concerned with particular occurrences that the Messiah or a miracle worker will bring about. Whatever the event predicted, the fact that its nature and the time of its happening are specified satisfies the third point on our list of conditions.

The second condition specifies strong behavioral commitment to the belief. This usually follows almost as a consequence of the situation. If one really believes a prediction (the first condition), for example, that on a given date the world will be destroyed by fire, with sinners being destroyed and the good being saved, one does things about it and makes certain preparations as a matter of course. These actions may range all the way from simple public declarations to the neglect of worldly things and the disposal of earthly possessions. Through such actions and through the mocking and scoffing of nonbelievers there is usually established a heavy commitment on the part of believers. What they do by way of preparation is difficult to undo, and the jeering of nonbelievers simply makes it far more difficult for the adherents to withdraw from the movement and admit that they were wrong.

Our fourth specification has invariably been provided. The predicted events have not occurred. There is usually no mistaking the fact that they did not occur and the believers know that. In other words, the unequivocal disconfirmation does materialize and makes its impact on the believers.

Finally, our fifth condition is ordinarily satisfied—such movements do attract adherents and disciples, sometimes only a handful, occasionally hundreds of thousands. The reasons why people join such movements are outside the scope of our present discussion, but the fact remains that there are usually one or more groups of believers who can support one another.

. . .

We can now turn our attention to the question of why increased proselyting follows the disconfirmation of a prediction. How can we explain it and what are the factors that will determine whether or not it will occur?

Since our explanation will rest upon one derivation from a general theory, we will first state the bare essentials of the theory which are necessary for this derivation. The full theory has wide implications and a variety of experiments have already been conducted to test derivations concerning such things as the consequences of decisions, the effects of producing forced compliance, and some patterns of voluntary exposure to new information. At this point, we shall draw out in detail only those implications that are relevant to the phenomenon of increased proselyting following disconfirmation of a prediction. For this purpose we shall introduce the concepts of consonance and dissonance.[1]

---

[1] The theory of dissonance and its implications are set forth in detail in a forthcoming book by Leon Festinger. [Editor's note: The book has since been published.]

Dissonance and consonance are relations among cognitions —that is, among opinions, beliefs, knowledge of the environment, and knowledge of one's own actions and feelings. Two opinions, or beliefs, or items of knowledge are *dissonant* with each other if they do not fit together—that is, if they are inconsistent, or if, considering only the particular two items, one does not follow from the other. For example, a cigarette smoker who believes that smoking is bad for his health has an opinion that is dissonant with the knowledge that he is continuing to smoke. He may have many other opinions, beliefs, or items of knowledge that are consonant with continuing to smoke but the dissonance nevertheless exists too.

Dissonance produces discomfort and, correspondingly, there will arise pressures to reduce or eliminate the dissonance. Attempts to reduce dissonance represent the observable manifestations that dissonance exists. Such attempts may take any or all of three forms. The person may try to change one or more of the beliefs, opinions, or behaviors involved in the dissonance; to acquire new information or beliefs that will increase the existing consonance and thus cause the total dissonance to be reduced; or to forget or reduce the importance of those cognitions that are in a dissonant relationship.

If any of the above attempts are to be successful, they must meet with support from either the physical or the social environment. In the absence of such support, the most determined efforts to reduce dissonance may be unsuccessful.

1

INTEREST GROUPS

To many citizens the term "interest group" or "pressure group" is the closest thing in the political dictionary to a four-letter word. For many years professional political scientists shared the same attitude. Convinced that these groups were the bastions of special interests (which in many cases they were and are), and therefore antidemocratic, students of government tended to ignore them in their research and writings. A reversal of this attitude has occurred only in the last two decades.

The arguments against pressure groups are fairly well known. What is not so widely understood is the useful set of functions that pressure groups perform in the political system. They provide many Americans with an added voice in Washington and the various state capitals. In addition they serve as a vital source of information to legislators. By providing this service, they can often save a harried senator or representative much time and effort. Finally, interest groups are often responsible for the initiation of what has turned out to be a vast body of useful laws such as consumer, civil rights, farm, trade, and labor legislation.

In the first selection Professor Mahood examines whether or not pressure groups are compatible with democracy, and in the second the oil-gas lobby is analyzed to determine what is its actual power in the political process.

PRESSURE GROUPS: A THREAT TO DEMOCRACY?

H. R. MAHOOD

There has been an increase in the amount, tempo and intensity of pressure group activity in recent decades. Many and various reasons may be given for this. Certainly the advantages of organization have become obvious to workers, farmers, Negroes and others in the attainment of their respective goals.[1] Population increase has given rise to more and newer aspirations which are encompassed and furthered by new organizations. Technological advances on many fronts have produced new and highly differentiated economic and social groupings with problems which may or may not be completely resolved through existing organizations. Also, the appearance of new organizations has threatened and endangered older ones bringing about realignments and consolidations among them. Finally governmental policy-making has contributed to the creation of groups. The Tennessee Valley Authority, for example, gave rise to various groups in the Tennessee River Valley on both the state and local level which benefited from the program. Likewise, the Rural Electrification Administration and its programs of public power stimulated a myriad of professional and business organizations connected with public power.[2] Such factors as these, then, have

---

Reprinted by permission of Charles Scribner's Sons from *Pressure Groups in American Politics*, pages 295–303, by H. R. Mahood. Copyright © 1967 Charles Scribner's Sons.
[1] V. O. Key, *Politics, Parties, and Pressure Groups*, 5th ed. (New York: Thomas Y. Crowell, 1964), develops the establishment and growth of some of the leading pressure groups in American politics and their activities.
[2] For a brief discussion of the impact of the Tennessee Valley Authority

been generative in the proliferation of pressure groups and their activities in American politics.

The multiplication and differentiation of pressure groups have been matched by a refinement of various techniques and greater use thereof to maximize political effectiveness. Groups are turning, for example, to more extensive use of television along with wider use of radio and the press. Coupled with these are greater use of the mails, attendance at a variety of organization conventions, dissemination of auto bumper stickers, wider personal contacts with public and private officials, use of billboards and any other media to both convince and exploit those susceptible to pressures. More and more of group budgets are expended not only on public media but also for the hiring and retention of certain functional specialists such as writers, researchers and public relations specialists.

Pressure groups have also continued to exploit the American political system which bestows certain advantages on them *vis-à-vis* government in their continuing competition for public power and support.[3] As previously mentioned, pressure groups have ready access to communications and other media. This access is more privileged and available to them than it is to government. Pressure groups also have more continuity both in policy and personnel, better paid personnel, more secrecy in operation and lower public visibility. They also have less public accountability and freer selection of targets for their pressures than government and its agencies have.

These events have greatly contributed to the growing political power and significance of pressure groups in the political system and their influence on the workings of that system. With their position and importance established, it is only

---

and the Rural Electrification Administration and their political stimulation on the local level, see Arthur M. Schlesinger, Jr., *The Politics of Upheaval* (Boston: Houghton-Mifflin, 1960), pp. 362–384.

[3] Donald C. Blaisdell, *American Democracy Under Pressure* (New York: The Ronald Press, 1957).

natural that they have become subjects of controversy. By being able to influence policies which not only affect their own members but also non-members and rival groups, they are alternately criticized and praised or viewed with suspicion, mistrust or approbation.

Some of the more serious criticisms leveled at pressure groups and their activities are first, that they are not democratically organized. Critics charge that the rank and file members have little to do with the selection of group officers and leaders and even less with policy-making. A small clique, it is argued, dominates the group hierarchy and operates at times in a manner totally indifferent to the hopes and aspirations of the membership as a whole.[4] Group meetings and conventions are rigged by leadership so as to allow little time and opportunity for the general membership to question policies or leaders. Little is known by the members in regard to total membership, financial affairs or operating procedures.

Second, groups are severely criticized because they put their own interests above the "public" interest. They tend to operate on the "Me First Principle." They are so blinded by their own narrow interests that they are totally incapable of realizing other legitimate interests may exist. They are simply incapable of rising above their own selfishness and working for the good of the entire nation.[5]

A third criticism of groups is their use of certain techniques. It is often expressed by group critics that they use questionable methods—bribing, deceiving, cheating, falsifying—in obtaining their objectives. By engaging in such unethical tactics, they engender suspicion and fear in the minds of public officials. Their use of pressure mail, telephone calls, telegrams and personal visits is further evidence of the lengths to which groups will go in order to get what they want.

---

[4] Grant McConnel, "The Spirit of Private Government," *American Political Science Review* (September, 1958), pp. 754–770.
[5] Stuart Chase, *Democracy Under Pressure* (New York: The Twentieth Century Fund, 1945), p. 4.

In the eyes of their detractors, these criticisms add up to a powerful indictment of pressure groups and their value to the American political system. They do more harm than good by dividing the American people through their tactics, continually confusing them with their slanted propaganda, and inhibiting effective governmental action by constantly badgering and harrassing public officials with conflicting claims.

Various proposals and remedies, both formal and informal, have been offered by critics to deal with the problems of pressure groups. The most prominent of the formal type, perhaps, has been regulation. Laws have existed on both the national and state levels for some time dealing with libel, bribery, slander and fraudulent use of mails. Also, toward the end of the nineteenth century, more and more states passed laws regulating lobbying activities by various private organizations. In 1874, Alabama outlawed bribery, and in 1877, Georgia wrote into its constitution a provision that "lobbying was a crime." In the 1890's, Massachusetts legalized public exposure of pressure tactics, and soon Wisconsin and New York followed its lead. Today other states such as Illinois, California, and Texas have enacted recent legislation regulating pressure activities in their own particular way.[6]

National regulation of pressure groups did not begin until 1946 when Congress passed the Congressional Reorganization Act (P.L. 79-601). Title II of this act called for regulation of certain types of political activity by pressure spokesmen. This law applied to "any person who solicits, collects, or receives money to be used principally to influence Federal legislation." Thus a lobbyist (or pressure spokesman) was required to register with the Clerk of the House of Represen-

---

[6] A recent approach to the regulation of pressure groups on the state level is that of California. For the recommendations of the California investigations see, California Legislative Assembly, Interior Committee on Governmental Efficiency and Economy, *Federal and State Laws on Lobbying* (Sacramento, 1950). Also the Reports of this Committee, 1955-57.

tatives and the Secretary of the State and file financial statements and other information regarding their employers and the lobbying they engaged in. Penalties were provided for non-compliance.

This law, however, did not impose any restrictions on the general activities of groups or their representatives. Nor did it impose any financial restrictions. It was simply making as a matter of public record many of the behind-the-scenes legislative operators, including lawyers, former congressmen and former federal officials who were perceptive in the ways of influencing legislation. It turned the public spotlight on many individuals who had operated either covertly and/or discretely through contacts with various key congressmen influential in the legislative process. Both the public and some congressmen had little knowledge as to who these persons were and even less of the money being spent by them and who they represented.

Although the passage of this law was helpful to the public and many congressmen in revealing certain lobbying techniques of pressure groups, it was not in force long before it became clear to many that the law was defective. Its vague phraseology, for example, raised questions as to who should register as a lobbyist. Further, the act made no provision for a central enforcement agency which would supervise compliance, investigate the accuracy of statements filed and publicize this information. In practice, both the Clerk of the House of Representatives and the Secretary of the Senate act as little more than depositories for filed statements. These offices have neither the facilities nor the staffs to properly analyze, verify and catalogue the filed information. Finally, recent criticism claims the law did not go far enough. In light of expanded activities by pressure groups before executive agencies, critics charge that the law should have originally covered executive lobbying. Because of these statutory shortcomings, it is small wonder that the lobbying law soon became involved in litigation. The definitive court interpreta-

LOBBY SPENDING FOR YEARS 1961-1965*

CATEGORY	1961 Reporting Groups	1961 Amount Spent	1962 Reporting Groups	1962 Amount Spent	1963 Reporting Groups	1963 Amount Spent	1964 Reporting Groups	1964 Amount Spent	1965 Reporting Groups	1965 Amount Spent
Business	171	$1,672,259	170	$1,836,126	153	$1,521,600	147	$1,361,427.81	154	$1,472,863.72
Citizens	52	494,175	50	531,002	51	707,333	57	1,065,197.29	64	836,113.02
Employee and Labor	40	892,569	37	945,206	36	1,130,124	33	945,071.32	31	1,094,782.86
Farm	22	367,238	22	412,524	21	405,849	23	365,471.81	25	419,633.65
Military and Veterans	10	133,735	6	141,991	5	140,180	6	154,493.05	7	167,634.81
Professional	17	426,120	19	344,455	20	318,519	21	331,616.11	23	1,493,384.96
Total	312	$3,986,096	304	$4,211,304	286	$4,223,605	287	$4,223,277.39	304	$5,484,413.02

* Congressional Quarterly Service, "Legislators and Lobbyists," (Washington, D.C.: Congressional Quarterly Service), p. 39. Figures for 1964 and 1965 were added to the original table.

tion of the law came in 1954 in the case *United States* v. *Harriss*.[7]

Another formal approach to the problems of pressure groups consists of measures to strengthen governmental organization. It is claimed by their critics, that pressure groups have become significantly influential because various governmental institutions have neither the strength nor the know-how to neutralize pressure penetration. Some congressmen are especially susceptible to group activities while others are not; some pressure groups have extensive legislative influence while others do not; and certain legislative procedures help some groups and hurt others. Congress needs proper reorganization and equipment to do a proper job in dealing with pressure activities. Countervailing powers within the legislature are needed to minimize pressures and protect the public interest.

Actually, some basic changes have already been made, for example, in congressional machinery. In 1946, recommendations in the Legislative Reorganization Act produced long-needed congressional reforms and reorganization.[8] Committee reorganization, professional staffing, public hearings and improved bill-drafting are indicative of congressional modernization and streamlining. Also, such thorny legislative problems as seniority, party discipline and filibustering are also under periodic review. Whether or not Congress, in-

---

[7] 347 U.S. 612 (1954). This case grew out of certain lobbying activities by a New York cotton broker, Robert M. Harriss. Harriss was charged in violation of the law being neither registered nor reporting his lobbying activities to influence legislation. A lower federal court ruled the lobbying law unconstitutional on the grounds that it was too vague and indefinite to meet the requirements of due process, that the registration and reporting requirements violated the First Amendment and that certain of the penalty processes violated the constitutional right to petition Congress. On appeal, the Supreme Court ruled in 1954 that the lobbying law was constitutional though construing it narrowly.

[8] Joint Committee on the Organization of Congress, *Report*, 79th Cong., 2nd Sess., September 2, 1946.

corporating all these and other contemplated changes, would be a formidable and effective barrier against incessant group pressures can only be an object of conjecture. . . .

At the same time pressure groups are active before the national legislature, they may also be bringing pressure on the executive. Like Congress, the executive branch has also undergone reorganization and strengthening since the end of World War II.[9] Recruitment policies have been changed and improved and salaries have been raised continuously to make them more competitive with private industry. The civil service system has continued to be extended. These policies have upgraded public service and thereby, attracted higher caliber people to government service. Is this type of establishment, however, to be completely impervious to group demands or merely designate which group demands can be incorporated into executive policies and which cannot?

One other formal approach to the pressure group problem is functional representation. This is an essentially positive approach whereas regulation and the strengthening of governmental institutions are essentially negative. The functional approach emphasizes the utility of pressure groups within the political system and the contribution they can make to it. Functional representation does exist today in France. An Economic and Social Council exists within the French governmental framework which represents the most important economic and social pressure groups within the nation. The Council has consultative and advisory powers on economic and social legislation.[10]

If functional representation was adopted in some form within our system, government and pressure groups would be

---

[9] See the two reports of a special commission chaired by the late President Herbert Hoover. Commission on Organization of the Executive Branch of the Government (Washington, D.C.: Government Printing Office, 1949, 1955).

[10] See E. Drexel Godfrey, Jr., *The Government of France* (New York: Thomas Y. Crowell, 1961), p. 58.

tied more closely together. Pressure groups would have a definite role to play and have a greater stake in the success or failure of various public policies. Their activities would be on a more regularized and open basis and they would be able to provide needed information and ideas for the legislative process.[11] At the present time, however, there appears to be little public sentiment for such a radical governmental change.

An informal method of pressure group management is the principle of "countervailing power" or the development of counterpressures. As illustrated by John Kenneth Galbraith, this principle operates within the business community.[12] According to Galbraith, the gradual concentration of American business created not only strong producers (or sellers) but also strong buyers who act as a countervailing force on the sellers. The strong buyers and sellers are a check on each other. Pressures stimulate counterpressures. This has become a significant pattern within our economic and social communities. Diverse and competing centers of private power are engaged in an eternal power struggle. Sometimes, for example, labor may countervail agriculture, or private utilities may counterbalance public utilities, or Negro activities may oppose those of Southern whites.

It is a mistake, however, to believe that countervailing power applies universally. Some groups, such as veterans, find little opposition to their activities. On the other hand, organized labor in southern states and communities has not been an effective counterforce to business, and organization drives have not produced the results labor leaders have sought.

---

[11] This type of representation was tried by Franklin Roosevelt during the days of the New Deal. The National Industrial Recovery Act attempted to incorporate economic groups more completely into government and give them responsibilities. See, for example, Arthur M. Schlesinger, Jr., *The Coming of the New Deal* (Boston: Houghton-Mifflin, 1958), pp. 87–118.

[12] John Kenneth Galbraith, *American Capitalism: The Concept of Countervailing Power* (Boston: Houghton-Mifflin, 1952).

Local attitudes and the political environment have been factors minimizing the applicability of countervailing power.

There is probably no single best approach to pressure group control. Certainly, existing statutory regulation is vague and too difficult to enforce to be meaningful. Any attempt, however, to write a stringent law might run afoul of First Amendment freedoms inherent in freedom of association. No consensus exists as to the threat posed by pressure groups to democracy and our governmental processes. Perhaps what is needed is a more positive approach to pressure groups and a government that is both receptive and discriminating to group demands. Pressure groups make important contributions to the American political process by (a) stimulating and formalizing the desires of thousands of American citizens, (b) transmitting these collective desires and aspirations to government at the appropriate level, (c) presenting needed and specialized information to national policy-makers, and (d) maintaining surveillance of policy-making centers so as to protect the interests of their memberships. The total effect of pressure groups and their activities upon government is one of amelioration.

Political pluralism has contributed to America's greatness. Our progress in economic, social, technological and cultural fields has been stimulated and expanded by pressure groups. Their operation is sometimes chaotic and sometimes selfish, but by the very fact that groups may pursue their interests so freely and openly is a sign that our political processes are in a healthy state.

OIL-GAS INDUSTRY IS POWERFUL LOBBY FORCE

FROM *CONGRESSIONAL QUARTERLY WEEKLY REPORT*

In the array of large and successful lobbies based in Washington, D.C., the oil-gas industry ranks as one of the most effective. Central to its success is the fact that since 1926, it has kept intact the 27.5 percent oil and gas depletion allowance despite constant condemnation and bitter legislative wrangling.

But Congressional staff members who have observed the industry and worked with it have told Congressional Quarterly that preserving the depletion allowance is only a part of the industry's overall effort—the most controversial and visible part. They say the industry is "up to its ears" in a number of other issues, including the establishment of natural gas rates, gas pipeline safety standards, oil import quotas, and many others.

One Congressional staff member described the industry's success by saying that it usually gets what it wants, and occasionally it has to settle for—in the phrase many lobbyists use to describe the successful outcome of a fight—"something we can live with."

But within the industry itself, CQ heard no claims of great success. In interviews with CQ, most spokesmen emphasized their problems—problems with the Federal Power Commission (FPC) over natural gas rates, problems with the Interior Department over oil imports, problems with Congress over establishing an import program, and other difficulties.

From *Congressional Quarterly Weekly Report*. Washington, D.C.: Congressional Quarterly Inc., November 29, 1968. Reprinted by permission.

This Fact Sheet describes the makeup and the lobbying objectives of the oil-gas industry as well as recounting past legislative battles in which the industry was heavily involved. It is the first in a series of CQ "profiles" on major lobbies.

Profile of the Industry

The oil-gas industry has several different segments—the large international oil and gas producing companies, the independent producers, the refiners, the pipelines, the transporters, the wholesalers and the retailers.

Some of these, such as Texaco Inc. and the Gulf Oil Corp. are world-wide operations, producing, refining and distributing all over the world. Some are small, independent firms with a few wells in one or two states, dependent only on sales of crude oil for a viable operation.

Some are independent refiners, with no source of independent supply other than purchases, no source of distribution except sales to wholesalers. Other independent refiners operate on a larger scale, with some of their supply coming from their own sources, and some of their sales made through their own outlets.

But when the transportation companies such as pipelines are added to the segments of the industry, and the retailing aspect is added, the huge size and geographical distribution and economic distribution becomes evident.

Several figures illustrate the size of the industry and its consequent strength. According to the Bureau of Mines, the value of crude oil as drawn from the wellhead in 1967 was $9,375,727,000. The value of natural gas at the wellhead was $2,898,741,000. The value of natural gas liquids, liquid fuels extracted from natural gas, was $1,179,936,000. Shipments from oil refineries were estimated at $20 billion annually. The employment figure given for the oil and gas industry in 1967 was 445,562, and this does not include the distribution of products, only production and refining.

Some of the industry's efforts, such as preserving the depletion allowance, affect the entire industry. Some, such as oil import quotas, pit domestic independent producers against the international oil companies that produce both in the United States and in foreign countries.

LOBBYING STRUCTURE

The segments of the industry are represented by their own associations in Washington; some big oil companies maintain year-round representation, and there are groups that represent more than one segment. The American Petroleum Institute (API) is considered the umbrella organization, watching over the interests of the entire industry. Powerful lobby groups representing various segments of the industry are the Independent Petroleum Assn. of America, the Independent Natural Gas Assn. of America, the Natural Oil Jobbers Council, the National Petroleum Refiners Assn., the Assn. of Oil Pipe Lines, the American Gas Assn., the American Public Gas Assn. and various regional associations representing both oil and gas interests. . . .

The biggest oil companies such as Standard Oil of New Jersey, Standard Oil of California, Gulf and Texaco, and some smaller (but still very large) companies have registered lobbyists in Washington.

These lobbyists work mostly on legislative or administrative agency matters that only affect their company—on matters which would not involve industry-wide problems.

Industry-wide problems, such as pipeline safety, or an occupational safety bill, would be handled by the umbrella association—the American Petroleum Institute or by pressure groups representing general business interests, such as the National Assn. of Manufacturers or the Chamber of Commerce of the United States.

Oil-gas industry companies are influential in both of the latter organizations, and have been effective in mobilizing them to seek the decisions the oil-gas industry wants. Notable examples are the water pollution control and occupational safety bills (S 3206, HR 14816) which were defeated in the 1968 session of Congress after vigorous lobby fights. . . .

It is thought that many persons who work for the industry in Washington do not register as lobbyists. This is due to a loophole in the 1946 Federal Regulation of Lobbying Act, which required persons to file reports of their lobby spending only if they obtain money for the principal purpose of engaging in lobbying of Congress and only if the lobbying involves direct communications with Members of Congress. . . .

In 1967, the API filed a report showing that it spent $33,199 for lobbying that year. The Assn. of Oil Pipe Lines reported lobby spending of $1,005 in 1967. The Independent Natural Gas Assn. of America reported it spent nothing for lobbying in 1967. Several individual companies reported lobby spending of relatively small amounts. . . .

CONGRESSIONAL POWER

Some critics of the industry have contended that oil "owns" Congress because of its enormous economic power and the fact that it operates in so many different states. The largest oil-gas states are Texas, Louisiana, California, Oklahoma, Wyoming, New Mexico and Kansas, but the industry is significant in others, including Illinois, Mississippi, North Dakota and Arkansas.

The industry states have chairmen of the two powerful Congressional committees which directly affect the oil-gas industry—the tax-writing House Ways and Means and the Senate Finance Committees. Rep. Wilbur D. Mills (D Ark.) is chairman of the Ways and Means panel, and Sen. Russell B. Long (D La.) is chairman of Senate Finance. Staff members on both committees told CQ they could not recall the last time the panels considered reducing the depletion allowance. Lobbyists, who generally shy away from headlines, consider it their greatest success if they can bottle up a bill in committee.

The importance to a big oil-gas state such as Texas of having representation on the Ways and Means Committee can be perceived by the House action July 30 appointing Omar Burleson (D Texas) as a member of that panel. Burleson resigned from the Committee on House Administration, where he was chairman; Foreign Affairs, where he was third-ranking Democrat; and from the Joint Committee on Library (chairman) and Printing (vice chairman), to move to Ways and Means.

An oil-state Member does not have to preside over a committee directly affecting oil and gas to exert influence in the industry's behalf. If he is chairman of another committee, the mere fact of his chairmanship, his power to push a bill in his committee that is sponsored by a friend who supports the depletion allowance, and to sit on a bill sponsored by an enemy of depletion allowance, is of great importance.

Texas has four House chairmanships, Appropriations, Banking and Currency, Veterans' Affairs and Agriculture.

Louisiana has Sen. Allen J. Ellender (D) heading the Agriculture Committee and Sen. J. W. Fulbright heading Foreign Relations. New Mexico has Sen. Clinton P. Anderson (D) heading the Aeronautical and Space Sciences Committee.

Although opponents of the depletion allowance have included such Senate powers as former Sen. Paul H. Douglas (D Ill. 1949–67), it had such potent supporters as former Sen. Robert S. Kerr (D Okla. 1949–63), who was often called "The Uncrowned King of the Senate." Kerr, as second ranking Democrat on the Finance Committee, always kept an eye out for his state's oil interests.

The industry also has Congressional strength through sheer numbers of Senators and Representatives from oil-gas states.

Natural Allies. The oil-gas industry is only one of many enjoying depletion allowances of varying percentages. Coal, clay, aluminum and many others also have percentage depletion allowances. Because of the geographical spread of these minerals across the nation, there is a mutual interest between oil state Senators and Representatives and those from the other mineral states to preserve the depletion allowance system.

Also, many oil and gas companies are diversified, owning industries totally unrelated to the parent business and located far from the producing states. This gives the oil-gas companies an opportunity to approach non oil-gas Senators and Representatives from states in which subsidiaries are located, to ask for support of the industry on the basis that what helps the parent company helps the subsidiary.

INDUSTRY-AGENCY RELATIONSHIPS

Much of the work of the trade associations representing the industry and/or its segments is before Federal regulatory agencies. The natural gas segment looks to the Federal Power Commission (FPC), which regulates gas prices. The independent oil producers look to the Interior Department's Oil Import Administration, which controls import quotas. Other segments have direct and important relationships with the multiple agencies which regulate American commerce.

Generally, the attitude among the industry is that the relationship is not good. Spokesmen for segments do not like to openly criticize departments they have to deal with continually. "We've disagreed with some decisions they've made," said one association's spokesman, in a discussion of industry-agency relationships.

A Congressional staff member who works with the industry and the agencies, however, was more explicit. He was particularly critical of the Interior Department, saying it had "turned a deaf ear" to the industry, and "frustrated" the industry's attempts to pursue its goals.

An Interior spokesman acknowledged that controls produce inequities and that "there is no question the program is in need of an overhaul." But he said that the Department is receptive to the presentations of the domestic producers.

"They are afraid we are going to constantly ease up on the quota," he said.

The quota is usually given as 1.1 million barrels a day, excluding residual oil, and is set by Presidential proclamation.

The Interior spokesman also said that Interior has "exceptionally good relationships" with the National Petroleum Council, a governmental body whose membership comes from the industry and advises Interior on petroleum policy, and the Foreign Petroleum Supply Committee, an industry committee with a government-appointed chairman.

Department of Defense. A Defense Department spokesman said the Pentagon is "considered the world's biggest buyer of petroleum products," and keeps a strong watch on all aspects of the industry, both domestic and international. Six oil companies were among the 100 contractors doing the most business with the Defense Department in fiscal 1968: Standard Oil Co. (New Jersey), 25th place; Standard Oil Co. (Calif.), 44th; Texaco, Inc., 46th; Asiatic Petroleum Corp., 49th; Mobil Oil Corp., 51st; and Gulf Oil Corp., 78th. . . .

NATIONAL PETROLEUM COUNCIL

The National Petroleum Council is a semi-governmental organization set up to provide the Interior Department with information sought by the Department on any matter relating to the petroleum industry. It does not act until it is asked for advice and recommendations by Interior, and its board has the authority to decline to act on a request. A noncouncil government spokesman described it as "the cushion between government and the industry."

INTRA-INDUSTRY RELATIONSHIPS

Because the oil-gas industry is not one huge monolith, but rather a complex collection of segments, it sometimes becomes difficult for the segments to work together.

"Everyone is looking at his own problem, not the industry's problem," one Congressional staff member said.

There is even some diversity on the depletion allowance, an objective so important to the industry that it is generally described as having universal support. But a spokesman for the oil jobbers said his segment of the industry believed the big independent production companies use it to subsidize their own marketing operations for oil, and so cut profits for jobbers.

The greatest diversity of view in the industry is over the oil import quota. The big companies, called the "majors," such as Standard Oil of New Jersey, Mobil, Texaco, Gulf and Standard of California, have sought to keep control of the quota in the hands of the Interior Department, where adjustments can be made administratively. The independent domestic producers have sought legislation establishing absolute limitations on the imports.

In a controversy such as this, when two segments of industry confront each other, the usual result is a standoff, because each side has the Congressional power to block the other.

But when segments are not in conflict they support each other, several spokesmen for various oil-gas segments said.

Continuing Fights

There are three major controversies which confront the industry continually. One is keeping the 27.5 percent depletion allowance intact. Another is oil import quotas. The third is federal regulation of natural gas prices.

DEPLETION ALLOWANCES

President Truman in 1950 said there was no tax provision "so inequitable" as the "excessive" oil-gas depletion allowance. The industry has maintained it is an offset for the exhaustion of oil and gas and was needed to ensure that companies are encouraged to invest in the risky venture of exploration and development of new oil-gas possibilities.

The depletion allowance allows oil and gas companies to deduct 27.5 percent of gross income from taxable income, providing the deduction does not exceed 50 percent of taxable income. According to Internal Revenue Service preliminary statistics for fiscal 1967, the allowance amounted to $3,053,548,000. Thus if the allowance did not exist, the industry would have had to pay taxes on an additional $3 billion.

The tax benefit actually began as an allowance limited to the recovery of costs, similar to depreciation. In 1926, however, it became a percentage allowance with no relation to costs, and in many cases permitted the kind of tax-free recovery far in excess of costs that prompted Mr. Truman to call it the most inequitable provision of the tax law.

The industry has been capable of mustering its combined vast strength to defeat all attempts to decrease the depletion allowance below 27.5 percent. Sen. William Proxmire (D Wis.), a leader in the fight against the allowance, tried to reduce it in 1967 by an amendment to the Investment Tax bill (HR 6950–PL 90–26), but was defeated by a voice vote. Previous attempts to reduce it were made by amendments to the Revenue Act of 1964 (HR 8363–PL 88–272), but were defeated by Senate roll-call votes of 33–61 and 35–57. . . .

Industry spokesmen said geography was more important than ideology in organizing forces to support the depletion allowance. For instance, both Texas Senators, Ralph W. Yarborough (D), a liberal, and John G. Tower (R), a conservative, support the allowance. The geographical influence affects many states because the industry operates across a wide area.

The fight shifted to the administrative level in 1968, when the Internal Revenue Service proposed changes that would increase tax receipts an expected $100 million a year. Industry spokesmen have condemned the proposal and are fighting it.

The industry was also watching closely and making its views known as the Administration prepared a final set of recommendations concerning tax reforms, which could include a change in the depletion allowance. . . .

IMPORT QUOTAS

The quota limiting the amount of crude oil imported into the United States is the bulwark of the domestic oil-producing industry. Without it, cheaper foreign crude would flood the country, and domestic producers say they would have to shut down production. So, preserving and strengthening the limits on imported crude is the biggest lobbying objective of the domestic industry.

Imports are regulated by the Interior Department, but the domestic producers want Congress to enact legislation fixing firm limits on imports. The "majors," companies such as Texaco and Gulf, which produce internationally, are opposed to legislation setting firm limits. They want to retain flexibility in the amount of oil that may be brought in. . . .

But according to spokesmen for the majors and for independent producers, both segments of the oil industry oppose proposed "free trade zones" which have been requested so that refineries can be built using imported oil. One request is for a free trade zone, an area where tariffs on imports are not charged, at Machiasport, Me. Occidental Petroleum Co. of Los Angeles planned to build a refinery using 300,000 barrels of imported crude oil a day. A bitter fight between Gulf Coast refining interests and Eastern interests has been going on for months over this request. Late in November, it did not appear that the issue would reach the point where Interior Secretary Stewart L. Udall would make a decision on the oil import request, and it was likely that the resolution of the fight would be in the next administration. . . .

NATURAL GAS PRICE REGULATION

From the time of the passage of the Natural Gas Act of 1938 until 1954, the natural gas segment of the oil-gas industry successfully opposed regulation of natural gas prices. Consumer interests historically have sought this regulation, because the price of natural gas at the wellhead determines its ultimate price to the consumer. After a 1954 court decision which authorized the FPC to regulate gas prices the FPC began active regulation. Congressional supporters of the industry regularly introduced legislation exempting the industry from regulation, but big city Congressional representation opposed it, and one has passed. . . .

The FPC regulated on a company-by-company basis, because of the different production costs at different wells, and this became a monumental task with a huge backlog. In 1960 the FPC started a legal effort to regulate on an area basis, and in 1968 the Supreme Court approved area regulation in the Permian Basin case. . . .

The industry continued to fight the price regulation administratively, in the FPC, and in the Congress, by strongly supporting bills introduced in each Congress to exempt it from regulation.

Although it is able to muster its usual Congressional strength, it is opposed by other powerful blocs, such as mayors' organizations which want low gas prices for the consumers in cities. The legislation also would naturally be opposed by large consumers of natural gas and by competitive sources of power, making the fight an intense battle between powerful interests.

CONGRESS

The Congress, perhaps more than any other of our constitutional branches of government, is something of an enigma. Is it truly the primary source of new laws or is it merely a cumbersome body whose sole function is that of negating the Office of the Presidency? Obviously, the chief responsibility of the Congress is legislative. Yet in today's setting approximately 80 percent of all proposed legislation emanates in one form or another from the administration, with Congress mainly delaying, negating, modifying, or bargaining. But Congress has other functions as well, one of them being to act as a check on the administration. Among its other functions are representing constituents and local interests and serving as an educational forum through public debate.

It could be argued that certain extraconstitutional developments, such as the congressional committee system and seniority, have turned Congress into a minority power institution. It could also be posited that in these current times Congress as a unit cannot function properly. The exact role that Congress should play in coming years and the precise reforms that should be undertaken to streamline the Congress remain moot.

In one selection Robert A. Dahl shows us a side of Congress

that we often miss—the congressman as an individual human being, with policy being the outgrowth of personality and beliefs, on the one hand, and political pressures on the other. In the second selection Congressman Richard Bolling presents us with a critical evaluation of the legislative branch of government and suggested reforms from the point of view of a practicing insider.

THE CONGRESSMAN AND HIS BELIEFS

ROBERT A. DAHL

His Private Preferences [1]

The Congressman is a rather ordinary person in some respects, not much wiser than the average small town lawyer, banker, doctor, or bartender, frequently confused, almost always harassed, excessively overworked, busy with an enormous variety of problems presented by his constituents, and sometimes called upon to make decisions on foreign policy that will affect man and his institutions over a large part of the earth's surface for generations to come.

All too often, those who see him as *homo politicus* (rather than the small town lawyer turned *homo politicus*) hold him to be animated by nothing more than the drive ascribed to him by Hobbes: ". . . I put for a general inclination of all mankind a perpetual and restless desire of power after power, that ceaseth only in death." From this assumption it is easy to pass on to a simplified, mechanistic interpretation of the politician, pressed relentlessly by his dominant drive for power, with an ear cocked only to the main chance.

But this is oversimple and overgeneralized. Politicians are

From *Congress and Foreign Policy* by Robert A. Dahl, copyright, 1950, by Harcourt Brace Jovanovich, Inc. and reprinted with their permission, pp. 10–19.

[1] By *private* preferences I mean his inner, highly subjective feelings of what he regards as desirable for self and others, as distinguished from his publicly articulated and discussed preferences. The two may coincide; they also may not.

complicated human beings with a considerable repertory of motivations. Doubtless one of the most important of these motivations is a desire for power or influence. But such a statement tells us very little as to *why* a politician desires power. To the understanding of his behavior, this "why" is crucial. It may be that he seeks power only under conditions acceptable to his "principles" (or if one prefers, acceptable to the demands of his super-ego). In this case his behavior may be quite different from that of a colleague whose imperious needs for deference and prestige are allayed by the simple act of holding public office. To say this is to say nothing more than what newspaper reporters at the state and national capitols have long recognized: how a legislator votes is partly determined by "what kind of a person he is."

Now if we were to observe *homo politicus* carefully and were to speculate about our observations, probably we should find it useful to distinguish between his personality, his character, his preferences, and his picture of reality. Let me say here a word about each of these except the last, which will be dealt with in the following section.

About the relationship between personality and character on the one side and political behavior on the other, very little is known even today, and I do not propose to speculate about this relationship in Congressmen.[2] It is, to be sure, a plausible hypothesis that some kinds of personality types find certain kinds of political behavior and attitudes more satisfying than others. And yet it is highly improbable that there is any simple one-to-one relationship between a Congressman's attitudes on foreign policy and his basic personality pattern, or that Congressmen with similar attitudes about foreign affairs tend to have similar kinds of personalities.

This terra incognita may be left, however, for exploration

---

[2] Perhaps the most thorough examination of the relationship between these factors and political behavior is to be found in the works of Harold Lasswell, particularly *Power and Personality* (Norton, 1948).

by others, while we advance to the slightly more accessible terrain referred to as the Congressman's "preferences." By his preferences, I mean his sense of what we would like to have happen as distinct—when it is distinct—from his sense of what is in fact happening in the world, which may be called his picture of reality. That is to say, his preferences govern the manner in which he tries to adapt his conduct to the world he discerns about him, and conversely, to adapt the world about him to his purposes.

The Congressman's preferences are shaped by his loyalties, his attitudes of deference and respect, his view of a desired future for himself and for those with whom he identifies himself, for his constituency, for his society, his country, the world, posterity.[3]

A recent study of the events surrounding passage of the Foreign Service Act of 1946 suggests the variety of private preferences that may go into a Congressional decision:

> *Personal factors . . . played some part in the Subcommittee acceptance of the basic structure and character of the draft bill. To Judge Kee it was an administration measure sponsored by a member of the President's cabinet; as such it deserved his support. To Mr. Richards it was a favored project of two fellow South Carolinians, Mr. Byrnes and Mr. Russell. As for Mr. Vorys, his interest in the Foreign Service and his conviction of the need for a non-patronage career service dated back to his work with the Disarmament Conference in 1922. At that time he had found a higher level of competence and devotion among the career diplomats and officials than among*

---

[3] To describe the individual's evaluations I use the word "preferences" rather than the older term "interests" or the newer term "values." On occasion, where the reference is to widely shared preferences of "basic" importance, the word "value" will be used; and because the phrase "interest group" has wide acceptability among political scientists, it is sometimes employed here.

> the patronage appointees on the staff of the U.S.
> delegation, even though he was himself a patronage
> appointee. To him, therefore, the Rogers Act and
> this proposed revision of it seemed wise.[4]

The influence of the legislator's private preferences is magnified whenever the other influences playing upon him are weak. Among the most important of these other influences are political parties and pressure groups. To the extent that party influence is weak, there is greater room for the expression of the legislator's private preferences as to the kind of foreign policy he would like the nation to have. At the very least, the limited force of party means that the private, nonparty preferences of the legislator influence his choice of the particular pressure to which he defers. When pressure groups are active, they can be extraordinarily effective. But on many issues of foreign policy they are not mobilized, or they cancel one another. On vital foreign policies, therefore, the Congressman is sometimes virtually a free agent.

Many Congressmen enjoy this role. They like to think of themselves as relying on their private preferences, which they call "principles," rather than on the "dictates" of party leaders, or the party program, or pressure groups, or occasionally even constituents. They call this "independence," and "independence" is highly regarded not only in Congress but evidently among the electorate. A high place is reserved in the American political tradition for the insurgents—Theodore Roosevelt, the La Follettes, George Norris, and the like. In emphasizing the supreme importance of one's own private conscience, the independent simply expresses in politics the religious attitudes of the Protestant sects that have so much shaped the American temper.

Not long after his election in 1948, Senator Paul Douglas

---

[4] Committee on Public Administration Cases, *The Foreign Service Act of 1946*, Washington, D.C. (mimeo.), 1949, p. 112.

expressed this set of attitudes thus: "Support one's party in all procedural matters everywhere. Argue substantive programs within party councils in the hope of gaining a majority within the party. But when the chips are down in the Senate, a Senator should vote his profound individual convictions on substantive matters regardless of who is with or against him." [5]

An observer who interviewed thirteen Congressmen to discover how they made up their minds on the repeal of the arms embargo during the special session in the fall of 1939 reported that twelve of them put their own "independent judgment" in first place. Only two listed "party considerations"—and these two put this influence in third place.[6] These Congressmen were, no doubt, grossly exaggerating their "independence." But what is significant is their evident agreement that "independent judgment" is a highly respectable influence in Congress.

If the Congressman likes to think of himself as "independent" of party and other pressures, why does Congress not break up into a multiplicity of different groups, shifting and reforming on every issue? How can we explain such homogeneity and consistency of voting groups as do exist? The answer is, in part, that Congress *does* tend to break up into voting groups that change from issue to issue. The historic weakness of the American party system is precisely that it has been unable to prevent this occurrence. Although we often pride ourselves on our two-party system in Congress, in some

---

[5] Paul H. Douglas, "Report from a Freshman Senator," New York *Times Magazine*, March 20, 1949, p. 74.
[6] Gleeck, *loc. cit.* The importance of the symbol of "independence" to the Congressman is confirmed by my own interviews. I was struck by the large number of Congressmen, of varying influence, who wished to emphasize that they had arrived at their decisions on the basis of their own "independent" judgment. Even party leaders tried to emphasize this quality in their own party—although not necessarily in the opposition. "Independence" is easily the most socially acceptable explanation of one's political decisions in the American milieu.

respects we have little more than a system of multiple parties operating under two labels.

The functioning of a two-party system is helped, however, because influences often tend to enlist in two camps. They polarize. What party loyalty by itself cannot accomplish is achieved by a rather formidable combination. Supporting one side, for example, one may find these allies: the President; executive experts interpreting and communicating events, who in turn may influence the views of newspaper editors and other publicists; party leaders in Congress; and possibly executive-stimulated pressures among constituents or private pressure groups. Lined up on the other side may be a variety of influences working together: hostility toward the President; interpretation and communication of events by newspapers and party staffs; party loyalty and leadership; and possibly pressure induced by important opinion leaders.

Thus in the period 1932–48, the accumulation of executive and party influences helped to produce a certain unity and consistency in Democratic voting on foreign policy issues. A lesser but nonetheless significant unity and consistency in Republican voting also resulted from the tendency for various influences to coincide, such as party, anti-presidential hostility, and judgment as to constituent opinion. . . .

Finally, foreign policy is only a part of a general Weltanschauung. Preferences about policy tend to be *persistent, consistent,* and *shared.* Attitudes that cause Senator Jones to vote in a particular way on one issue persist into subsequent issues. Likewise, Jones strives for a behavior that is internally consistent from his own point of view: he tries to bring his attitudes on domestic issues into some kind of subjective harmony with his attitudes on foreign issues; his various attitudes on foreign issues also tend to take on a certain subjective consistency. And because Jones is a product of a cultural milieu shared by others, his views, too, tend to be shared by others.

Thus, if one were to observe Congressional voting on foreign policy issues over a period of time, one might detect a number of different "clusters" of more or less persistent attitudes, held by groups frequently cutting across the more obvious lines of party and region. It seems likely, for example, that in the years 1933–48, at least three critical sets of attitudes underlay the activities of many Congressmen. These were: attitudes toward international violence; attitudes concerning collaboration of the United States with other nations or international organizations; and attitudes toward the domestic status quo. There were, to be sure, many minor variations, but for schematic purposes one might divide the attitudes toward violence into pacifist (rejection of violence) and militant (acceptance of violence); attitudes toward collaboration into isolationist (rejection) and internationalist (acceptance); and attitudes toward the domestic status quo into reformist (rejection) and conservative (acceptance). Given the various possible combinations, it is easy to see why, indeed, politics does make strange bedfellows.

While it would be tedious to explore all the permutations of these six key preferences, three combinations may be taken for illustrative purposes: the pacifist-isolationist-reformist, the pacifist-internationalist-reformist, and the militant-internationalist-reformist. Congressional supporters of the New Deal were largely drawn from these three groups, operating in an uneasy alliance with militant-internationalist-conservatives from the South. These New Deal groups tended to vote together on questions of domestic reforms. But on international questions they often tended to fall apart, even under the meticulous guidance of party leaders in Congress and the White House.

The first group was isolationist because of its pacifism; its members looked upon war as a destroyer of life and welfare; isolationism in foreign affairs and social security at home were both devices for protecting the welfare of the "victims" of modern social arrangements. The second group, unlike the first, was internationalist because it was pacifist; it looked upon international collaboration as a way of avoiding violence. Its members therefore tended to break away from support for "internationalist" action whenever such a commitment might involve violence. This in turn would tend to foster an alliance between the militant internationalists, both reformist and conservative. It was this alliance that President Roosevelt increasingly relied upon as, after 1937, he moved toward foreign policies of the militant-internationalist type.

Thus we see how the persistency, consistency, and sharing of attitudes about certain broad classes of issues helped to create clusters in Congress much more inclusive than the individual Congressman, but less inclusive than the party.

So far, the Congressman's preferences have been treated as if they were something detached from his view of reality. Such a sharp delineation, if insisted upon, would almost certainly be nonsense. For it is highly probable that the Congressman, like most other mortals, in some degree adapts his view of what *ought* to be to his view of what *is;* and conversely, he adapts his view of what *is,* albeit unconsciously, to his view of what *ought* to be. For example, Congressman Vorys supported the Foreign Service Act of 1946 because he valued competence and devotion in the public service—and also because his view of reality, shaped by his experience at the Disarmament Conference in 1922, seemed to confirm his belief that the principles of the Act were likely to produce the competent and devoted public servants he desired.

THE PICTURES IN HIS HEAD

Congressman X is a small town lawyer who originally went into politics in Illinois in the well-founded hope that a little campaigning would build up his clientele. He was sent to a small rural grade school, attended a high school in a nearby town, studied at a denominational college in Ohio, and earned his law degree by correspondence. He was a little too young for service in the First World War; his brother, a sergeant in the infantry, was killed three days after arriving at the front. Most of his life, Congressman X has read little other than small town newspapers and the Chicago *Tribune*. His personal experiences, his relationship with people, his cultural milieu, the images that have stuck in his mind from reading the newspapers—all these have given him what I have called his view of reality. These "pictures in his head," to use Walter Lippmann's graphic expression of two decades ago,[7] he now summons up in what he finds is a confused and yet familiar kind of intellectual newsreel, as he ponders how he is to vote on the first European recovery bill. He finally votes against the bill, as he had voted against proposals of a similar stripe ever since the bill to repeal the arms embargo at the special session of Congress in 1939. He is no longer so sure as he once was of the validity of the old familiar jumble of snapshots in his mind that represent "England," "Europe," "Socialism," "Allies." Radio commentators he has sometimes listened to, his reading of the New York *Times* (which he felt it his duty to begin perusing during the war as events were happening he felt he ought to know more about), the speeches of some of his acquaintances on the Foreign Affairs Committee, and the evident discontent of many of his constituents in the last campaign have all combined to give him doubts. But the familiar snapshots are the only ones that hang together in some kind of sense-making arrangement. So he votes against the bill.

Congressman Y grew up in South Carolina, the son of a cotton exporter. Like John C. Calhoun before him, he went North to Yale College; he took his law degree at Harvard just before the First World War, worshiped Wilson, enlisted in the Air Corps but missed going overseas, developed a furious

---

[7] *Public Opinion*, Macmillan, 1930. This volume is still in many ways the best introduction to the problem of rationality in public policy-making.

youthful hatred for Senator Lodge, and during his years as a small town lawyer in his home state discovered in his local library the books provided by the Carnegie Endowment for International Peace, which confirmed his feeling that American rejection of the League was a tragic blow to world unity. Elected to the House, he supported "internationalism" on those infrequent occasions when the House debated subjects relevant to such an issue. During the recent war he spoke frequently for a permanent United Nations and was overjoyed upon American entry. In Washington he has consistently read the New York *Times* and the Washington *Post*. The "pictures in his head" under the caption "foreign affairs" were most neatly arranged, perhaps, shortly after the end of the war in Europe. Since that time they have become somewhat jumbled and indistinct. He is not without serious doubts about ERP. But after a five-minute speech in which he parades the same set of familiar word pictures he has employed on previous occasions, he casts his vote in favor of the bill.[8]

Now it is not too much to say that whoever, or whatever, put the pictures in the heads of Congressman X or Congressman Y substantially determined his decision about ERP. To be sure, if other pressures—the President, the party leaders in Congress, his constituents—pile up sufficiently, the Congressman, despite his private view of reality and the policy consequences that seem to flow from that view, may support a policy contrary to the one suggested by his own view of reality. But unless these pressures overwhelm him (and whether they do so is, in the last analysis, a matter of his own preferences) he will try to achieve some kind of adjustment between his private preferences, public policy, and the pictures in his head. For his concept of reality—his idea of what is happening, what is likely to happen, what is capable of happening—indicates to him what policies will help him to achieve his preferences, given the "objective" situation as he sees it.

---

[8] Y, like his colleague X, is purely fictional.

THE ROAD TO REFORM

RICHARD BOLLING

In the many years that I have been a Member of Congress, the House has revealed itself to me as ineffective in its role as a coordinate branch of the federal government, negative in its approach to national tasks, generally unresponsive to any but parochial economic interests. Its procedures, time-consuming and unwieldy, mask anonymous centers of irresponsible power. Its legislation is often a travesty of what the national welfare requires. It does not even fulfill one of its possible functions —that of being "the grand inquest of the nation," in William Pitt's phrase.

Other House Members, who have traveled the same road and shared the same experiences, have similar views. After frustrations, setbacks, and compromises, we have taken heart from time to time from new developments: the large liberal majority in the Eighty-sixth Congress, the emergence of an able, modern-minded man as chairman of an important committee or as a party officer, the defeat or retirement of some of the notorious boodlers, social Darwinists, and incompetents, or the arrival of promising new Members. But, again, expectations have been disappointed. It has seemed that at last the House Members must rise in anger and dismay and demand a return to the fair procedure, responsible leadership, and awareness of national tasks that have distinguished the House in the past.

From the book *House Out of Order* by Richard Bolling. Copyright, ©, 1964, 1965, 1966 by Richard Bolling. Published by E. P. Dutton and Co., Inc., and reprinted with their permission, pp. 221–225.

Now we have less hope that Congress will reform itself. The burden is too great for a few enlightened and energetic Members to bear alone. The impetus for the effective reform of the House will have to come from outside pressures.

There have been signs interpreted as growing voter awareness of the deficiencies of Congress. After the Eighty-eighth Congress failed to pass civil rights legislation in its first session and had engaged in a fratricidal battle over foreign aid, a poll taken by the public-opinion analyst Louis Harris early in 1964 indicated that 65 per cent of the sampling voted "no confidence" in the job the Congress had done to date.

But some months later, after the particularly productive first session of the Eighty-ninth Congress passed much long-overdue legislation, voter disapproval turned to approbation. It seemed clear that if the American voters had any knowledge of the basic deficiencies of Congress, it was at best superficial. They, in effect, endorsed the same faulty power structure and organization of Congress which they had so soundly condemned short months earlier. That the legislative program was passed simply because of the overwhelming Democratic majorities in both houses, and despite the way the House and Senate were organized, obviously was overlooked. With no Barry Goldwaters on the Republican ticket to produce future Democratic landslides, the basic flaws in House organization will once more emerge and the need for reform will become evident.

There is no possibility that reforms will be achieved as a result of recommendations of the Joint House–Senate Committee on the Organization of Congress established in 1965. The very terms of the resolution creating the committee denied it the right to make recommendations that would achieve true basic reform. Consequently, though some minor improvement may result from the committee's recommendations, the fundamental fault will remain: the maldistribution of power resulting from the way the House organizes itself. And the possession and distribution of power is really what practical politics is about. This is particularly true of legislative politics, which is more confused, complicated, and hidden than any other kind of politics.

Proposals for reform are very numerous. Some are gimmickry; some are superficial; a few are fundamental. Of the last, fair apportionment, after a timely Supreme Court decision and several congressional refusals to override that decision, will in a few years be substantially achieved. The other really important reforms, such as getting the problem of money in politics under control and attacking the problem of conflicts of interest of Members of Congress, will not come until after the basic reform of the House is achieved.

Even the lesser but still fundamental problems, such as a fair treatment of the minority party in the distribution of time in debate, and their need for more adequate staff for their committee work, remain.

But it is idle to suppose that any fundamental reforms can be accomplished without a drastic revision in the power structure of the House. What is the power structure of the House? It can be discerned by studying how the House functioned on the 1959 labor bill and on recent civil rights legislation. How can this power structure be altered? A study of the manner in which it evolved historically provides clues.

When Joseph Cannon, Speaker of the House, was stripped of many of his powers in 1911, he said: "The Speaker does now believe, and has always believed, that this is a government through parties, and that parties can act only through majorities."

The Democrats controlled the House for thirty-one of the thirty-five years from the end of 1931 through 1966. During this period it has been more conservative than any President, even a Republican one, and more conservative than the Senate.

The entire function of the House is determined by the effective action of a majority. Yet the majority of House Democrats has not had effective control of the House. Even the Democrats' own party whip system is symptomatic of the unrepresentative nature of the House. Party whips—the Members responsible for organizing voting of party Members on the House floor—are selected from eighteen geographical areas of the country and are supposed to represent fairly the broad interests of the voters of these zones. But the zones are not based at present on any formula of equal representation by state, region, or population. Some zones consist of several states, others of only one state. If we examine the populations of these zones, we find, according to a late 1965 estimate, that the whip zones in the South average out at about 8.5 million inhabitants, while zones in the West average about 12.6 million. House Democrats who clamor for equal representation in electoral districts tolerate a whip system that does not represent populations equitably.

Basic flaws in party organization are reflected in the present power structure of the House. They are entirely the responsibility of House Democrats, and the Democrats alone have the means at hand to correct them.

The Republican Members of the House are preponderantly conservative. In a responsible and representative way, House Republican leaders make certain that their party's seats on the powerful committees are filled by Members who reflect their conservative views. There are no Republican liberals— with one possible exception—on the three more powerful committees, Appropriations, Rules, and Ways and Means. The John Lindsays of the party are given lesser committee assignments.

The Democratic Members of the House are, for the most part, moderate to progressive in their outlook. Nevertheless, this majority of Democrats accepts without argument the myth of the inviolability of seniority, permitting conservative Democrats, a numerical minority, to retain many of the most powerful committee positions. Thus the majority of House Democrats permits the power that rightfully belongs to them to be wielded by a minority of conservatives whose only affiliation with the Democratic party is the party label they use at election time. With the help of Republicans, this minority wing on the floor of the House sometimes subverts the objectives and defies the spirit of the Democratic party as a whole.

However, the course of the Congress and its success or failure is established before the first session is gaveled to order. Just before each Congress convenes, the Democratic members of the House gather in caucus to distribute the tools of power —committee assignments and chairmanships. It is in the caucus that the moderate to liberal majority allows the power of the party to be dissipated among the conservative minority.

It is, of course, gratifying to the Republicans to see the Democrats put conservative foxes in charge of liberal chicken coops, appointing to high committee posts members who reflect Republican rather than Democratic views on great national issues.

The history of the House and the development of its present power structure suggests ways of accomplishing some necessary reforms. Few liberal Democrats seem aware that the cast-iron seniority system is a comparatively new development; until 1911 the Speaker had the power to appoint chairmen and members of all committees. Liberal Democrats also overlook the fact that the power of their elected Committee on Committees (the Democratic Members of Ways and Means) to fill committee vacancies is a power delegated by the House Democratic caucus.

The place to reform the procedures of the House is not in study commissions or on the floor of the House, but in the House Democratic caucus. It is here that methods could be adopted by a majority of House Democrats to assure an assignment of committee seats that will reflect the liberal views of the majority. At the same time the power of the party's titular leader could be increased. Three important goals for the Democrats are to enhance the authority of the Speaker; make sure that Democratic membership on legislative committees is representative; and to increase the individual responsibility of each Democrat toward his leaders.

The House has functioned effectively, aside from times of national emergency, only when there was general agreement on policy objectives and on the avenues to achieve them. And this state of affairs has come about when two conditions existed: (1) when the majority party functioned through its caucus, as in the time of Clay and in the time of Speaker Champ Clark and Oscar W. Underwood, his majority leader, from 1913 to 1916; (2) when the Speakership was held by strong and aggressive men such as Reed and Cannon.

To suggest a return to either is surely to bring down on one's head the cry of "King Caucus" or "Czar Speaker." There is no reason, however, why the two approaches cannot be combined in a fashion that eliminates the objections against either.

DOMESTIC POLITICS AND ECONOMICS

One of the most significant changes that has taken place in the function of American government since World War II has been in the relationship between the government and the economy. Although the United States has never had a pure laissez-faire economic system, it is only thirty to forty years since the federal government became responsible for maintaining the economic health of the nation. Thus, in 1946 Congress pledged itself to sustain a state of full employment, and in his book on the United States Presidency, the late Clinton Rossiter noted that one of the modern President's functions was that of keeper of the prosperity. Therefore if a recession occurs, blame for this woeful event falls upon those in Washington and their fiscal policies. Both liberals and conservatives are aware of, and rarely criticize, the government-economic partnership.

Today the government not only regulates the economy, but it also actively participates in it. This fact can be best illustrated by the following piece of information: The federal government is the single largest purchaser of petroleum products in the United States, as well as the largest single owner of cars, aircraft, land, and buildings.

In sum, our political and economic systems have become so

interrelated that in reality they are inseparable, despite our ingrained beliefs in the virtue of private enterprise.

In the following two readings, John Kenneth Galbraith examines the structural nature of the political-economic relationship, and Berkley Rice analyzes the effect of economic events upon the nation and the scientific community.

CHANGE AND THE INDUSTRIAL SYSTEM

JOHN KENNETH GALBRAITH

A curiosity of modern economic life is the role of change. It is imagined to be very great; to list its forms or emphasize its extent is to show a reassuring grasp of the commonplace. Yet not much is supposed to change. The economic system of the United States is praised on all occasions of public ceremony as a largely perfect structure. This is so elsewhere also. It is not easy to perfect what has been perfected. There is massive change but, except as the output of goods increases, all remains as before.

As to the change there is no doubt. The innovations and alterations in economic life in the last seventy years, and more especially since the beginning of World War II, have, by any calculation, been great. The most visible has been the application of increasingly intricate and sophisticated technology to the production of things. Machines have replaced crude manpower. And increasingly, as they are used to instruct other machines, they replace the cruder forms of human intelligence.

Seventy years ago the corporation was still confined to those industries—railroading, steamboating, steel-making, petroleum recovery and refining, some mining—where, it seemed, production had to be on a large scale. Now it also sells groceries, mills grain, publishes newspapers and provides

---

The New Industrial State. Copyright © 1967 by John Kenneth Galbraith. Reprinted by permission of the publisher, Houghton Mifflin Company, pp. 1–4.

public entertainment, all activities that were once the province of the individual proprietor or the insignificant firm. The largest firms deploy billions of dollars' worth of equipment and hundreds of thousands of men in scores of locations to produce hundreds of products. The five hundred largest corporations produce close to half of all the goods and services that are available annually in the United States.

Seventy years ago the corporation was the instrument of its owners and a projection of their personalities. The names of these principals—Carnegie, Rockefeller, Harriman, Mellon, Guggenheim, Ford—were known across the land. They are still known, but for the art galleries and philanthropic foundations they established and their descendants who are in politics. The men who now head the great corporations are unknown. Not for a generation have people outside Detroit and the automobile industry known the name of the current head of General Motors. In the manner of all men, he must produce identification when paying by check. So with Ford, Standard Oil and General Dynamics. The men who now run the large corporations own no appreciable share of the enterprise. They are selected not by the stockholders but, in the common case, by a Board of Directors which narcissistically they selected themselves.

Equally it is a commonplace that the relation of the state to the economy has changed. The services of Federal, state and local governments now account for between a fifth and a quarter of all economic activity. In 1929 it was about eight per cent. This far exceeds the government share in such an avowedly socialist state as India, considerably exceeds that in the anciently social democratic kingdoms of Sweden and Norway, and is not wholly incommensurate with the share in Poland, a Communist country which, however, is heavily agricultural and which has left its agriculture in private ownership. A very large part (between one-third and one-half) of public activity is concerned with national defense and the exploration of space. This is not regarded even by conservatives as socialism. Elsewhere the nomenclature is less certain.

Additionally, in the wake of what is now called the Keynesian Revolution, the state undertakes to regulate the total income available for the purchase of goods and services in the economy. It seeks to insure sufficient purchasing power to buy whatever the current labor force can produce. And, more tentatively and with considerably less sanction in public attitudes, it seeks, given the resulting high employment, to keep wages from shoving up prices and prices from forcing up wages in a persistent upward spiral. Perhaps as a result of these arrangements, and perhaps only to test man's capacity for feckless optimism, the production of goods in modern times has been notably high and remarkably reliable.

Previously, from the earliest appearance of capitalism until the beginning of Hitler's war, expansion and recession had followed each other, at irregular intervals, but in steady procession. The business cycle had become a separate subject of economic study; the forecasting of its course and the explanation of its irregularities had become a modest profession in which reason, divination, incantation and elements of witchcraft had been combined in a manner not elsewhere seen save in the primitive religions. In the two decades following World War II, there was no serious depression; from 1947 until this writing (1966) there has been only one year in which real income in the United States has failed to rise.

Three further changes are less intimately a part of the established litany of accomplishment. First, there has been a further massive growth in the apparatus of persuasion and exhortation that is associated with the sale of goods. In its cost and in the talent it commands, this activity is coming increasingly to rival the effort devoted to the production of goods. Measurement of the exposure, and susceptibility, of human beings to this persuasion is itself a flourishing science.

Second, there has been the beginning of the decline of the trade union. Union membership in the United States reached a peak in 1956. Since then employment has continued to grow; union membership in the main has gone down. Friends of the labor movement, and those who depend on it for a livelihood, picture this downturn as temporary or cyclical. Quite a few others have not noticed it. There is a strong presumption that it is deeply rooted in related and deeper change.

Finally, there has been a large expansion in enrollment for higher education together with a somewhat more modest increase in the means for providing it. This has been attributed to a new and penetrating concern for popular enlightenment. As with the fall in union membership, it has deeper roots. Had the economic system need only for millions of unlettered proletarians, these, very plausibly, are what would be provided.

DOWN AND OUT ALONG ROUTE 128

BERKLEY RICE

Arnold Limberg, Wayne Lees, Phil Blum and David Gernes don't know each other, but they should, for they have much in common. They are all scientists or engineers who live within a few miles of each other in Lexington, Mass., a prosperous, well-groomed suburb of Boston. They are all married, with two children, two cars and comfortable homes. To the extent that salary represents any measure of a technical man's worth, they are all competent, successful men, who until recently were earning more than $15,000 a year. This year, they all acquired a new experience in common—they've been fired.

Of course, no one uses such a crude word as "fired" any more. These days one is "laid off," "displaced," "surplused" or "temporarily furloughed, pending recall." Whatever the corporate euphemism, it applies equally to an alarming number of engineers and scientists in the Greater Boston area. Like the massive layoffs in the West Coast aerospace industry, most of those in this area have been caused by cutbacks in Federal spending for defense and space. But unlike the huge assembly lines on the West Coast, which turn out planes, missiles and other big items of military hardware, most electronics and research firms around Boston specialize in complex systems which require relatively few production workers. As a result, the layoffs here have hit the highly skilled technicians as badly as the man on the production lines.

From *Down and Out Along Route 128*, by Berkley Rice. *The New York Times Magazine*, November 1, 1970. © 1970 by The New York Times Company. Reprinted by permission.

While no Ph.D. bread lines have formed as yet, the problem of technical unemployment has become a community one. Retail sales are off, the real estate market has softened considerably and mortgage payments are running behind. At a recent farewell dinner given by a departing employe of a Lexington electronics firm which has laid off several hundred men this year, three of the five guests had also been laid off by other firms. At the September board meeting of the Couples' Club of Lexington's Hancock Congregational Church, the discussion concerned jobs, rather than church affairs. One engineer, laid off a few months ago, was doing research in his basement; another had just been laid off for the second time this year by Raytheon; one had been laid off after nearly 20 years with his company; the wife of another engineer who expected to be dropped soon, said, "We just live from day to day."

Similar remarks can be heard these days at dinner parties, church meetings and country clubs in Needham, Wellesley, Newton, Waltham, Weston, Lincoln, Concord, Bedford, Burlington and other suburbs that border Boston's Route 128. In the age of the computer, Route 128 has become Boston's "Golden Horseshoe," and the East Coast center of the electronics industry. Most major electronics corporations have headquarters, or at least plants, here, and hundreds of smaller companies with exotic or cryptic names huddle together in sterile concrete clusters which P.R. men call "industrial parks." In nearby Cambridge, dozens of small research firms have sprung up in the last 20 years, many of them spin-offs of research done at M.I.T. and Harvard, and often tied in some way to the larger firms out on 128.

By 1969, nearly 50,000 professional engineers and scientists worked in the Cambridge-128 area, forming one of the greatest concentrations of technical talent in the country. In the past year and a half, at least 10,000 of them have been laid off. The number of technical men collecting unemployment benefits has tripled in the last year, and state officials estimate that many more have not filed because of pride, or hope that a job will turn up soon. To a statistician, figures like these mean that technical unemployment in this region has reached epidemic proportions. The plague has caught graduates hired last June from engineering schools, as well as Ph.D.'s with 20 years of loyal service. Actually the Ph.D.'s often go first, because they're expensive, highly specialized, and, in some cases, beginning to slow down. The young engineers generally work harder for considerably less money.

Bad as conditions are, they seem to be getting worse. Dozens of empty buildings along Route 128 are available for lease. Many small firms facing failure have already been taken over by larger companies. Others, like National Radio of Melrose, have gone into bankruptcy. The plague has struck the new glamour companies like Viatron, a computer firm that has dropped from more than 1,000 men to less than 300, as well as established national firms like Sylvania. After having already laid off several hundred men this year, Sylvania has just announced the "phasing out" of its semiconductor divisions, which employ about 1,200 men, mostly in the Greater Boston area. In a statement now familiar to Boston's financial reporters, Sylvania president Garland Morse said the company would try to place some men in its other divisions, and he consoled the rest: "We are not unmindful of the impact this action will have on our employes."

In addition to laying men off, some firms have tried to reduce their budgets by cutting salaries 10 per cent. Others have tried to "increase productivity" by getting more work out of the men they've kept. Making them work evenings and weekends represents a painless form of belt-tightening for the companies, since engineers, as "professionals," do not receive overtime pay. In most cases the survivors hardly need to be urged to work harder. "There's a lot of talk about 'pulling together' to save the company," says a still-employed physicist, "but it's actually to save our jobs."

At the larger firms, the only way to be sure who's still around is to check the latest company phone directory. The tense atmosphere among those waiting to see who gets laid off next has led to some fairly black humor. A metallurgist at TYCO Laboratories who was recently given three months' notice soon found many of his colleagues avoiding him as though he had contracted some virulent disease. One of his remaining friends gave him a gift of a leper bell, so that he could warn everyone away when he came down the halls. In the company cafeterias, a standard joke these days runs: "Hey, when are you going downtown for your hack license?" Worst of all are the farewell luncheons for those laid off. "They're really pretty gruesome," says an engineer who has attended several for his colleagues. "There're usually about 20 or 30 guys from the department. They all get up and say what a great guy he was, and he gets up and tells them how much he enjoyed working with them and everything. *Eeyuch!*"

Raytheon, the giant of the local electronics industry, has had the most farewell luncheons lately. Like other large corporations that have had to merge or close down troubled divisions, Raytheon has essentially dismantled its Space and Informations Systems Division in Sudbury.

The Missile Systems Division in Bedford, its biggest plant, has been hurt by cutbacks or "stretch-outs" on its contracts for the A.B.M., SAM-D and Hawk missile programs. (Despite such troubles, Raytheon managed to increase its sales for 1969 to a record $1.28-billion, of which about half came from Government defense and space contracts.)

Such troubles at Raytheon have a tremendous effect on the technical labor market since it is by far the largest employer in this region, and one of the biggest in New England. Before the first cutbacks came in 1969, Raytheon had more than 30,000 men working in plants in Lowell, Andover, Bedford,

Burlington, Lexington, Waltham, Wayland, Sudbury and Norwood. Over the past year or so this labor force has dropped by 3,500.

Raytheon may be bigger than the other firms along Route 128, but its dependence on military contracts is typical. While the general recession may be responsible for some of the cutbacks along 128, the basis for the area's previous prosperity has always been defense and space contracts. The names of the largest firms in the industrial parks of the Golden Horseshoe read like a list of the country's biggest defense and space contractors: Raytheon, R.C.A., AVCO, General Electric, Western Electric, Sperry Rand, Sylvania, Control Data, Litton. Much of their Government contract money filters down to the smaller firms in the area. They buy electronic components, subcontract research projects, and hire dozens of M.I.T. and Harvard professors as consultants.

To coordinate all this activity, and to handle the billions of dollars in contracts that go to these firms, the Department of Defense has established its own electronics and research headquarters here. The Air Force, the country's largest buyer of electronic equipment, has stationed its Electronics Systems Division at Hanscom Field in Bedford, a five-minute ride from 128. Out of its 1969 budget of $400-million, E.S.D. alone spent $160-million on contracts to Massachusetts firms. In addition to the Air Force E.S.D., the Defense Department has several other major research installations in this area: the Air Force Cambridge Research Lab, Lincoln Lab and MITRE Corporation, all conveniently close to E.S.D. headquarters at Hanscom Field, plus the Instrumentation Lab (recently renamed Draper Lab) at M.I.T. Together, the budgets of these four research centers totaled more than $200-million in 1969, much of it spent on contracts to local research and engineering firms. Even more important to the local job market, they employ about 6,800 personnel, more than half of whom are civilian scientists and engineers.

In addition to cutting back on contract funds, the Government has also begun "reducing" personnel at its local research centers. Rumors have been circulating for months about impending mass layoffs, and there have even been rumors about a possible transfer of the Air Force E.S.D. headquarters. While the Defense Department continually denies such rumors, public and corporate officials around here are justifiably nervous. Many of them feel the severity of the Federal cutbacks in this area are due more to political spite than simple economics. They claim the Nixon Administration is deliberately punishing Massachusetts Senators Edward Brooke and Edward Kennedy for their lack of support on the A.B.M., the Haynsworth-Carswell nominations and other crucial legislative matters. As proof, they cite the case of last summer's closing of NASA's 800-man Electronics Research Center in Cambridge. In December, 1969, in response to rumors about the center's future, the Administration assured Senator Brooke, who in turn assured his constituents, that there were no plans to close the center down. A few weeks later, just before Christmas, The Boston Herald broke the news of the center's closing.

Of more than 400 scientists and engineers who were put out of work by June, fewer than half have since been retained by the Department of Transportation, which has taken over the facility. A few of the younger, more adaptable men found jobs elsewhere with NASA and other Federal agencies. The rest were simply laid off. Their names automatically go on priority lists for Federal job openings, but with the current contraction in Federal research projects, these lists offer little hope. More than 100 of those laid off are still out of work.

. . .

While the electronics industry in general has been badly hurt by defense and space cutbacks, the research labs have suffered the most damage. Faced with a shortage of funds, both the Defense Department and the companies have pretty much dropped their long-range research projects. According to one senior research scientist: "You can count on the fingers of one hand the number of companies around here still supporting their own in-house, long-range research programs. They just can't afford to spend money on any work that isn't going to pay for itself right away."

A journey along Route 128 illustrates this hard-nosed policy. AVCO's Everett Research Lab, which had just moved into an expensive new building, laid off about 200 men last spring—a 30 per cent cut. "It all happened very fast," recalls one of the survivors: "One weekend, a few of the top people went through the names of everyone in the lab. Monday morning the list went up, and the number two man in the lab, who had helped pick the guys to be laid off, found his own name at the top of the list. They chopped off a lot of Ph.D.'s and some really skilled engineers. A lot of them are still out of work now, after six months. The place is kind of spooky now. Lots of secretaries' desks with no secretaries, shopping baskets full of telephones, empty offices. The ones who are left are really breaking their backs now—partly because the place is badly undermanned, and partly because they're scared to death of losing their own jobs."

At E.G.&G., a Bedford firm specializing in nuclear-testing devices for the Atomic Energy Commission, a 50 per cent staff cut has virtually wiped out several research departments. When I asked him how the company decided which men to drop, one department head told me: "They don't usually tell you whom to lay off. They just tell you your department doesn't have enough contract money to support its personnel budget. Those who are working on contract projects are relatively safe. The ones who aren't, who are supported by in-house funds, are in trouble. Ordinarily many good people are on in-house funds between contracts, but now they have become a luxury. The ones who are kept on are the ones who can go out and drum up business. Once we've got the contracts, we can always go out and hire a lab full of good scientists and engineers, particularly these days."

THE PRESIDENCY

Any President must fulfill many different functions, constitutional or otherwise, at the same time. Often these roles find themselves in conflict. Most of us, at one time or another, become involved in dialogues concerning our agreement or disagreement with a given move on the part of a given President. But do we take the time to consider the entire context? How much latitude does the President have as an individual and to what extent is he circumscribed by his office?

Certainly there have been different views of the proper role of the Presidency entertained by both scholars and Presidents. In the modern age, however, one might argue that the multiplicity of decisions, foreign and domestic, that confront any President, the speed with which events occur, and the limited amount of time within which decisions must often be made serve to aggrandize the already awesome powers of the chief executive. One could also argue with equal facility that as a result of the technological nature of modern society the President must rely more and more on the federal bureaucracy and that, for the very same reasons just mentioned, Presidential power must therefore be further increased.

Louis W. Koenig's analysis of and prescriptions for the

Presidency for the 1960s are even more meaningful as we enter the 1970s, whereas Tom Wicker's journalist's eye captures for us the dilemmas of the modern Presidency in very human terms.

PERSPECTIVES ON PRESIDENTIAL POWER

LOUIS W. KOENIG

President John F. Kennedy, according to Theodore Sorensen, his valued counselor, was a man "subject to moods" and at times discouraged by his inability "to get everything done as quickly as he would like to get it done." The source of Kennedy's discouragement was the far-stretching chasm between the ideal of a vigorous, creative Presidency he envisaged in his gallant 1960 campaign and the reality of the complicated, restraint-bound, frustrating office he discovered after his inauguration. The Presidency of John Kennedy's campaign speeches was the office that would "get this country going again," an organ of bold leadership in a fast-changing world, the mover and shaker of legislation fit for the urgent, controversial problems of the day.

In a press conference of June 27, 1962, with his term nearing its midpoint and the end, therefore, of a span that ordinarily is the most fruitful part of a Presidential tenure, Kennedy indulged, with the reporters' encouragement, in an off-the-cuff evaluation of his official experience, all the more candid because it was spontaneous. He acknowledged, with a tinge of sadness, that even with a one-third majority in both houses of Congress, he lacked, as he put it, a "working majority." Even though Democrats at the time outnumbered Republicans 263 to 174 in the House of Representatives and 64 to 35 in the Senate, with one Republican vacancy, he could not command

---

From *The Chief Executive* by Louis W. Koenig, © 1964 by Harcourt Brace Jovanovich, Inc., and reprinted with their permission, pp. 3–13.

sufficient support from his own party nor wean away enough Republicans to move difficult bills through Congress and onto the statute books. The President was goaded into his notice of a lack of a "voting majority" by the fact that a week before his press conference his farm bill had been lost in the House, with forty-eight Democrats voting against it. "We should realize," he told the reporters, "that some Democrats have voted with the Republicans for twenty-five years, really since 1938, and that makes it very difficult to secure the enactment of any controversial legislation."

The President on that June day looked to the approaching November Congressional elections with hopes that the Democratic Congressional majority might be increased. Kennedy did not get his "working majority," but fared better than most Presidents, whose Congressional strength traditionally sags in midterm elections. Although the new totals of 258 Democrats and 177 Republicans in the House meant a net Democratic loss of four seats, the President enjoyed a net gain of three Representatives who promised to support his program. In the Senate the Democrats gained four seats. In the House, where the President's troubles were greatest, he still required between ten and forty Republican or Southern Democratic votes on controversial issues. A year after the election and a year and a half after the press conference, when the tragedy of his assassination struck, Kennedy still was deprived of legislation he deemed important—public school aid, civil rights legislation, medical care for the aged, the establishment of a cabinet-level urban affairs department, the barring of arbitrary use of literacy tests as qualifications for voting, the establishment of standby authority to lower taxes, the withholding of taxes on dividend and interest income at the source, and the permanent strengthening of the unemployment insurance system. Kennedy's principal victory in nearly three years of office, and probably the only one that deserves to be called major, was the Trade Expansion Act of 1962. The balance of political power between the White House and Congress in the Kennedy years was so even that the President could not with any certainty secure the controversial legislation he wanted and the country needed. The President and the nation were the victims, in the phrase of James MacGregor Burns, of "the deadlock of democracy."

President Kennedy's frustrations were not confined to the domestic scene. Conflict and rejection often blocked him from achieving his purposes in foreign affairs. His plans for United States and multi-national control of nuclear weapons were spurned by the French. He proposed to reduce United States troops in Europe and Berlin, but the allies refused to fill the vacuum with their own forces, so he resigned himself to the status quo. He put to work a State Department group to make a fearless review of the policy toward Red China, but after the study was reported, Kennedy, staring political reality full in the face, put the project aside. "We live in a world," Sorensen said, in explanation of Kennedy's moods, "which is full of setbacks to the hopes of a man who has a good many ideals, who would like to make a contribution during the short time he's on the scene. So he's bound to have his moments of discouragement."

As President, Kennedy labored mightily and often brilliantly against the obstacles. He was "in the thick of the battle," as he promised in the campaign he would be, pressing legislators for their votes, arguing and pleading with Allied leaders and taking his message to their peoples, campaigning unstintingly to increase the number of Congressional Democrats, breasting the torrent of executive business with his extraordinary command of fact and deep involvement in decision, instilling vitality and urgency into administrative effort, and rallying around him a staff whose outstanding competence bears comparison with that of any Presidency. Yet when the record of the late President is compiled and weighed, the gulf between the Presidency he hoped for in 1960 and the Presidency he attained is striking. Kennedy—the contours of historical judgment are already emerging—will be remembered more for the ideals and innovative methods he brought to the great office than for achievement in program and policy. The Presidency and its world were something less than responsive to his commanding talent and high purpose. "Has your experience in the office matched your expectations?" Kennedy was asked in 1962 in a year-end interview. "Well, I think . . . the problems are more difficult than I had imagined they were," he replied. The Presidency, for which he had so long and so skillfully campaigned, in no little way let him down.

As much as if not more than most American chief executives, Kennedy was the victim of the chasm between the Presidency as it appears, or is imagined, and the Presidency of reality. The imagined Presidency is vested in our minds with more power than the Presidency really has. The real Presidency is what the Presidency effectively is in the present, what it can do in a given situation. The imagined Presidency is a euphoric impression of its past, present, and future, and is grounded partly in reality and partly in fancy. It exaggerates the office's strength, encouraged by the substantial power it actually possesses, the prestige built in its past, and the pomp that surrounds it. The imagined Presidency underestimates the limitations of power and environment the office suffers. It equates past Presidential success, the nation's might, and expectations of how the world should go, with available Presidential power.

The chief executive of the world's most advanced technological nation, which produces 40 percent of the world's wealth and sustains a military establishment of unsurpassed destructive capabilities, is bound to bask in an aura of reflected power, no matter what the inherent power of his office may be. Our view of what the Presidency can do is shaped by what it has done. It is an office whose finest triumphs are better remembered than its failures. It is a gallery of our heroes: Washington launching the republic despite economic weakness and foreign hostility; Andrew Jackson asserting union against nullification and implanting political and economic democracy; Abraham Lincoln leading the union through the crucible of civil war; Theodore Roosevelt, Woodrow Wilson, and Franklin D. Roosevelt raising high the banner of economic and social reform; and Wilson and the second Roosevelt triumphing in two wars. The Presidency is a place where men faced with horrendous challenge have achieved unexpected growth and responded with unexpected effectiveness. Lincoln, James K. Polk, and others, held in poor esteem when they took up their duties, grew enormously in stature after brief exposure to the trials of office. "Go thou and do likewise," we are ready to instruct any present incumbent.

The Presidency appears all the more imposing because it is the center of our expectations. Just as he is to the Sioux Indians, the President is in a sense the Great Father to us all. We look to him because he has unlimited power to make proposals for action. He can, if he chooses, espouse any cause, from simplified spelling to the soil bank, and whatever he says will be heard and noticed. The one figure in our public life elected by and responsible to a national constituency, he better than anyone can bring problems forward, define the possible solutions, and advocate the one most likely to achieve the chosen end. But woe to him if trouble does not fade and the clouds do not roll back. He often will fail because some of us expect him to do things he cannot do: to maintain a posture of victory in any war the country is associated with, to secure from the investment of foreign aid a return of friendship and loyalty, and to organize an administration of invariable efficiency. The President cannot extract conformity with United States objectives with absolute success from traditional allies whose wealth, and therefore independence, is on the rise. He cannot, merely by his own acts, keep the economy whirring at high speed, puncture ballooning unemployment, and fasten tight the lid on inflation. He cannot, by a wave of his hand, assure Americans a life of peace, contentment, and security.

He does not, as Sidney Hyman has suggested, "have God's autonomous powers to make mountains without valleys as the mood strikes him." The difference between what some of us imagine the Presidency to be and what it really is leads to disappointment, frustration, and attack.

The appearance of Presidential power is enhanced by the color and pageantry of the office, the adaptation to American needs of the monarchical principle. The President reigns as well as rules. Like the flag, he is the symbol of national unity, a focal point of loyalties, and the ceremonial chief of the nation. He approaches with the accompaniment of "Hail to the Chief"; he decorates war heroes, dedicates parks and post offices, and performs prodigious social feats on the scale of Theodore Roosevelt who on New Year's Day in 1902 shook hands with eight thousand people.

The appearance of Presidential power is increased by the sweeping appreciations that are accorded it, like Harry S Truman's when he declared that "The Presidency of the United States of America has become the greatest and most important office in the history of the world." Its might is inherent in the epithets sometimes flung at Presidents in mid-tenure like "that man in the White House" Franklin D. Roosevelt and "Mad Tom" Jefferson. The appearance of power glows more strongly when a hero-figure like Dwight D. Eisenhower and a hero-glamour-figure like Kennedy occupy the White House. The appearance of power is conveyed in Eisenhower's astounding electoral victory margin of 9.5 million votes in 1956 and by the equally astounding popularity of John Kennedy, whose ratings in the public opinion polls at times outdid those of his predecessor. But mere popularity, both those Presidents would testify, does not achieve policy.

The appearance of the Presidency as an office more powerful than it really is has led to ill-advised attempts to reduce its presumed effectiveness by drastic surgery. One of the most menacing of these attempts has succeeded, the Twenty-Second Amendment, adopted in 1951, which was hawked with cries that it was imperative to prevent the President from becoming a dictator, even though no such dictator had appeared in the long experience of the American Presidency. In actuality, as public discussion made clear, the amendment was a reflection upon Franklin D. Roosevelt, who was driven by the urgencies of World War II into accepting, and by no means willingly, an incumbency of four terms. The amendment is a tragedy whose full dimensions are yet to be known; it badly inhibits the President's power in his second term and shifts the balance in the legislature's favor.

Spurred by the success of the Twenty-Second Amendment, the foes of Presidential power launched the Bricker amendment, also of the 1950's. Appearing in its long career in several forms and pushed by tireless promoters, the amendment would in effect have prevented the chief executive from making treaties and executive agreements with foreign governments. It would have largely shut down the Presidency in foreign affairs. Other amendments are floated periodically by those afflicted with the high fever of the imagined Presidency. They propose to limit income tax assessments to 25 per cent, to transfer federal welfare functions to the states, and other such things, all of which either directly or indirectly could do the Presidency great harm.

The glory and power of the Presidency have been a favorite theme of those who, over the decades, have been charged with the task of introducing the chief executive on great occasions to make an address. Former President William Howard Taft recalled one day in a lecture at Columbia University how those who formerly presented him, by way of exalting the occasion, frequently cited him as one "who exercised greater governmental power than any monarch in Europe." This of course was a day when monarchs still were thriving. Taft declared to his university audience,

> *I need hardly point out the inaccuracies of this remark, by comparing the powers of the President of*

> *the United States with those of the rulers of countries in which there is not real popular legislative control. The powers of the German Emperor, of the Emperor of Austria, and the Emperor of Russia are far wider than those of the President of the United States.*

Those who introduced President Taft on the public platform were confused by the difference between the appearance and the reality of Presidential power. The real Presidency exists in a world of circumscribed powers whose limits are becoming increasingly confining. That the Presidency should be a tightly limited office was part of its original conception. Distrustful of power and fearful of tyranny, the Founding Fathers instilled the principles of checks and balances and separation of powers into the Constitution. The arrangement of the executive and Congress, as Woodrow Wilson put it, reflected "the Whig Theory of political dynamics, which was a sort of unconscious copy of the Newtonian Theory of the universe." Neither Congress nor the executive was to become the dominant force, but each shared the power of the other, whether making laws, appointments, or treaties, and each therefore could check the other's assertion.

From the beginning and throughout Presidential history, the chief executive has been able to maintain no important policy, domestic or foreign, without Congressional support in the form of laws and money. Neither is there any dependable way under the Constitution in which the President can bring Congress to provide this wherewithal against its will. A complex of forces that prompts Congress to resist or oppose the President much of the time prevails. Because the method of electing the President differs from the method of electing Congress, their constituencies, concerns, and viewpoints differ. The President and Vice President alone are chosen by the nation. Senators and Congressmen, in contrast, are essentially local officers responsible to the voters of a single state or Congressional district. Congress does not choose the President and is therefore not beholden to him, and cannot be bullied by him. Only once in four years are the President and members of the House of Representatives elected simultaneously, and even on that occasion only one-third of the Senate is elected. At the President's midterm the House and another one-third of the Senate are chosen, usually with local issues predominating. The outcome more often than not worsens the President's own party support in both Congressional houses. At no point in his four-year span does the President face a Senate wholly elected during his tenure, owing to the Senate's six-year-term and system of staggered elections. Presidents come and go, but the most powerful legislators—the chairmen of the standing committees—stay on, often rolling up tenure of a third of a century and more.

The likelihood is that a President who seeks legislation promoting social and economic reforms, as Kennedy did, will face a hard wall of opposition from the legislative leaders of his own party. These are the committee chairmen who have risen by seniority because they come from "safe" districts, which are situated chiefly in Southern or rural Northern areas. Both areas tend toward conservative outlooks and therefore produce conservative legislators. Theodore Roosevelt, advancing the reforms of his Square Deal, had to work principally through conservative Senators Eugene Hale and Nelson Aldrich in the Senate and Speaker "Uncle Joe" Cannon in the House, who "distrusted anything that was progressive." "We succeeded in working together," Roosevelt wrote of their relationship, "I pushing forward and they hanging back," not a promising juxtaposition, on its face, for cooperative endeavor. Speaker Cannon's estimate of his dealings with Theodore Roosevelt is an admirable indication of the President's common plight in legislative relations. "He was a good sportsman," said Cannon, "and accepted what he could get so long as legislation conformed even in part to his recommendations."

Although the Founding Fathers did not foresee political parties, their rise has in no significant way hampered the intended effect of checks and balances. Parties are not a dependable force for cooperation between the legislative and executive branches. The party functions effectively as a national organization only once every four years, when control of the White House is at stake. Otherwise, the party is a confederation of largely autonomous state and local organizations, where sectional cleavages and factional differences are commonplace. The President, in fact, invests much time maintaining unity between the squabbling factions. The President and the legislators, although they wear the same party label, are nominated by different party organizations as well as being chosen by different electorates, an arrangement hardly conducive to unity. There is no known common standard of party loyalty, and no party caucus, as in Great Britain, which joins the executive with the legislators of his party in the enterprise of an accepted policy program. Indeed the Presidency and Congress may simply be vantage points of the party's rival factions. Thus Eisenhower in the Presidency was faced with an array of standing committee chairmen, holders of the supreme legislative policy posts, who were identified overwhelmingly with the Taft wing of his party, which had fought his nomination unremittingly. Eisenhower may have beaten Robert Taft for the nomination, but Taft got the enormous consolation prize of the United States Congress.

The President is checked by the opinion of the people in general or, when they organize, by their opinion as pressure groups. American pressure groups possess enormous economic, ethnic, and sectional diversity. What pleases the Democratic Italian voters of New York may be anathema to Democratic Negro voters of Los Angeles or Democratic Protestants of the Middle West. A policy that delights Republican hard-money bankers in New York may disgruntle Republican wheat farmers in Kansas. The President has the Solomon-like task of mediating between the groups with all their hopes and fears, of weighing the political situation as a whole, and of safeguarding the public interest. He is both a great and good engine of the aspirations of the groups and a brake upon them when they seek too much at the expense of the nation and other groups. The relationship is also, to a degree, reciprocal. A President, particularly a Democratic President, must pay heed to groups that because of their voting power function as veto groups. Pressuring for new advantage and meaning to keep gains already achieved, they weigh and criticize his plans and act according to their lights. He earns their votes only if they judge him to be sufficiently the vehicle of their purposes. Among Lyndon Johnson's earliest callers after his accession to the Presidency were the leaders of organized labor and Negro civil rights groups, the two veto groups on whose favor his political future most depends.

Impressed from his own full and intimate knowledge of the limitations the chief executive toils under, Harry S Truman once observed, "The principal power that the President has is to bring people in and try to persuade them to do what they ought to do without persuasion. That's what I spend my time doing. That's what the powers of the President amount to." Given the interdependence of its powers, the Presidency is an intensive experience in practical politics. To lead, to win support, to achieve, the President must practice with skill and ardor the arts of political persuasion. Woodrow Wilson noted before taking up the Presidency, "We have all been the disciples of Montesquieu, but we have also been practical politicians." The President must woo, cajole, threaten, and even wage war on party leaders, legislators, and chieftains of the veto groups. He must bring the several parts of government and the private groups into harmonious effort to accomplish shared objectives. He alone in our political life can do it.

George Washington discovered the necessity for practical politics promptly upon taking up the Presidential office. The new government, he wrote, was to be one "of accommodation as well as a government of laws." The President's political means cover a wide gamut: blandishments, favors, bargains, compromises, and the assertion, when necessary, of naked pressure. Herbert Hoover, aiming to secure tariff reform legislation, met with the legislative leaders and made public appeals. When these proved unavailing, he granted a rare recognition by entertaining Senator William E. Borah alone at dinner to woo him, and, varying his attack, dispatched a sharp message to Senator Reed Smoot, who was guiding the bill in the Senate: "No flexible tariff, no tariff bill." Again failure on both counts, whereupon Hoover entertained all the Republican leaders at breakfast, but without success. When he learned that the House-Senate conference committee had watered down the flexible provisions nearly to the point of drowning them, Hoover responded with equal ferocity. "I wrote out the provision I wanted," he said. "I sent word that unless my formula was adopted the bill would be vetoed. The result was a complete victory."

To get his controversial measures enacted, whether in foreign or domestic affairs, the President, because of the unreliability of his own party, must build a special coalition for his purpose from both major parties. The coalitions keep forming and breaking up as their purpose is achieved. Moving on to new objectives, the President must develop a new combination of support. To make his way, the President must know when to spend and when to hoard his influence, and how to build it. He must realize, as Richard Neustadt has suggested, that the essence of his persuasive task is to convince the legislators whose support he courts "that what the White House wants of them is what they ought to do for their sake and on their authority." In playing the political game, the President occupies certain of the best vantage points in the political system. His power of publicity, his veto, his power over budget and expenditure, his power of appointment are means that exist nowhere else in the political structure. For all the limits upon his power, he is the supreme unifying force in our diffuse political system and pluralistic society. He better than anyone else can act affirmatively and flexibly. But his great rival, Congress, also enjoys distinction. No other body can cast the negative so readily, so conclusively, and in so many ways.

But the President, if he shall write his name large on the pages of history, must do more than excel at practical politics. He must use political power to advance great ends. His shining hours occur in the Fourteen Points of Wilson, in the social purposes of Lincoln and the Roosevelts, and in the assertion of principle of Grover Cleveland against the test of events. He must rise to moments as Cleveland did when pressing the House Speaker to support an administration measure; Cleveland found him hesitant and fearful of the consequences to his future. "Mr. Speaker," Cleveland exclaimed, "what is your political future weighed in the balance against the fortunes of the country? Who are you and I compared with the welfare of the whole American people?" The Speaker surrendered. But the President who, like Cleveland, chooses to enter the roaring furnace where political necessity and principle converge, subjects himself to the burning anguish that reaches its highest intensity in the Presidency itself. One day Cleveland invited a visitor, Dr. Wilton M. Smith, to listen to the draft of a speech. Cleveland, as he read on, worked up into a high pitch of emotion. He exclaimed, turning suddenly on his visitor,

> *Doctor, I suppose at times you won't approve of many things I do, but I want you to know that I am trying to do what is right. . . . Sometimes the pressure is most overwhelming, and a President cannot always get at the exact truth; but I want you to know that I am trying to do what is right.* I am trying to do what is right.

Tears welled in the big President's eyes; he blew his nose hard, and paced the room.

The President wears many chains. Since there are no more hours in the President's day than in any other man's, he needs aides and assistants for the massive affairs of the executive branch. Upon their information, skill, initiative, and loyalty much of his administration's success depends. But the vast executive bureaucracy, as Presidents have found, can be a slumbering giant, slow to act, unimaginative and uncreative, and disloyal to his purposes in its alliance with pressure groups which oppose him. Aides who earn his confidence acquire in time influence of their own, and become, to a degree, independent of their chief.

In the far reaches of foreign affairs, the President faces problems and trends he cannot control that are not running in his country's favor: the rising strength of its enemies, the independence of its allies, the recalcitrance of new nations, the spread of nuclear weapon capability. With the horror of general war at his elbow, he must conduct foreign affairs with a restraint unknown to his predecessors. President Kennedy acknowledged the weight of these realities when he declared,

> *We must face the fact that the United States is neither omnipotent nor omniscient, that we cannot always impose our will on the other 94 per cent of mankind, that we cannot right every wrong or reverse every adversity, and that therefore there cannot be an American solution for every world problem.*

In domestic affairs the President seems destined to struggle indefinitely with intractable problems: a steadily expanding hard core of unemployment, adjustments to the new technology which may require redefinitions of social attitudes toward work and leisure, a complex of adjustments in relations between the races which compose American citizenry, a deepening dependence of society, government, and therefore the Presidency upon intellectuals. His power ends where their knowledge stops.

Certain of the machinery of the Presidency has had little or no repair since the Founding Fathers originally constructed it in 1787. The electoral college is a creaky affair from whose capacity for disaster the country has already had narrow escapes, and given the law of probabilities we are due for further crises. Presidential inability is a problem the Founding Fathers left unsolved, and the nation, in continuing to neglect such incapacity, invites disaster. The succession law is rightly a subject of constant complaint.

The President and the Presidency, in a word, are in a race without letup against change and emergency. The office has indeed adjusted, too, and remarkably so, but the nice question remains: Has it been adapted sufficiently to stay with the race; can it give the nation, the world, and mankind creative and forceful responses for the towering problems of the 1960's?

ALONE AT THE TOP AND MASTER OF NOTHING

TOM WICKER

Senator John F. Kennedy addressed the National Press Club eleven months before he was elected President, and gave the following view of the kind of man needed in that office:

> *Whatever the political affiliation of our next President, whatever his views may be on all the issues and problems that rush in upon us, he must above all be the chief executive in every sense of the word. He must be prepared to exercise the fullest powers of his office—all that are specified and some that are not . . . the President is alone, at the top.*

In the same speech, the erudite young Senator quoted Woodrow Wilson's famous dictum that "the President is at liberty, both in law and conscience, to be as big a man as he can . . . His office is anything he has the sagacity and the force to make it . . . His capacity will set the limit."

In the long campaign that followed, Kennedy never deviated from this expansive idea of the office and the opportunity confronting the man who would be elected in November, 1960. And in that campaign, he stood for nothing if he did not stand for federal aid to education and for an increase in, and an expansion of the coverage of, the minimum wage.

In the massive record of his campaign statements, more than

From *JFK and LBJ*, by Tom Wicker. Reprinted with omissions by permission of William Morrow and Company, Inc. Copyright © 1968 by Tom Wicker.

two pages are required merely to index his remarks on education. He did not simply advocate federal aid, he promised it:

> *Unless we have a good and increasing educational system, we are not going to have a strong democratic society . . . America needs the Democratic party because the Democratic party intends to help the states build classrooms and pay for the teachers which are necessary if we are to have an educational system second to none. And America cannot afford schools which are second to anyone . . . We will permit every American child to receive the kind of education which will produce the skills and creativity which a growing America desperately needs . . . A Democratic administration will act in 1961.*[1]

Exactly one month to the day after he was inaugurated, Mr. Kennedy sent his education program to Congress with the confident message that it would provide a "new standard of excellence" available "to all who are willing and able to pursue it."

In his campaign, he was no less positive or stirring on the subject of the minimum wage; in office, he was even more prompt to move in this field than he was in sending up his education bill.

On August 29, 1960, to reporters in the Capitol, he had said: "I intend to take this fight to the American people. I am sure that they will support me in November in my goal of a minimum living standard of $1.25 an hour for millions of Americans who work in the large enterprises of our country."

And a month later, on September 29, in Buffalo, in one of the most ironic footnotes to the campaign and events to follow, Kennedy declared ringingly: "As long as the average wage for

---

[1] This is a composite of quotations from campaign speeches by Senator John F. Kennedy at Eugene, Ore., on Sept. 7, 1960; Oakland, Calif., Sept. 8, 1960; Charleston, W. Va., Sept. 19, 1960; and Cleveland, Ohio, Sept. 25, 1960.

laundry women in the five largest cities is 65 cents an hour for a 48-hour week . . . there is a need for our party."

Again and again, candidate Kennedy repeated such pledges as he raced across the United States. It was about as surprising, therefore, as the reappointment of J. Edgar Hoover, that President Kennedy asked in his first Economic Message, February 2, 1961, for a minimum wage increase. One month after his inaugural, he sent a special message to Congress asking a program of federal aid to education.

Thus it was that the new President—in his campaign and in his first actions—identified himself, as on few other issues, with aid to education and an increased minimum wage. These were old and familiar propositions in American politics; if the new President really meant, in the words of Wilson, "to be as big a man" as he could be—to be in his own phrase "the chief executive in every sense of the word"—then here was the place to begin. On no other issues had he more thoroughly committed himself; on none did he more passionately paint the need; on none could he either move his program ahead more decisively for the whole, or be held more strictly to account.

Scarcely two years later, Theodore C. Sorensen, the President's brilliant and tough-minded special counsel, one of the prime shapers of his domestic legislative proposals, told an audience at Columbia University: "While it should not be impossible to find an equitable constitutional formula to settle the church-school aid problem, it is difficult for that formula to be suggested by the nation's first Catholic President."

And Kennedy himself wrote in 1963, in his foreword to the book publication of Sorensen's Columbia lectures, a far different view of the Presidency than he had offered the National Press Club in 1960:

> *The President . . . is rightly described as a man of extraordinary powers. Yet it is also true that he must wield those powers under extraordinary limitations—*

> *and it is these limitations which so often give the problem of choice its complexity and even poignancy. Lincoln, Franklin Roosevelt once remarked, "was a sad man because he couldn't get it all at once. And nobody can." Every President must endure a gap between what he would like and what is possible.*[2]

What had happened in the intervening years, to cause this heightened regard for the limitations of the office Kennedy had sought so eagerly, with such confidence that it would confide its greatness to a man who would not shrink from it?

What happened, of course, is the story of the Kennedy Administration. But that story was influenced, in no small part, by events that took place at the outset, particularly the episodes of the minimum-wage and aid-to-education battles. And those episodes, like the larger story, were in great part shaped by circumstances that existed the day John Kennedy took office—by the human and political context circumscribing that particular man as he took the oath on the Capitol steps on January 20, 1961. It might have been a context that he, more than any other, had fashioned; but he could not control the minds, experience and imaginations of others, as they sought to see it for themselves.

But the frustration that would reach John Kennedy, that would cause him, finally, to see the White House in terms of its limitations rather than its opportunities, had origins even earlier than that, in the very nature of things. He might have envisioned himself being "alone, at the top" but, like Wilson, he would find out that not even a President moves free of human entanglement, human needs, human illusions; not even a President can be independent of those around him.

Kennedy learned at least that lesson right at the start. It

---

[2] The Sorensen quotation is on page 53, and the Kennedy quotation is in the foreword, of *Decision-Making in the White House: The Olive Branch or the Arrows*, by Theodore C. Sorensen, Columbia University Press, 1963.

was taught to him, as it had been to some of his predecessors, by the Committee on Rules of the House of Representatives. And the committee's challenge to his power disclosed much about the difficulties that lay ahead—about the world in which John Kennedy would seek to be as big as he could.

. . .

Almost four years earlier, when the Kennedy Administration was young and Lyndon Johnson had believed he could play a part in it, he had written on his return from Asia that the United States must be ready to decide whether it was willing to commit major forces to the defense of South Vietnam.

"We must remain master of that decision," he told Kennedy.

Johnson lost that mastery on February 7, 1965. He lost it because the event he set in motion that day—the "retaliation" he launched in such confidence of both its power and its restraint, in such certainty that it was both "limited" and "fitting"—acquired a life of its own, ugly and growing. From it flowed consequences no one had foreseen, consequences foreign to American experience and expectation, demanding new responses, permitting no evasion, imposing their own realities, until in the end Lyndon Johnson was not the master of anything; he was the creature of personality and circumstance.

So, Lyndon Johnson, trusting what he knew and confident of his country and kind, drifted into war. He had seen the people of which he was so intrinsically a part—"the farmer in Iowa, the fisherman in Massachusetts, the worker in Seattle, the rancher in Texas"—all harboring the same hopes and fears, all gathered before him in the Great Tent he had erected in his vision and his dreams. He had carried out a rainy night's pledge at the University of Texas and achieved a Consensus that, for a moment, really did "end obstruction and paralysis and liberate the energies of the nation for the work of the future." He had gone a long way, from the dust of the hill country to the loneliest peak of American political power and opportunity. And then, like Roosevelt before him, he had reached too far, believed too much, scaled the heights only—in the blindness of his pride—to stumble and fall.

He could call upon history to vindicate him, and in the rich and recurring irony of the endless adventure, perhaps it would. But not history nor all the king's men could give back to Lyndon Baines Johnson of Texas that moment for which he had waited all of his life.

FOREIGN POLICY

The scientific analysis of the decision-making process has presented students of that phenomenon with a new understanding of the dynamics of the process and the variables that enter into it. Foreign policy is one form of decision-making. Some argue that it can be understood in terms of a strategic bargaining game, while others claim that foreign policy is best viewed as a function of the historical evolution of power politics.

Whichever approach one takes, one should realize that there are many component parts to any decision: the President, Congress, the bureaucracy, mass media, public opinion, pressure groups, and the like. Decisions, especially in the arena of international relations, are never made in a vacuum, though this does not necessarily imply that the cues that other nations put forth are always properly perceived.

One element of the decision-making apparatus in foreign-policy formulation is the decision-makers themselves—those who are charged with the responsibility for the consequences of any particular decision. By examining the case of James Forrestal, the first American Secretary of Defense, Arnold A. Rogow raises a number of potentially disquieting but nonetheless relevant questions concerning the individual foreign-policy maker who must operate under growing stress and strain and within a framework of myths and assumptions, while at the same time coming out with swift, realistic, and reasonable advice and action. In the other selection, the noted newsman Elie Abel graphically describes the dynamics of the decision-making context, pointing up its strengths and weaknesses, as seen in one of the most significant tests of foreign-policy making in recent times, the Cuban missile crisis.

JAMES FORRESTAL

ARNOLD A. ROGOW

My interest in Forrestal . . . relates less to the fact that he was a distinguished American public servant—he was certainly that—than to his significance in any study of the relationship between personality, especially personality disorders, and politics. Forrestal was not the first high official to become mentally ill, but he is the highest-ranking American official to have committed suicide. The tragedy that ended his life in May, 1949, underscores the observation that we need to know much more about the tensions and frustrations of high office. And if it be doubted that the Forrestal case proves the point, perhaps it is enough to refer briefly to some other officials whose medical histories reflect stress and strain in high office.

Since 1900 two American Presidents (excluding McKinley) have died in office, one was incapacitated before the expiration of his term, and one was forced to curtail seriously his activities as a result of heart illness. There is a body of opinion which holds that illness and exhaustion affected decisions made by Presidents Woodrow Wilson and Franklin D. Roosevelt during their last years in the White House.[1] More recently ulcers, hypertension, coronary disease, and "exhaustion" have affected or terminated the political careers of Generals George C.

Reprinted with permission of The MacMillan Company from *James Forrestal* by Arnold A. Rogow. Copyright © 1963 by Arnold A. Rogow.

[1] The medical histories of Wilson and Roosevelt are given chapter-length treatment in Noah D. Fabricant, M.D., *13 Famous Patients* (Philadelphia: Chilton Company, 1960).

Marshall and Walter Bedell Smith, former Secretaries of State Hull, Stettinius, Byrnes, and Acheson, Under Secretary of State Sumner Welles and Deputy Secretary of Defense Robert A. Lovett.

Needless to say, the "tension diseases" are not exclusively American. The British list of those who have suffered incapacitating physical or mental illness while in office includes Anthony Eden, Ernest Bevin, Stafford Cripps, Neville Chamberlain, Stanley Baldwin, Ramsay MacDonald, and Andrew Bonar Law.[2] Russian victims of stress are hardly less numerous; perhaps the best known are Joseph Stalin (hypertension and paranoia), Andrei Y. Vishinsky (duodenal ulcer), and Nikita Khrushchev (hypertension).

"Is the fate of the world—*our* fate," Burnet Hershey asked in June, 1949, "in the hands of sick men?"[3] One month after Forrestal's death the question was timely, and also timely was a congressman's remark that "The secret malady of a statesman can be as disastrous as his secret diplomacy." In the light of what we know now about the behavior of Hitler and Stalin,[4] it may be permissible to suggest that a statesman's "secret malady" can be more disastrous than secret diplomacy.

---

[2] In two articles in *The Practitioner*, Dr. Hugh L'Etang has dealt with illness of senior British and French military officers in both world wars, and with the medical histories of Wilson, Roosevelt, Harry Hopkins, Forrestal, MacDonald, Bevin, Cripps, and others. See his "The Health of Statesmen and the Affairs of Nations," *The Practitioner*, January, 1958; and "Ill Health in Senior Officers," *The Practitioner*, April, 1961. I am indebted to these articles and to their author for many valuable insights and suggestions.

[3] *The Nation*, June 18, 1949.

[4] Of a number of books concerned with Hitler's behavior and personality development, one of the most important is Alan Bullock, *Hitler: A Study in Tyranny* (New York: Harper & Brothers, 1953). Less has been published about Stalin, but Khrushchev's report to the 20th Congress of the Soviet Communist Party may be read with profit. His report was published in the United States as *The Crimes of the Stalin Era: A Special Report to the 20th Congress of the Soviet Union*, February 24–25, 1956, supplement to *The New Leader*, July 16, 1956.

In the 1960's, when the survival of civilization may depend upon sanity in high places, the question is especially urgent and the remark well worth pondering.

Unfortunately, in Washington, and no doubt in London, Paris, Bonn, and Moscow as well, there is a mental-health mythology that turns aside such a question or at least regards it with suspicion. The mythology . . . holds in essence that Very Important Persons do not become mentally ill, or at any rate not while they are in office. Thus the invariable rule is that VIP's never experience anything more than "exhaustion" and the exhaustion, of course, reflects the fact that they overworked themselves in the nation's service. Only many years later—and sometimes not then—is it discovered that the "exhaustion" was an incapacitating psychosis. This does not deny the reality of a physical and mental fatigue that may precede or accompany a psychosis and require an extended rest or change of job. It remains true, however, that there is no psychosis clinically known as "exhaustion."

Nevertheless, the official mythology remains hostile to the question "Is our fate in the hands of sick men?" and even if it welcomed such a question there would still be difficulties. Understandably, no living government official wishes to be regarded as a psychotic or neurotic, and few want the public to know that they suffer from ulcers, heart disease, hypertension, and other ailments. The families of those who are dead are hardly more willing to have the physical or mental decline of the deceased made a matter of common knowledge. Where Very Important Persons are concerned, it is almost as if a confession of illness were a confession of weakness, and a confession of weakness a confession of failure.

The popular suspicion of psychiatry as an occult science, the tendency to regard the "headshrinker" as a modern version of the witch doctor, also play a role. If in some circles it is fashionable to discuss one's analysis, in Washington circles it is awkward and may even be costly to admit that one is making regular visits to a psychiatrist. Far from agreeing that public officials would benefit from psychoanalysis or psychotherapy, the public is more apt to conclude that those who require a psychic massage at any time in their lives are unfit to hold office. In effect, a known psychiatric patient has as much chance of being elected President as a known homosexual or alcoholic.

This does not deny the very real problems involved in diagnosing, treating, and curing personality disorders. Differences among psychiatrists regarding theory and therapy are sharp and frequently acrimonious; the outsider, listening to psychiatrists and psychoanalysts argue a case, is sometimes tempted to exclaim "Physician, heal thyself!" And even if there is agreement, can any psychiatrist be certain that a depressed and suicidal patient is cured, able to return to the family and job, capable of resuming a normal life? If the job is a political position of the highest importance, if the patient has responsibility for decisions that affect the course of history, the psychiatrist must be courageous indeed to recommend resumption of appointive or elective office. And even more courage is required on the part of appointing officials or voters who have some knowledge of the situation if his recommendation is to be accepted.

The widespread feeling that exploration of the psyche may be more art than science is reflected in the relative paucity of biographies that base themselves on psychoanalytic insights and formulations. Despite pleas that historians and social scientists make more use of psychoanalytic concepts, pleas similar to that issued by Harvard historian William L. Langer in 1957, few biographies and biographical studies cast even a glance in Freud's direction.[5]

---

[5] The outstanding exceptions in recent years have been Alexander and Juliette George, *Woodrow Wilson and Colonel House: A Personality Study* (New York: John Day, 1956); Erik Erikson, *Young Man Luther: A Study in Psychoanalysis and History* (New York: W. W. Norton, 1958); Alex Gottfried, *Boss Cermak of Chicago* (Seattle: University of Washington Press, 1962).

While it is true that not all great men require a psychiatric biography, any more than all men require a psychiatrist, there are many distinguished heroes and villains in history whose biographies—to paraphrase the expression quoted earlier—lacking psychiatric insights, tend to be taxidermic. One thinks immediately of Alexander Hamilton and Aaron Burr, of John Stuart Mill and William Gladstone, of Elizabeth I and Catherine de Medici. In certain instances, the most suggestive treatment of an important personage has appeared in the form of a novel, for example, the novels that were inspired by the careers of Ramsay MacDonald and Huey Long.

But despite the difficulties that arise in efforts to analyze motives and probe the unconscious, such efforts must continue to be made if there is ever to be any reliable answer to the question "Is our fate in the hands of sick men?" The question will never be a welcome one, but it would be foolhardy to pretend that it does not exist. The illnesses of Wilson and Roosevelt, the suicides of James Forrestal and John Winant, draw attention to the question, and so do the recent novels and films that concern themselves with the possibility of annihilation as a consequence of illness or error. The film *Dr. Strangelove,* reads a full-page advertisement in *The New York Times,* is

> *A Nightmare Comedy in which a psychotic Air Force General triggers an ingenious, foolproof and irrevocable scheme, unleashing his Wing of B-52 H-Bombers to attack Russia.*
>
> *The President of the United States, unable to recall the aircraft, is forced to cooperate with the Soviet Premier in a bizarre attempt to save the world.*[6]

---

[6] *The New York Times,* Western Edition, February 18, 1963. See also Eugene Burdick and Harvey Wheeler, *Fail-Safe* (New York: McGraw-Hill, 1962) and Fletcher Knebel and Charles W. Bailey, *Seven Days in May* (New York: Harper & Brothers, 1962).

Such books and films do not establish the existence of "psychotic" Air Force generals, much less demonstrate that our fate is being decided by "sick men." But their popularity—many of the books have been best-sellers—tends to confirm the impression that there is a good deal of anxiety about the physical and mental condition of our leaders.

. . . Forrestal's illness and suicide were not inevitable; the illnesses and suicides of other world leaders are not inevitable; and it is not inevitable that the world community become ill and commit suicide. But there will be other Forrestals and other wars if attempts are not made to prevent, detect, treat, and cure those illnesses that affect rational mental processes in decision-making environments. The Forrestal case, in and of itself, does not indicate with certainty what steps need to be taken, although certain proposals are advanced. . . . More knowledge, more discussion, and more case studies are necessary if citizens everywhere are to have some assurance that the policy process does not suffer from the contamination of illnesses that affect the mind.

In the meantime, the question "Is our fate in the hands of sick men?" becomes ever more relevant, and anxiety about the answer becomes ever more widespread. Perhaps it is well to remember that certain sicknesses, whether physical or mental, personal or national, are contagious. Some of them can also be fatal.

POSTSCRIPT

ELIE ABEL

Twenty-three days passed. The same Russians who had built the missile bases now smashed the concrete footings with electric hammers, plowed up the ground and loaded their missiles on ships bound for the Black Sea and Baltic ports whence they had come. But Castro refused to give up the Ilyushin bombers which, unlike the missiles, were under his control. The ships of Admiral Ward's task force remained on station in the Caribbean. General Power kept his loaded B-52s in the air. Key West was still bulging with troops. The President, advised by Tommy Thompson that Khrushchev would yield in the end, stepped up the pressure. At the United Nations, and also in private meetings of Robert Kennedy with Dobrynin, the Russians were told time and again that unless they removed the bombers the President would feel free to take military action; the no-invasion deal was off so long as a single offensive weapon remained on Cuban soil.

On November 20—Robert Kennedy's thirty-seventh birthday—Dobrynin called on the Attorney General. "I have a birthday present for you," he said. It was another letter from Khrushchev to the President, agreeing to remove the bombers. Robert Kennedy asked the Soviet Ambassador to point out the significant passages in Khrushchev's text. Dobrynin marked them carefully. Then he marched up and down the Attorney

From the book, *The Missile Crisis,* by Elie Abel. Copyright, ©, 1966 by Elie Abel. Reprinted by permission of J. B. Lippincott Company, pp. 209–216.

General's office, re-enacting the scene in Khrushchev's office as he had observed the First Secretary and Chairman of the Soviet Council of Ministers dictating other important messages in the past. A new bargain was struck: the President, Robert Kennedy assured Dobrynin, would issue his no-invasion pledge within thirty days if the bombers started moving out. The President, that same day, announced Khrushchev's promise to remove the bombers, adding that all known launching sites in Cuba had now been dismantled and the missiles sent back to the Soviet Union. In the circumstances, the President gave orders to terminate the quarantine. All told, nineteen Soviet merchant ships and six belonging to other Communist-bloc countries had passed through the screen of American destroyers; apart from twenty-three ships registered in other countries that were sailing under Soviet-bloc charters and seven belonging to friendly nations—three Greek, two British, one Spanish, and one Italian. The quarantine had been in force exactly twenty-seven days.

It was Fidel Castro, not Khrushchev, who had balked at the settlement terms. "Whoever comes to inspect Cuba," he shouted, "must come in battle array." U Thant had tried halfheartedly to bring him around, flying to Havana on October 30. He had returned the following day with nothing to show but his notes of an interminable Castro harangue directed against the Russians no less than the Americans. Thant's approach to Castro was apologetic. The Acting Secretary General had talked at times as if he represented forty-five nonaligned countries instead of all the United Nations—Russia and the United States included. "We hold this matter of inspection to be one more attempt to humiliate our country, and for that reason we do not accept it," Castro said. "I understand perfectly the sentiments of Your Excellency," Thant murmured. Throughout the conversation Thant behaved as if he were carrying out a distasteful duty forced upon him by the United States. If he saw fit to mention that the Soviet Union also was party to the U.N. inspection plan, an essential element in the Kennedy-Khrushchev agreement to wind up the crisis, excerpts of the conversation published afterward by the Cuban Government ignored that point. Castro had complained bitterly that the Russians treated him like a vassal, not allowing any Cuban to set foot on the missile bases, and—when the pressure became too much for them—agreeing to remove the missiles without asking his leave. No foreign government had the right, he argued, to speak in Cuba's name. There could be no inspection without Cuban consent and he refused to give it.

Khrushchev found himself in a tight box of his own construction: Castro was sulking, Kennedy threatening, and the Red Chinese were crowing over his "capitulation" to the imperialists. In Havana, posters proclaiming Cuba's eternal friendship for the Soviet Union were ripped from the walls. Street urchins sang a mocking couplet:

> *Nikita, Nikita,*   (Nikita, Nikita,
> *Lo que se da*   That which is given
> *No se quita.*   Is not taken back.)

Peking encouraged Castro to go on thumbing his nose at Moscow. The Chinese coined a Mao-Marxian syllogism to doubly denounce Khrushchev. It was sheer "adventurism," Peking said, to have put missiles into Cuba in the first place—a judgment millions in other countries could accept; but to take them out under American pressure amounted to simple "capitulationism."

As in other awkward moments—the moment in 1956, for example, when Budapest rebelled against Russian overlordship—Khrushchev sent for Anastas Mikoyan. On November 2, after a brief stopover in New York, the wily Mikoyan flew to Havana. His unquestioned talents as Moscow's great persuader were of no effect in Cuba. He pleaded, argued, threatened, but Castro would not be moved. For days on end, Castro simply ignored his distinguished visitor. "Mikoyan discovered that Castro was the first satellite he couldn't dominate," said one American who kept in close touch with the U.N. negotiations. "When he returned to New York he told us all about the beautiful beaches and the wonderful agricultural stations he had seen in the new Cuba. But it was quite obvious that he failed with Castro." While Mikoyan was in Havana, his wife died in Moscow. He missed the funeral, staying on to wrestle with Fidel as the Kremlin had directed. In the end the missiles were inspected at sea on their way out of Cuba. Russian captains cheerfully pulled back the tarpaulins while United States destroyers alongside them kept their running tally. They counted forty-two missiles altogether being removed to Russia. Navy reconnaissance planes followed the ships back across the Atlantic to make sure they did not change direction.

The sticking point for Khrushchev was the Ilyushin bombers. These had been a gift. They were now Cuban property and Castro would not hear of surrendering them. While Mikoyan grappled with Castro in Havana, John McCloy met repeatedly with Kuznetsov—in New York, at his own home in Stamford, Connecticut, or at the Soviet delegation's Glen Cove, Long Island, estate. Both McCloy and Stevenson soon wearied of the long, fruitless conversation with Kuznetsov. The Ilyushins in any case were obsolescent planes and the Russians, some suggested, may have been justified in arguing that they were not part of the original bargain. Some sentiment developed in the U.S. negotiating team to let Khrushchev wriggle off the hook. But the President, giving personal attention to the detailed reports of each negotiating session, refused. Instead, whenever a new snag developed, he would fire off one more letter to Khrushchev and step up the pressure, sending word through one emissary or another that if the bombers were not promptly removed the United States Air Force would have to destroy them on the ground. Tommy Thompson's reading had been that once Khrushchev backed down on the missiles, at whatever cost to his own prestige, he would not forever go on balking at the removal of some overage bombers as well. The President acted on Thompson's advice to the end. As for the Russians, they had been given reason to believe that if a fire-fight started the Washington "hawks" might overpower the "doves," invade Cuba and get rid of Castro. They did not care for the prospect. "We were happy to leave them believing that could happen," one of the American negotiators recalled. Again, Thompson's reading of the Kremlin auguries proved triumphantly accurate. On November 19 Castro caved in, agreeing not to obstruct the removal of the bombers. The following day Dobrynin delivered his "birthday present" to Robert Kennedy. Mikoyan left Cuba on November 25 with something accomplished, after all. And, on December 6, the last of the Ilyushins, neatly crated on the deck of a Soviet ship, sailed home.

To each of the Executive Committee members Kennedy in gratitude presented a silver plaque in the form of a calendar for the month of October 1962, the thirteen crisis days etched more deeply than the rest. There was no inscription, only the initials J.F.K. at the upper right and the recipient's initials at the left. No inscription was needed.

On December 12, 1962, speaking before the Supreme Soviet, Nikita Khrushchev attempted to set down certain lessons of the Cuban missile crisis. He put the question:

> *Which side triumphed, who won? In this respect one may say that it was sanity, the cause of peace and security of peoples, that won. Both sides displayed a sober approach and took into account that unless such steps are taken as could help to overcome the dangerous development of events, a World War III might break out.*
>
> *As a result of mutual concessions and compromise, an understanding was reached which made it possible to remove dangerous tension, to normalize the situation.*
>
> *It is, of course, true that the nature of imperialism*

> *has not changed. But imperialism today is no longer what it used to be when it held undivided sway over the world. If it is now a 'paper tiger,' those who say this know that this 'paper tiger' has atomic teeth. It can use them and it must not be treated lightly. . . .*
>
> *Of course, this was a critical time and the Government of the United States understood the possible development of events. . . .*
>
> *Both sides made concessions. We withdrew ballistic rockets and agreed to withdraw IL-28 planes. This gives satisfaction to the Americans. But both Cuba and the Soviet Union received satisfaction too: the American invasion of Cuba has been averted, the naval blockade lifted, the situation in the Caribbean is returning to normalcy.*

President Kennedy preferred not to philosophize about the missile crisis, though he was frequently asked after the event to state his own conclusions. In a joint interview with the three television networks on December 17, the President talked of one lesson.

> *I think, looking back on Cuba [Kennedy said]; what is of concern is the fact that both governments were so far out of contact, really. I don't think that we expected that he [Khrushchev] would put the missiles in Cuba, because it would have seemed such an imprudent action for him to take, as it was later proved. Now, he obviously must have thought that he could do it in secret and that the United States would accept it. So that he did not judge our intentions accurately.*
>
> *Well now, if you look at the history of this century, where World War I really came through a series of misjudgments of the intentions of others, certainly World War II where Hitler thought . . . that the British might not fight. . . .*
>
> *When you look at all those misjudgments which brought on war, and then you see the Soviet Union*

> *and the United States, so far separated in their beliefs . . . and you put the nuclear equation into that struggle; that is what makes this . . . such a dangerous time. . . . One mistake can make this whole thing blow up.*

The President's crucial achievement, once the crisis had started, was to make Khrushchev understand that he must withdraw—by showing him the nuclear abyss to the edge of which he had blundered and pointing a way back without disgrace. In the nuclear age, every President has the power to make war, with or without a Congressional declaration. Every President has the power to surrender a vital interest, with or without Senate ratification. To this extent, megaton technology has annihilated the clock and amended the Constitution. Kennedy succeeded in steering a safe course between war and surrender, remembering always that Khrushchev too was a politician, who must never be put in the position of risking discredit at home. Kennedy put the lesson this way in his American University speech the following summer:

> *Above all, while defending our own vital interests, nuclear powers must avert those confrontations which bring an adversary to the choice of either a humiliating retreat or a nuclear war.*

It is, perhaps, a fitting epitaph.

THE JUDICIARY

When one describes the federal judiciary, most discussion centers around the Supreme Court. Unlike most other tribunals, the United States Supreme Court is actively concerned with decisions that may overturn laws enacted by the popularly elected branches. In this sense the Court acts as a superlegislature.

Though some may claim that the practice of judicial review runs counter to democracy, this argument is, at best, moot because the American form of government is not a pure democracy. Rather it is a republic with built-in mechanisms of minority control such as the electoral college and the committee system in Congress. Therefore the real question that must be asked is, "Which branch of government has done the most to enhance democratic procedures?" On this point the Supreme Court certainly scores well.

Another important attribute of the Court is that it is a political institution. Political considerations enter into the naming of Court justices (witness the recent Fortas, Haynesworth, and Carswell episodes), as well as in the decisions of various justices. While some judges can transcend their earlier political beliefs and prejudices, it is apparent that a larger number do not.

Because of the Court's political nature, as well as its broad powers in the legislative process, the Court occupies a position of great strength in the American political system. This latter point is stressed in the selection written by Leo Pfeffer. In the second piece, *New York Times* reporter Anthony Lewis gives the background of a landmark Supreme Court decision, *Gideon* vs. *Wainwright*.

A MOST INGENIOUS PARADOX

LEO PFEFFER

For as long as there have been public schools in the United States, countless numbers of children have been accustomed to start the school day by reciting a prayer or listening to a teacher or pupil read a few verses from the Bible. In thousands of schools all over the nation, when classes resumed after the summer recess of 1963, the school day began without recitation of a prayer or a reading from the Bible. Those public school principals who thought it appropriate to inform the children of the reason for the change, told them that in June the United States Supreme Court had declared that public school Bible reading and prayer recitation were unconstitutional and must be stopped.

In 1894, the Congress of the United States enacted, as it had done on previous occasions, an income tax law, and millions of Americans painfully but dutifully prepared income tax returns and mailed them in to the government with check enclosed. Suddenly, on May 21, 1895, all these Americans stopped mailing tax returns and checks to the government, not to resume this unpleasant duty for almost twenty years. The reason? On May 20, 1895, the Supreme Court had declared the income tax law unconstitutional.

Our Supreme Court is not quite a unique institution; a few countries (Australia, for example) have liked what it has been doing and have established similar Supreme Courts for them-

From *This Honorable Court*, by Leo Pfeffer. Copyright © 1965 by Leo Pfeffer. Reprinted by permission of Beacon Press, pp. 3–10.

selves. But nowhere else can anything like it be found. If the Parliament of Great Britain were to enact a law imposing an income tax upon Englishmen or requiring teachers to lead their children in prayer, it is inconceivable that any court in Britain would dare to consider whether Parliament had the power to do what it did, much less to decide that it had no such power.

Nor do the publicized decisions handed down by the Supreme Court resemble the kind of decisions one would generally expect from a court of law. To the average American, a court is a forum that decides controversies between individuals, such as claims for damages arising out of an automobile accident or a suit to collect for goods sold and delivered, or criminal proceedings ranging from homicide to passing a red light. The Supreme Court, being principally a court of appeals, would not be expected to hear witnesses and hold jury trials. But like the appeal courts of the states, one would expect it to hear appeals from jury and other lower court trials and to reverse those decisions that it finds to have been erroneous.

The Supreme Court does not consider itself a tribunal whose purpose it is to correct the mistaken judgments of lower courts. It will not take an appeal simply because the lower court's decision may have been erroneous. To a disappointed litigant it may appear to be shocking that—as he is told by his lawyer—though the law is definitely on his side and the lower court made an egregious error of law in deciding against him, nevertheless he must pay money he really does not owe or may not receive money legally due him simply because the Supreme Court will not bother itself to right an obvious miscarriage of justice. Where a criminal case is involved the sense of shock will be even greater. The fact that an innocent man can go to jail or even to the death chamber is not of itself sufficient reason for the Supreme Court to accept an appeal. In the 1920's few non-lawyers could understand why the Supreme Court would not consider an appeal in the

Sacco-Vanzetti case and permitted the execution of two persons who millions of Americans believed were innocent of the crime of which they were convicted. While the Sacco-Vanzetti case arose in a state (Massachusetts) court, it is equally true that the Supreme Court will not intervene in a federal case, whether civil or criminal, merely because the lower court may have decided the case wrongly.

This does not mean that a litigant in a federal lower court has no recourse if the judge decides a case incorrectly. In our American judicial system every litigant generally has at least one right of appeal. In the states he appeals either to an intermediate appellate court or directly to the state supreme court. In the federal system he appeals to the circuit court of appeals. But if any of these courts decides the case incorrectly, that fact is not of itself sufficient to invoke the jurisdiction of the United States Supreme Court.

The reason for this is a simple, practical one. One Supreme Court, consisting of nine men, could not possibly undertake to correct the errors that might be contained in the innumerable decisions of the numerous state supreme and federal circuit courts. There is just no practical alternative to allowing the decisions of these courts to stand in well over 95 per cent of the cases they handle. This is not nearly as bad as it may at first glance seem. There must be an end to litigation at some point, and even if the Supreme Court accepted every appeal brought before it, the loser in every case would be assured by his lawyer that the Supreme Court was wrong but that there simply was no higher tribunal to which an appeal could be taken.

Efforts are made to bring only a minute fraction of decided cases before the Supreme Court and of these the Court accepts only a small fraction to hear and decide. Unlike state supreme courts, the United States Supreme Court, for all practical purposes, is master of its own calendar; that is, it is not required to hear any appeal it does not wish to hear. The cases that the Court does agree to hear and decide are those of great public importance, cases which directly or indirectly affect large segments of the population. A decision that Congress may or may not enact an income tax or compulsory military service law, or that a state may or may not set up separate public school systems for whites and Negroes, or that prayers may not be recited in public schools, obviously affects millions of Americans. While not all or perhaps not even most of the Court's decisions affect so many persons directly, the Court will rarely take a case unless the principle at issue is of great public importance. The numerous Jehovah's Witnesses cases, for example, directly affected only a tiny religious sect; but the principles of freedom of religion and speech formulated in those decisions concerned the whole American nation.

The majority of Supreme Court decisions are not what are generally called constitutional law decisions. They are decisions in which the Court interprets the numerous laws Congress enacts in a variety of fields—tax laws, copyright laws, bankruptcy statutes, maritime laws, labor relations acts, and a host of similar enactments of Congress. These decisions are generally technical; they are rarely reported outside of trade journals or legal publications. Yet dull, specialized and technical as they may be, they are important to the American public generally.

Take one illustration. Every American adult male knows that it costs but one dollar to look sharp, feel sharp and be sharp, and for that same dollar you may also get not only a safety razor but six double-edged blades and a neat carrying case. This great luxury is purchasable at such a low price only because the patents on safety razors have expired and manufacturers are free to enter into the competitive market on equal terms. Before the patents expired, the price of a safety razor alone was generally not less than five dollars. There is nothing more dull, technical and completely non-understandable to the layman than a decision under the patent law, but millions of American consumers may be affected in their pocketbooks by how a particular patent law case is decided by the Supreme Court. (A patent is issued only for inventions or improvements that are "novel," i.e., original. When Fuller was Chief Justice, towards the end of the nineteenth century, the Court had to decide on the "novelty" of a patent for a triangular piece of cloth to be sewn in the crotch of men's underwear for reinforcement. "Not a man in the Court," the Chief Justice said, "but had seen his mother sew that kind of a patch in his drawers." Needless to say, the patent was thrown out, and commercially made reinforcements could thereafter be purchased at a considerably lower price.)

It is in hearing and deciding cases under federal statues that the Supreme Court acts most like one would expect a court of law to act. The high courts of the states act that way and so too do the high courts of foreign countries. But decisions such as these are almost never reported on the front pages of the general press and do not often find their way even into the back pages. When the average American today thinks of the Supreme Court it is in terms of decisions outlawing racial segregation in the public schools or declaring unconstitutional gerrymandering in favor of rural over urban and suburban voters, just as his father in the 1930's thought of it in terms of decisions nullifying the NRA and other legislative efforts of the New Deal, his grandfather in the 1890's in terms of decisions outlawing federal income tax laws, and his great-grandfather in the ante-bellum days in terms of the Dred Scott decision.

These are the Court's constitutional law decisions. They are the most dramatic of the Court's actions, the ones in which it invokes the superior authority of the Constitution to check action by Congress, the President or the states. The uniqueness of the Supreme Court as a judicial tribunal is to be found in these decisions, and lies in the fact that in other countries (except the few that emulate us) decisions such as these are not made by the judicial arm but by the political arms of the government. In other countries it is the cabinet and the parliament, not the courts, that decide with finality questions regarding election districts or the rights and burdens of political dissenters or racial and religious minorities. In the United States, on the other hand, as early as 1832, de Tocqueville noted that practically every political question sooner or later becomes a judicial question.

The truth of the matter is that when the Supreme Court decides constitutional questions such as these it is not really a court of law at all, at least not in the usually accepted sense. It uses all the forms and trappings of a court of law and on the surface its decisions look like those usually handed down by conventional law courts. But if form is brushed aside and a square look is taken at the reality of the situation, the conclusion is inescapable that in these cases the Court acts not as a judicial but as a political organ of government. In short, it is supreme, but it is not really a court.

Generally it is assumed that when, after considerable debate, both houses of the federal or a state legislature pass a measure and the President or the governor signs it, the debate is over and we have a law. But, in reality, the legislative process is not at an end and the debate is not over. It may, and frequently does, simply shift to another building. From the legislative chambers the proposal went to the White House or the Executive Mansion of the governor. Now it comes to the marble palace occupied by the Supreme Court. It is only after a majority of the Court agrees that there ought to be a law that it can be said with reasonable finality that there is one. If the first two decisions, by the legislative and the executive, that there ought to be a law are political decisions—and who would deny that they are?—is it unfair to say that the third is likewise political? What is there to distinguish the first two steps from the third? (Before 1937 the Court's power to declare laws unconstitutional was generally exercised only in cases affecting business or property interests, and rarely in those involving civil or personal rights. Since 1937 the converse has been true, but the question is the same in both types of cases.)

The conventional answer is that only the Court passes on

the constitutionality of a law. But the members of the legislatures, federal and state, and the President and the governors, no less than the members of the Supreme Court, all take an oath to support the Constitution. Unless we are prepared to charge them with deliberately violating their solemn oaths, we must assume that before voting for the measure or signing it they had considered its constitutionality and had in good faith reached the conclusion that it was constitutional. How is that different from what the Supreme Court does?

Another conventional answer is that the legislature and the executive are concerned with the measure's wisdom whereas the Court is concerned only with its constitutionality. But the difference between constitutionality and unconstitutionality is a difference in degree, just as is the difference between wisdom and unwisdom. An unwise law may not for that reason alone be unconstitutional, but a very unwise law is. Unreasonable or arbitrary laws, the judges say, are unconstitutional; but "unreasonable" and "arbitrary" are simply legalistic jargon for very unwise, and what to a majority of the Court may be very unwise may be profoundly sagacious to a majority of Congress or of a state legislature. There is nothing wise or unwise but a majority vote makes it so.

True, a legislator, federal or state, will vote against a bill and the President or governor will veto it if he thinks it unwise, while a member of the Supreme Court will vote against it only if he thinks it very unwise, or very, very unwise. But a member of Congress has only a one five-hundred-and-thirty-fifth negative vote, while a member of the Court has a one-ninth negative vote, so it is not unreasonable that a more stringent standard should be in operation when the member of the Court casts his negative vote. The President does have a 100 per cent negative vote; but his exercise of it can be overruled by two-thirds of Congress, while the negative vote of the Court majority can be overruled, at least theoretically, only by the slow, tortuous and rare process of constitutional amendment.

If one could examine the consequences of the Supreme

Court constitutional law decisions divorced from the rather cumbersome judicial machinery that grinds out the decisions, the conclusion appears inescapable that these decisions are part of a single political-legislative process along with the decisions of the legislatures and of the executives. To the non-lawyer there would appear to be little difference whether the required judicial approval of an act of the legislature is considered an independent step or the third step in a three-step process, the first two of which are the enactment by the legislature and approval by the President or governor.

Aside from their practical consequences, evidence of the political nature of Supreme Court decisions with a constitutional background can be found in the style and language of the decisions themselves. The average opinion of a state court in a commercial or property law case is written with a legalistic style that repels the non-lawyer, to whom it is generally completely unintelligible, as it often is to a lawyer who does not specialize in the field of law involved in the case. The Supreme Court's constitutional law opinions, on the other hand, are quite readable and understandable to the layman. They read like political essays rather than legal documents. They are often reprinted in whole or substantial part in the New York *Times* and there is hardly a book of readings in political science used in college which does not contain large portions of such opinions.

Two decisions, both highly controversial, will suffice to illustrate this point. In 1951, in the case of *Dennis* v. *United States,* the Court upheld the conviction under the Smith Act of the top leaders of the Communist party in the United States. Justice Clark, who had been Attorney-General when the prosecution was begun, disqualified himself. The remaining eight judges voted six to two that the Smith Act was constitutional but they needed five separate opinions to state their views. This itself is an indication that the Court's constitutional law decisions are in a class different from the conventional decisions of a court of law. Almost never in a case involving commercial law or real property does one find such fragmentation of reasoning among the judges.

The difference is even more clearly indicated by the substance of the five opinions. Of those in support of the convictions, Jackson's may be taken as illustrative. To him the Communist party was not to be equated with the traditional American radical parties for whose protection the freedom of speech guarantee was placed in the Bill of Rights. The Communist party, he said, is realistically a state within a state, an authoritarian dictatorship within a republic. It demands constitutional freedoms for itself but not for its members, to whom it simultaneously denies freedom to dissent, to debate and to deviate from the party line. Therefore, he said, traditional guarantees of freedom of speech and of association are not applicable and do not prevent prosecution of the leaders for unlawful conspiracy, as "there is no constitutional right to 'gang up' on the Government."

Justice Douglas' opinion is illustrative of the reasoning of the dissenting Justices. (The other was Black.) To Douglas there was no authority given by the Constitution to distinguish among different types of unorthodox movements and political heresies; the guarantees of freedom of speech and of association protect them all equally. Only if there is a clear and present danger that the government will be overthrown unless preventative action is taken may these freedoms be impaired. As for that, while "Communism on the world scene is no bogeyman, Communism as a political faction or party in this country plainly is." Douglas expressed doubt "that there is a village, let alone a city or county or state which the Communists could carry."

The second decision was the 1954 case of *Brown* v. *Board of Education*, in which the Court, this time unanimously, overruled an 1896 decision and held that compulsory racial segregation in the public schools is unconstitutional. The reason was that the Fourteenth Amendment requires the states to treat all persons equally, and segregation by law has a detrimental psychological and educational affect on Negro children by creating in them a sense of inferiority which affects their motivation to learn and retards their educational and mental development.

For our purpose it is not material whether Jackson or Douglas was right, or perhaps more right, in respect to the threat of American Communism to our republic, or whether the 1896 or the 1954 Court correctly evaluated the effects of racial segregation. My point is that judgments such as these are not the type that the conventional court of law is called upon to make. Realistically they are not legal judgments but political or political-sociological judgments. When the Supreme Court makes judgments such as these it is not simply deciding a controversy between the two litigants before it but it is shaping the nature of American political, moral, economic and cultural patterns in a radically different way than the ordinary court does when it decides a question of business or property law. In a realistic sense the Supreme Court is legislating or at least participating in the legislative process.

GIDEON'S TRUMPET

ANTHONY LEWIS

In the morning mail of January 8, 1962, the Supreme Court of the United States received a large envelope from Clarence Earl Gideon, prisoner No. 003826, Florida State Prison, P.O. Box 221, Raiford, Florida. Like all correspondence addressed to the Court generally rather than to any particular justice or Court employee, it went to a room at the top of the great marble steps so familiar to Washington tourists. There a secretary opened the envelope. As the return address had indicated, it was another petition by a prisoner without funds asking the Supreme Court to get him out of jail—another, in the secretary's eyes, because pleas from prisoners were so familiar a part of her work. She walked into the next room and put the envelope on the desk of an assistant clerk of the Supreme Court, Michael Rodak, Jr.

Mr. Rodak, among other duties, concerns himself with what the Supreme Court calls its Miscellaneous Docket. This is made up mostly of cases brought by persons who are too poor to have their court papers printed or to pay the usual fee of one hundred dollars for docketing a case in the Supreme Court—bringing it there. A federal statute permits persons to proceed in any federal court *in forma pauperis,* in the manner of a pauper, without following the usual forms or paying the regular costs. The only requirement in the statute is that

---

From *Gideon's Trumpet,* by Anthony Lewis. Copyright © 1964 by Anthony Lewis. Reprinted by permission of Random House, Inc., pp. 4–10.

the litigant "make affidavit that he is unable to pay such costs or give security therefor."

The Supreme Court's own rules show special concern for *in forma pauperis* cases. Rule 53 allows an impoverished person to file just one copy of a petition, instead of the forty ordinarily required, and states that the Court will make "due allowance" for technical errors so long as there is substantial compliance. In practice, the men in the Clerk's Office—a half dozen career employees, who effectively handle the Court's relations with the outside world—stretch even the rule of substantial compliance. Rule 53 also waives the general requirement that documents submitted to the Supreme Court be printed. It says that *in forma pauperis* applications should be typewritten "whenever possible," but in fact handwritten papers are accepted.

Gideon's were written in pencil. They were done in carefully formed printing, like a schoolboy's, on lined sheets evidently provided by the Florida prison. Printed at the top of each sheet, under the heading Correspondence Regulations, was a set of rules ("Only 2 letters each week . . . written on one side only . . . letters must be written in English . . .") and the warning: MAIL WILL NOT BE DELIVERED WHICH DOES NOT CONFORM TO THESE RULES. Gideon's punctuation and spelling were full of surprises, but there was also a good deal of practiced, if archaic, legal jargon, such as "Comes now the petitioner. . . ." It seemed likely to Rodak that Gideon had a copy of the Supreme Court Rules.

The first of the documents in the envelope was a two-page affair headed "Motion for leave to proceed in forma pauperis" and including the notarized affidavit that the statute requires. A quick check indicated to Rodak that this prisoner had substantially complied with the rules. He appeared, for example, to have met the requirement that criminal cases be brought to the Supreme Court within ninety days of the lower court decision. Gideon had applied to the Florida Supreme Court for a writ of habeas corpus—an order freeing him on the ground that he was illegally imprisoned. He enclosed a copy of that application and of a brief order of the Florida court denying it. The Florida ruling against him, which he wanted the Supreme Court of the United States to review, was dated October 30, 1961, less than ninety days before.

There was very little in what he had sent to the Court to portray Clarence Earl Gideon the man. His age, his color, his criminal record if any—not even these basic facts appeared, much less any details for a more complete portrait. Because the case came from the South, one's assumption might have been that he was a Negro. He was not.

Gideon was a fifty-one-year-old white man who had been in and out of prisons much of his life. He had served time for four previous felonies, and he bore the physical marks of a destitute life: a wrinkled, prematurely aged face, a voice and hands that trembled, a frail body, white hair. He had never been a professional criminal or a man of violence; he just could not seem to settle down to work, and so he had made his way by gambling and occasional thefts. Those who had known him, even the men who had arrested him and those who were now his jailers, considered Gideon a perfectly harmless human being, rather likeable, but one tossed aside by life. Anyone meeting him for the first time would be likely to regard him as the most wretched of men.

And yet a flame still burned in Clarence Earl Gideon. He had not given up caring about life or freedom; he had not lost his sense of injustice. Right now he had a passionate— some thought almost irrational—feeling of having been wronged by the State of Florida, and he had the determination to try to do something about it. Although the Clerk's Office could not be expected to remember him, this was in fact his second petition to the Supreme Court. The first had been returned for failure to include a pauper's affidavit, and the Clerk's Office had enclosed a copy of the rules and a sample affidavit to help him do better next time. Gideon persevered.

Assistant Clerk Rodak, knowing and caring nothing for any of this, stamped Gideon's papers and gave them a number—890 Miscellaneous, meaning that the case was the 890th entered on the Miscellaneous Docket in the October Term, 1961. (Supreme Court terms, which usually run from October into June, are formally designated by the month in which they begin.) On a green file card a secretary typed the number and the title of the case: Clarence Earl Gideon, petitioner, versus H. G. Cochran, Jr., Director, Division of Corrections, State of Florida, respondent. Then the papers were put into a large red folder and tied with a string. (Red is the color for Miscellaneous cases; regular prepaid cases, on what is called the Appellate Docket, go into blue folders.) The Gideon folder was dispatched to the file room, one floor down, by an electric dumbwaiter.

Sometimes Rodak or his colleague in the Clerk's Office, Edward Schade, looking over the confused and often unintelligible prisoners' petitions that come before them, will spot one with an impressive legal claim. Their view has nothing whatever to do with the action the Supreme Court may take, since only the nine justices act for the Court and they do not discuss the merits of cases with the employees in the Clerk's Office. Still, just in the office, it enlivens things to say once in a while: "Here's one that I'll bet will be granted."

No one said that about *Gideon v. Cochran,* No. 890 Miscellaneous, October Term, 1961. In the Clerk's Office it had no ring of history to it. It was just one of nine *in forma pauperis* cases that arrived in the mail on January 8, 1962. Four others were, like Gideon's, criminal cases from the state courts—from Iowa, Washington, New York and Illinois. Two were appeals from federal convictions. One was a civil case, a claim by an unhappy and unaffluent author that someone had plagiarized his copyrighted play. The last was so confused that the Clerk's Office was unable to put it in any category at all.

Gideon's main submission was a five-page document entitled

"Petition for a Writ of Certiorari Directed to the Supreme Court State of Florida." A writ of certiorari is a formal device to bring a case up to the Supreme Court from a lower court. In plain terms Gideon was asking the Supreme Court to hear his case.

What was his case? Gideon said he was serving a five-year term for "the crime of breaking and entering with the intent to commit a misdemeanor, to wit, petty larceny." He had been convicted of breaking into the Bay Harbor Poolroom in Panama City, Florida. Gideon said his conviction violated the due-process clause of the Fourteenth Amendment to the Constitution, which provides that "No state shall . . . deprive any person of life, liberty, or property, without due process of law." In what way had Gideon's trial or conviction assertedly lacked "due process of law"? For two of the petition's five pages it was impossible to tell. Then came this pregnant statement:

"When at the time of the petitioners trial he ask the lower court for the aid of counsel, the court refused this aid. Petitioner told the court that this Court made decision to the effect that all citizens tried for a felony crime should have aid of counsel. The lower court ignored this plea."

Five more times in the succeeding pages of his penciled petition Gideon spoke of the right to counsel. To try a poor man for a felony without giving him a lawyer, he said, was to deprive him of due process of law. There was only one trouble with the argument, and it was a problem Gideon did not mention. Just twenty years before, in the case of *Betts v. Brady*, the Supreme Court had rejected the contention that the due-process clause of the Fourteenth Amendment provided a flat guarantee of counsel in state criminal trials.

Betts v. Brady was a decision that surprised many persons when made and that had been a subject of dispute ever since. For a majority of six to three, Justice Owen J. Roberts said the Fourteenth Amendment provided no universal assurance of a lawyer's help in a state criminal trial. A lawyer was constitutionally required only if to be tried without one amounted to "a denial of fundamental fairness." The crucial passage in the opinion read:

"Asserted denial [of due process of law] is to be tested by an appraisal of the totality of facts in a given case. That which may, in one setting, constitute a denial of fundamental fairness, shocking to the universal sense of justice, may, in other circumstances, and in the light of other considerations, fall short of such denial. In the application of such a concept there is always the danger of falling into the habit of formulating the guarantee into a set of hard and fast rules the application of which in a given case may be to ignore the qualifying factors. . . ."

Later cases had refined the rule of *Betts v. Brady*. To prove that he was denied "fundamental fairness" because he had no counsel, the poor man had to show that he was the victim of what the Court called "special circumstances." Those might be his own illiteracy, ignorance, youth, or mental illness, the complexity of the charge against him or the conduct of the prosecutor or judge at the trial.

But Gideon did not claim any "special circumstances." His petition made not the slightest attempt to come within the sophisticated rule of *Betts v. Brady*. Indeed, there was nothing to indicate he had ever heard of the case or its principle. From the day he was tried Gideon had had one idea: That under the Constitution of the United States he, a poor man, was flatly entitled to have a lawyer provided to help in his defense.

Gideon was tried on August 4, 1961, in the Circuit Court of the Fourteenth Judicial Circuit of Florida, in and for Bay County, before Judge Robert L. McCrary, Jr. The trial transcript begins as follows:

> *The Court: The next case on the docket is the case of the State of Florida, Plaintiff, versus Clarence Earl Gideon, Defendant. What says the State, are you ready to go to trial in this case?*

Mr. Harris (William E. Harris, Assistant State Attorney): *The State is ready, your Honor.*

The Court: What says the Defendant? Are you ready to go to trial?

The Defendant: I am not ready, your Honor.

The Court: Did you plead not guilty to this charge by reason of insanity?

The Defendant: No sir.

The Court: Why aren't you ready?

The Defendant: I have no counsel.

The Court: Why do you not have counsel? Do you not know that your case was set for trial today?

The Defendant: Yes sir, I knew that it was set for trial today.

The Court: Why, then, did you not secure counsel and be prepared to go to trial?

The Defendant answered the Court's question, but spoke in such low tones that it was not audible.

The Court: Come closer up, Mr. Gideon, I can't understand you, I don't know what you said, and the Reporter didn't understand you either.

At this point the Defendant arose from his chair where he was seated at the Counsel Table and walked up and stood directly in front of the Bench, facing his Honor, Judge McCrary.

The Court: Now tell us what you said again, so we can understand you, please.

The Defendant: Your Honor, I said: I request this Court to appoint counsel to represent me in this trial.

The Court: Mr. Gideon, I am sorry, but I cannot appoint counsel to represent you in this case. Under the laws of the State of Florida, the only time the court can appoint counsel to represent a Defendant is when that person is charged with a capital offense. I am sorry, but I will have to deny your request to appoint counsel to defend you in this case.

The Defendant: The United States Supreme Court says I am entitled to be represented by counsel.

> *The Court: Let the record show that the defendant has asked the court to appoint counsel to represent him in this trial and the court denied the request and informed the defendant that the only time the court could appoint counsel to represent a defendant was in cases where the defendant was charged with a capital offense. The defendant stated to the court that the United States Supreme Court said he was entitled to it.*

Gideon was wrong, of course. The United States Supreme Court had not said he was entitled to counsel; in *Betts v. Brady* and succeeding cases it had said quite the opposite. But that did not necessarily make Gideon's petition futile, for the Supreme Court never speaks with absolute finality when it interprets the Constitution. From time to time—with due solemnity, and after much searching of conscience—the Court has overruled its own decisions. Although he did not know it, Clarence Earl Gideon was calling for one of those great occasions in legal history. He was asking the Supreme Court to change its mind.

CIVIL LIBERTIES
AND CIVIL RIGHTS

Implicit in the question of civil liberties and civil rights is a constant tension between the rights of an individual, on one hand, and those of society, on the other. If absolute individual liberties are upheld, anarchy results. Conversely, if only the rights of society are respected, an oppressive condition of superconformity, and possibly even a police state, may emerge. As a result, an important task of legislators and judges is to strike a balance and encourage conditions in which both "law" (that is, justice) and order will result.

The tradition of individual liberties and rights can be traced in America to sources such as the Bill of Rights, the Virginia and Kentucky Resolutions, and the Fourteenth Amendment. Yet it has been mainly since World War II that the most progressive strides have been made in this field. Through decisions of the Supreme Court (*Miranda, Brown, Gideon*), Presidential actions, and certain acts of Congress (Civil Rights Acts of 1957, 1964, 1965), the rights of Americans are more protected today than at any time in this century.

While there may exist a certain amount of revulsion at decisions that "increase" rights of alleged criminals (actually they only explain what has always existed), it must be remembered that the acid test of a society that claims to be democratic is in its treatment of the weak and poorly regarded individual, not in the way it can rally support to popular causes.

In the following selections, political philosopher William Ebenstein examines the nature of individual rights, while former Supreme Court Justice Abe Fortas discusses the problem of dissent.

INDIVIDUAL FREEDOM

WILLIAM EBENSTEIN

The best introduction to the problem of individual liberty is still John Stuart Mill's essay *On Liberty* (1859). Mill wrote his essay at a comparatively civilized time, when there seemed to be little need for it. Yet he foresaw that illiberal forces would gain in influence, and he hoped that men would then turn to *On Liberty*. Though Mill modestly disclaimed originality other than that which "every thoughtful mind gives to its own mode of conceiving and expressing truths which are common property," the essay has grown in stature as time goes on, because many of Mill's predictions have come true, and much that he has to say is still valid today.

As Alexis de Tocqueville had done in his *Democracy in America* (1835–1840), Mill attacked the idea that the evolution of government from tyranny to democracy necessarily solves the problem of individual liberty. *Tyranny can be exercised by one, by a few, or by the majority,* and the latter is potentially the worst of all, since it commands the widest moral support, whereas oppression by one or a few is mainly physical. The power of public opinion in a democracy often exercises more restraint and repression against dissidents than a dictator exercises by physical means in a dictatorship. Protection against political tyranny is therefore not enough. It must be supplemented by protection against social tyranny, which

---

William Ebenstein, *Today's Isms*, 6th ed., © 1970. Reprinted by permission of Prentice-Hall, Inc., Englewood Cliffs, New Jersey, pp. 187–195.

leaves fewer means of escape, "penetrating much more deeply into the details of life, and enslaving the soul itself."

Mill sees that the natural tendency of man is not to be tolerant and open-minded, but to impose his views on others, and that lack of power is frequently the major cause of tolerating dissent. It makes little difference how numerous the dissenting minority is: "If all mankind minus one, were of one opinion, and only one person were of the contrary opinion, mankind would be no more justified in silencing that one person, than he, if he had the power, would be justified in silencing mankind."

Silencing an unorthodox opinion is not only wrong but harmful, because it robs others of an opportunity to get acquainted with ideas that may be true or partly true. "All silencing of discussion," Mill argues, "is an assumption of infallibility." Therefore Mill states that, unless *absolute freedom of opinion*—scientific, moral, political, and theological—is guaranteed, a society is not completely free.

No individual can grasp more than a fragment or portion of truth; no society can speak for all mankind; finally, whole eras are no more infallible than individuals. History is full of opinions held by one age as the last truth, only to be considered false and absurd by subsequent ages.

Just as liberty is not complete unless it is absolute, so discussion must be completely unhampered, and free discussion must not be ruled out when "pushed to an extreme," because the arguments for a case are not good unless they are good for an extreme case. Mill is aware of the argument that some opinions are so useful and important to society that they must be excluded from public discussion and criticism, but he answers that the "usefulness of an opinion is itself a matter of opinion."

Mill does not accept the "pleasant falsehood" that truth inevitably triumphs over persecution; history "teems with instances of truth put down by persecution." In the history of religion in the West, for example, there are numerous sects and churches that have been successfully suppressed, and Mill therefore concludes that "persecution has always succeeded, save where the heretics were too strong a party to be effectually persecuted."

Moreover, *the greatest harm of persecution is inflicted not on those who dissent from established beliefs, but on those who do not,* because the mental development of the latter is stifled by the fear of expressing unorthodox or dissenting views. In an atmosphere of cowed uniformity there may be a few exceptional great thinkers but not an intellectually active people. "No one can be a great thinker who does not recognize that as a thinker it is his first duty to follow his intellect to whatever conclusions it may lead."

Moreover, dogmatism robs truth of its vigor and vitality and is more likely to destroy truth than keep it alive. For its own health, truth needs to be "fully, frequently, and fearlessly" discussed. If possible at all, the opposing opinion should be expressed by someone who really believes in it. Only in the constant process of being challenged can truth grow and remain healthy. "Both teachers and learners go to sleep at their posts, as soon as there is no enemy in the field."

The necessity for the fullest expression of opinion may be based on three grounds. First, the silenced opinion may be *wholly true,* in which case its suppression is wholly unjustified. Second, the silenced opinion may be *partly true and partly false,* as most opinions tend to be, in which case "it is only by the collision of adverse opinions that the remainder of the truth has any chance of being supplied." Third, even if the silenced opinion be *wholly erroneous,* it should not be suppressed, because its very challenge of truth prevents the latter from degenerating into dogma and prejudice.

The purpose of individual liberty is personal self-development. It is the privilege of every person to interpret experience in his own way, and his moral faculties can only be brought into play when he is obliged to choose between alternatives. A person who merely follows custom and tradition makes no choice, nor does he who lets others make his decisions for him. *Different persons should be permitted to lead different lives;* the principle of liberty thus inevitably implies that of variety and diversity.

It should be noted that the progress of industrial civilization does not make it easier for men and women to remain individual personalities, because increasingly "they now read the same things, listen to the same things, go to the same places, have their hopes and fears directed to the same objects, have the same rights and liberties, and the same means of asserting them." People who do the same things tend to think the same thoughts.

This standardization has progressed enormously in the last hundred years; the radio, television, and movie industries have added new dimensions of prefabricated opinion. The number of daily papers is steadily declining in Britain and the United States (there are hundreds of cities and towns with only one daily paper) and the number of newspaper readers is constantly increasing, so that more and more people are reading fewer and fewer papers. Moreover, standardization has now reached the point where not only is identical news coverage published in thousands of papers, but even editorials, purporting to present the viewpoint of the local paper's editor, are actually "canned," prepared in a New York or Washington agency and then "farmed out" all over the country.

Mill reminds those who are willing to repress individual liberty for the sake of a strong state that the worth of a state is no more than the worth of its individual citizens. When the state "dwarfs" its men and reduces them to docile instruments, it will find that "with small men no great things can really be accomplished."

Mill is still the best guide to liberty based on reason. Yet *On Liberty* is more than a century old, and it cannot be expected to give clearcut answers to the problems that baffle us today. In particular, Mill did not deal with the problem of revolutionary movements in a democracy.

In the United States, the curbing of revolutionary movements by legal means is based on the Smith Act of 1940, Section 2 of which makes it unlawful for any person knowingly or willfully to "advocate, abet, advise, or teach the duty, necessity, desirability, or propriety of overthrowing or destroying any government in the United States by force or violence, or by the assassination of any officer of such government." In 1948, eleven communist leaders were indicted for violation of the Smith Act. The trial, one of the most important political trials in American history, lasted more than nine months and required almost 16,000 pages to record. Finally, the Supreme Court took up the case and decided against the communist leaders on June 4, 1951.

The main constitutional issue involved was *whether the Smith Act violated the First and Fifth Amendments*. The First Amendment provides that Congress shall make no law "abridging the freedom of speech, or of the press; or the right of the people peaceably to assemble, and to petition the government for a redress of grievances." Under the Fifth Amendment, no person "shall be deprived of life, liberty, or property, without due process of law." By a majority of six to two, the Supreme Court held the Smith Act constitutional.

A central concept in the conflicting opinions of the Court was the *clear and present danger* doctrine, as expressed by Mr. Justice Holmes in 1919: "The question in every case," Holmes wrote, "is whether the words used are used in such circumstances and are of such a nature as to create a clear and present danger that they will bring about the substantive evils that Congress has a right to prevent. It is a question of proximity and degree."

Writing for the majority in the case of the communists, Chief Justice Vinson declared that the communists *did* create a clear and present danger in recommending the overthrow of the government by force and violence. Chief Justice Vinson even went beyond the "clear and present danger" doctrine by accepting a narrower concept of *probable danger:* "In each case [courts] must ask whether the gravity of the 'evil,' discounted by its improbability, justifies such invasion of free speech as is necessary to avoid the danger." In a concurring opinion, Mr. Justice Jackson denied that the clear-and-present-danger doctrine could properly be applied to the case; otherwise communists plotting a revolutionary conspiracy would be protected during its period of incubation, and the government could move "only after imminent action is manifest, when it would, of course, be too late."

In his dissenting opinion, Mr. Justice Black emphasized that the communist leaders were not charged with any nonverbal acts designed to overthrow the government and that the outlawry of verbal expressions of revolution constitutes a drastic qualification or complete repudiation of the clear-and-present-danger doctrine. Mr. Justice Douglas, in his dissenting opinion, conceded that "the freedom to speak is not absolute," and accepted, in general, the Holmesian principle. However, whereas Holmes left the meaning of his principle rather vague, Douglas quoted approvingly Mr. Justice Brandeis in *Whitney* v. *California* (1927) that "no danger flowing from speech can be deemed clear and present, unless the incidence of the evil apprehended is so imminent that it may befall before there is opportunity for full discussion." Following Brandeis, Douglas argued that free speech *has* destroyed communism in the United States and that it is "inconceivable" that advocates of communist revolution in the United States would have any success. Under the Brandeis doctrine, it might be one thing to preach publicly against conscription when there is ample opportunity to rebut pacifism in public debate and quite another thing to preach pacifist doctrine outside a draft board, when such opportunity to rebut does not exist.

The Brandeis doctrine was expressed much earlier by Thomas Jefferson, who was willing to "tolerate error so long as reason is left free to combat it." In his first inaugural address Jefferson said that "having banished from our land that religious intolerance under which mankind so long bled and suffered, we have yet gained little if we countenance a political intolerance as despotic, as wicked, and capable of as bitter and bloody persecutions." Going into the fundamental question of how to deal with those who advocate basic change, Jefferson had this to say: "If there be any among us who would wish to dissolve this Union or to change its republican form, let them stand undisturbed as monuments of the safety with which error of opinion may be tolerated where reason is left free to combat it."

Jefferson was willing to allow even antirepublican (or antidemocratic, as we would say today) doctrines, not only on the basis of rational argument but also because he had tremendous faith in a free America, "the strongest government on earth." It is possible that our present wavering with regard to the Jeffersonian doctrine coincides with something deeper: a loss of self-confidence in the strength of liberty and the growing fear that antidemocratic propaganda, if unchecked, might gain too many converts.

There are indications of a return to more traditional American concepts. Virtually reversing its position of 1951, the Supreme Court ruled on June 17, 1957, in the case against fourteen west coast communist leaders that a distinction must be made "between advocacy of forcible overthrow as an abstract doctrine and advocacy of action to that end," and that "mere membership or the holding of office in the Communist Party" did not constitute sufficient evidence of the intent to overthrow the government by force. While this decision did not explicitly invalidate the constitutionality of the Smith Act, it marked, at least, a return to the clear-and-present-danger doctrine that had been strongly modified, if not abandoned, in 1951. In any case, the 1957 decision of the Supreme Court reestablished the traditional democratic concept under which all doctrines, including revolutionary ones, may be lawfully advocated and propagated. In other words, the validity of democracy is no longer a taboo issue that must not be challenged.

Under the Internal Security Act of 1950 (known as the McCarran Act), the Communist party was required to register with the government. In 1961, the Supreme Court held that this requirement was constitutional, but in 1964 and 1965 it effectively nullified the practical value of this position, for it ruled that neither the Communist party nor individual party members could be compelled to register, since this would be compulsory self-incrimination forbidden by the Fifth Amendment. The net effect of these (and other) decisions since 1957 has been to allow the Communist party to come out into the open more and more. In 1966, the party held its eighteenth national convention—the first since 1959. Yet despite the considerable freedom enjoyed by communists in recent years—due mainly to the liberal interpretation of existing laws by the courts and law enforcement agencies—the membership of the Communist party has remained stable at the low figure of about fifteen thousand. Above all, the party has failed to make any significant progress in penetrating its three prime targets: Negroes, Mexican-Americans, and labor unions.

In the protection of traditional liberties, the judiciary has held up best in the contemporary crisis. In 1955, for example, the United States Court of Appeals upheld the "natural right" of American citizens to travel abroad, thus denying the Department of State the authority to decide arbitrarily who may undertake such travel. Since that decision, upheld in a similar case by the Supreme Court in 1958, the government can deny the issuance of a passport only after due process of law, whereas until that time it could, and did, make such vital determinations on its own discretion. Although the Fifth Amendment does not specifically mention the right to travel, the Supreme Court held in 1958 that it is part of the "liberty" protected by the Fifth Amendment against infringement without due process of law. In 1964, the Supreme Court declared unconstitutional the provision of the McCarran Act under which Communists were forbidden to apply for passports. The court ruled that the government has the right to restrict travel under special circumstances on grounds of national security but that it could not forbid all Communists from traveling to all countries where passports are required. The government must show in each specific case why denial of a particular trip to a particular Communist is required by considerations of national security. In 1967, the Supreme Court ruled that a person could not be denied employment in a defense plant solely on the ground of membership in the Communist party.

In education too, the Supreme Court has had to reconcile individual liberty with national security. In 1957, the Court dealt with an important aspect of academic freedom. Professor Paul Sweezy, after lecturing at the University of New Hampshire on economics, was questioned by the state's attorney general about his political activities and beliefs. He denied the charge that he had ever been a member of the Communist party but refused to give any information about his teaching or his political opinions and associations. As a result, he was held to be in contempt by the New Hampshire Supreme Court. The United States Supreme Court decided that Professor Sweezy's conviction was invalid and added the warning that government should be "extremely reticent" to tread in the areas of academic freedom and political expression: "No one should underestimate the vital role in a democracy that is played by those who guide and train our youth. To impose any strait-jacket upon the intellectual leaders in our colleges and universities would imperil the future of our nation."

THE RIGHT AND
THE LIMITATIONS

ABE FORTAS

*"A function of free speech . . . is to invite
dispute. It may indeed best serve its high purpose
when it induces . . . unrest . . . or even
stirs people to anger."*

—MR. JUSTICE DOUGLAS

THE RIGHT

In the United States, under our Constitution, the question is not "may I dissent?" or "may I oppose a law or a government?" I *may* dissent. I *may* criticize. I *may* oppose. Our Constitution and our courts guarantee this.

The question is: *"How* may I do so?"

Each of us owes a duty of obedience to law. This is a moral as well as a legal imperative. So, first, we must seek to know which methods of protest are lawful: What are the means of opposition and dissent that are permissible under our system of law and which, therefore, will not subject us to punishment by the state and will not violate our duty of obedience to law?

There is another question. Are there occasions when we, with moral justification, may resort to methods of dissent, such as direct disobedience of an ordinance, even though the

---

From *Concerning Dissent and Civil Disobedience*, by Abe Fortas. Copyright © 1968 and 1970 by Abe Fortas. Reprinted by arrangement with The New American Library, New York, N.Y., pp. 27-40.

methods are unlawful? This is the perplexing philosophical question with which I shall deal in Part II of this discussion.

From our earliest history, we have insisted that each of us is and must be free to criticize the government, however sharply; to express dissent and opposition, however brashly; even to advocate overthrow of the government itself. We have insisted upon freedom of speech and of the press and, as the First Amendment to the Constitution puts it, upon "the right of the people peaceably to assemble and to petition the Government for a redress of grievances."

I say, with confidence, that nowhere in the world—at no time in history—has freedom to dissent and to oppose governmental action been more broadly safeguarded than in the United States of America, today. I say this even though I recognize that occasionally our officials depart from freedom's path.

This right to dissent may be exercised by the use of written and spoken words; by acts, such as picketing, which are sometimes referred to as "symbolic speech" because they are means of communicating ideas and of reaching the mind and the conscience of others; and by "peaceable" mass assembly and demonstrations. Ultimately, the basic means of protest under our system is the ballot box: the right to organize and to join with others to elect new officials to enact and administer the law.

These freedoms have long been celebrated. Our history and literature, as well as our law reports and legislative records, are crowded with moving and eloquent language reiterating the sanctity of dissent and the sacredness of the right to express it freely.

Our record as a nation demonstrates the validity of our commitment to freedom.

We are a great nation, I think, largely because of our protection of the freedom to criticize, to dissent, to oppose, and to join with others in mass opposition—and to do these things powerfully and effectively.

The Limitations

"Sic utere tuo ut alienum non laedas."
(*So conduct yourself that you will
not injure others.*)

—A MISLEADING MAXIM

There are limitations, however, even on the freedom of speech. The state may prescribe reasonable regulations as to when and where the right to harangue the public or to assemble a crowd may be exercised. It may require a permit for a mass meeting. But it can't use this housekeeping power for any purpose except to reduce the public inconvenience which any large assemblage involves.

And it is not true that anyone may say what's on his mind anytime and anywhere. According to the famous dictum of Justice Holmes, no one may falsely cry "Fire" in a crowded theater and thereby cause a panic. This is so even though the person's action may have been prompted by the highest motives.

He may have been alarmed and outraged by the lack of proper regulations to deal with fires in public places. He may have exhausted all other means to bring about the reform. He may have shouted "Fire" in the crowded theater only after all other measures failed, and only to dramatize the need and to secure necessary governmental action in the public interest.

But good motives do not excuse action which will injure others. The individual's conscience does not give him a license to indulge individual conviction without regard to the rights of others.

The man distressed at the inadequacy of fire regulations may speak in the public square; he may print and circulate pamphlets; he may organize mass meetings and picketing for the same purpose. He may denounce the city fathers as dunces, corrupt tools of the landlords, or potential murderers of innocent people.

He may even be able to call upon the courts to compel the government to act as he thinks it should. Our system provides a uniquely wide range of remedies in the courts which the citizen may invoke against his government.

Eventually, he and others may vote the government out of office.

But—and here is the point—he may not use means of advancing his program which, under the circumstances, will cause physical injury to others or unreasonably interfere with them.

Most of us would agree with Holmes that freedom to speak does not include falsely crying "Fire" in a crowded theater causing a panic, but the illustration does not solve the problem of defining the limits of permissible protest. Even with Holmes' help, the line between the permissible and the prohibited remains hard to draw.

Speech, including symbolic speech such as picketing, never exists in limbo. It always occurs in a particular place and in particular circumstances. Even if *what is said* does not create a "clear and present danger" of physical injury to others, the place where the speech is uttered, the size of the crowd, and the circumstances may convert the lawful into the unlawful.

For example, if the participants unlawfully prevent the movement of traffic or if they unlawfully and needlessly trespass on private property, the fact that their speech is constitutionally protected will not necessarily shield them from arrest for the traffic violation or the trespass. The words may not occasion punishment, but the attendant circumstances may.

Even the application of this simple proposition is difficult. In *Brown v. Louisiana,* the Supreme Court divided five to four on a question of this sort. CORE had decided to protest segregation of public library facilities in the parishes of East and West Feliciana and St. Helena, Louisiana. Negroes were excluded from the three libraries serving the parishes. The parishes operated two bookmobiles. One was red, the other blue. The red bookmobile served only white persons. The blue bookmobile served only Negroes. Residents of the parishes could revive library service by presenting registration cards. The cards issued to Negroes were stamped "Negro." A Negro holding a card could receive library service. But only from the blue bookmobile.

On a Saturday morning, during regular library hours, five adult Negro men, members of CORE, entered the segregated library building. They asked the librarian for a book: *The Story of the Negro* by Arna Bontemps. The librarian told them it was not on the shelves. They remained in the reading room as a protest against the segregation of the library. They were quiet and orderly. They were asked to leave. They politely refused.

CORE had given the sheriff advance notice of the proposed sit-in. The sheriff and some deputies arrived in ten or fifteen minutes from the time the men entered the library. The protesters were arrested. They were tried and convicted of disorderly conduct under a Louisiana statute.

On appeal, five of the nine members of the United States Supreme Court voted to set aside their conviction. There were differences of opinion even among the five as to the precise basis of the decision. The opinion which I wrote was joined only by the Chief Justice and Mr. Justice Douglas. It concluded that the protesters were engaged in the peaceful exercise of First Amendment rights. My opinion said that these rights clearly include the right to protest the unconstitutional segregation of public facilities by "silent and reproachful presence, in a place where the protestant has every right to be. . . ."

Justices Brennan and White agreed with the result that we reached, but wrote separate opinions. The five of us agreed, however, that the conviction of the protesters violated the Bill of Rights of the federal Constitution.

Four members of the Court disagreed. They did not quarrel with the proposition that the Negroes were privileged to enter the segregated library building, or that they were entitled, as members of the public, to library service. But they thought that by remaining in the library as a protest after they had asked for a book and had been informed it was not available, the Negroes were expressing their protest in an inappropriate and unauthorized place, and, accordingly, their action was not protected by the First Amendment.

In the minority's view, eloquently expressed by Mr. Justice Black, the Negroes had no right to be in the library after they had completed their business. Remaining there after their library business was completed, according to the minority of the Justices, was not a constitutionally protected form of protest, even though they entered the premises lawfully, remained there during regular hours only, and peacefully and quietly expressed their protest against the segregation of the library itself.

In substance, the difference between the majority and minority turned on their respective judgments as to whether a peaceful, orderly protest is ever protected by the First Amendment if it is held in a public library. The majority said it is protected if it does not interfere with others and takes place when the protesters have a right to be present.

The result might very well have gone against the protesters if they had stayed in the library after the regular hours during which it was open to the public. If they had done so, a majority and not a minority of the Court might have agreed that this conduct was not constitutionally protected.

The fact that they were sitting-in to protest segregation might not have protected them if they had violated reasonable regulations applicable to all, without discrimination. Their sit-in would not then have been merely an instance of symbolic speech. It would have been symbolic speech accompanied by violation of a lawful and appropriate regulation designed reasonably to regulate the use of a public facility by everybody.

Burning draft cards or even American flags has been defended as a form of protest. Some people say that this should be permitted as symbolic speech. It is urged that it is nothing more than a picturesque or dramatic form of expressing protest.

But the problem is much more difficult than this. A punishable offense is not excused solely because the conduct is picturesque, even if its purpose (to protest) might be unassailable. As my discussion of the library sit-in case shows, if the protest involves violation of a *valid law,* the fact that it was violated in a "good cause"—such as to protest segregation or war—will not ordinarily excuse the violator.

The law violation is excused only if the law which is violated (such as a law segregating a public library) —only if *that law itself* is unconstitutional or invalid. In the library sit-in case the protesters violated a segregation ordinance. This ordinance was unconstitutional and its violation could not be constitutionally punished. But if the law violated by the sit-in had been a lawful and reasonable regulation of library hours, the outcome might well have been different.

The burning of draft cards or American flags involves direct violation of law. Laws forbidding the burning or desecration of the national flag have existed for many years, and it is hardly likely that anyone would seriously contest their constitutionality or legality. In the case of draft cards, however, it has been vigorously urged that the federal law prohibiting mutilation or burning of draft cards serves no real purpose and was recently enacted by the Congress merely to punish dissent. For this reason, it is said, the law is an unconstitutional burden on the right of free speech. Therefore, it is argued, the draft card burning should not be held to involve a violation of law. A case involving this question is awaiting decision by the Supreme Court and I cannot comment upon it. But the point that I make is that if the law forbidding the burning of a draft card is held to be constitutional and valid, the fact that the card is burned as a result of noble and constitutionally protected motives is no help to the offender.

I can illustrate the principle involved by reference to a

problem that has arisen a number of times in connection with mass picketing. In *Cox v. Louisiana,* the Supreme Court reversed convictions for mass picketing even though the demonstration took place just outside of the courthouse and cells where civil rights activists, previously arrested, were incarcerated. But if the demonstrators had insisted upon blocking access to the courthouse, or had entered its doors and disrupted the work going on in the courthouse in order to stage a demonstration inside, or had refused to march or demonstrate in a way that allowed pedestrian or auto traffic to proceed, the result might have been different. The fact that they were engaged in a protest would not give them immunity from arrest and prosecution for their law violation.

This necessarily brief and general discussion discloses the difficulty and subtlety of the legal issues involved in determining whether a particular form of protest is or is not protected by the Bill of Rights. The reason for the difficulty is that, unavoidably, the Constitution seeks to accommodate two conflicting values, each of which is fundamental: the need for freedom to speak freely, to protest effectively, to organize, and to demonstrate; and the necessity of maintaining order so that other people's rights, and the peace and security of the state, will not be impaired.

The types of protests and the situations in which they occur are of infinite variety, and it is impossible to formulate a set of rules which will strike the proper balance between the competing principles. The precise facts in each situation will determine whether the particular protest or activity is within the shelter of the First Amendment or whether the protesters have overstepped the broad limits in which constitutional protection is guaranteed. It is, accordingly, hazardous to set out general principles. But here are a few principles that in my opinion indicate the contours of the law in this subtle and complex field where the basic right of freedom conflicts with the needs of an ordered society:

1. Our Constitution protects the right of protest and dissent within broad limits. It generously protects the right to organize people for protest and dissent. It broadly protects the right to assemble, to picket, to stage "freedom walks" or mass demonstrations, if these activities are peaceable and if the protesters comply with reasonable regulations designed to protect the general public without substantially interfering with effective protest.

2. If any of the rights to dissent is exercised with the intent to cause unlawful action (a riot, or assault upon others) or to cause injury to the property of others (such as a stampede for exits or breaking doors or windows), and if such unlawful action or injury occurs, the dissenter will not be protected. He may be arrested, and if properly charged and convicted of law violation, he will not be rescued by the First Amendment.

3. If the right to protest, to dissent, or to assemble peaceably is exercised so as to violate valid laws reasonably designed and administered to avoid interference with others, the Constitution's guarantees will not shield the protester. For example, he may be convicted for engaging in marching or picketing which blocks traffic or for sitting-in in an official's office or in a public or private place and thereby preventing its ordinary and intended use by the occupant or others. It is difficult to generalize about cases of this sort, because they turn on subtleties of fact: for example, Did the public authorities confine themselves to requiring only that minimum restriction necessary to permit the public to go about its business? Were there facilities available for the protest which were reasonably adequate to serve the lawful purposes of the protesters, and which could have been used without depriving others of the use of the public areas?

Despite the limits which the requirements of an ordered society impose, the protected weapons of protest, dissent, criticism, and peaceable assembly are enormously powerful. Largely as a result of the use of these instruments by Negroes, the present social revolution was launched: by freedom marches; organized boycotts; picketing and mass demonstrations; protest and propaganda. And by the use of the powerful instruments of dissent by people opposed to the war in Vietnam—by dissent expressed in the press, from the pulpit, on public platforms, and in the colleges and universities—issues of vast consequence have been presented with respect to the war in Vietnam, and, without doubt, national decisions and the course of that war have been affected.

The events of the past few years in this nation dramatically illustrate the power of the ordinary citizen, armed with the great rights to speak, to organize, to demonstrate. It would be difficult to find many situations in history where so much has been accomplished by those who, in cold realism, were divorced from the conventional instruments of power. Negroes and the youth-generation held no office. They did not control political machines. They did not own vast newspapers or magazines or radio or television stations. But they have caused great events to occur. They have triggered a social revolution which has projected this nation, and perhaps the world, to a new plateau in the human adventure. They have forced open the frontier of a new land—a land in which it is possible that the rights and opportunities of our society may be available to all, not just to some, in which the objectives of our Constitution may be fully realized for all; and in which the passion and determination of youth may be brought to the aid of our pursuit of the marvelous ideals that our heritage prescribes.

How wonderful it is that freedom's instruments—the rights to speak, to publish, to protest, to assemble peaceably, and to participate in the electoral process—have so demonstrated their power and vitality! These are our alternatives to violence; and so long as they are used forcefully but prudently, we shall continue as a vital, free society.

BUREAUCRACY

Perhaps the least understood portion of American government is the bureaucracy. To the average American the term "bureaucrat" conjures up an image of a small balding man who occupies a desk in a vast government building, and spends the day endlessly pushing a pencil or shuffling papers in a meaningless charade of self-importance.

While this stereotype may be valid occasionally, one must not lose sight of the fact that modern government is government by bureaucracy. Today the federal government alone employs about six million civilian and military personnel. Modern America therefore has developed a political system in which the bureaucracy has become an unofficial, but very real, fourth branch of government. Wielding the power to diminish, augment, delay, or even disregard the laws and/or orders given by the other parts of the federal government, the bureaucracy clearly has become a major force in the decision-making process.

While bureaucracy is officially neutral, in reality it is a highly political tool that cooperates or conflicts with interest groups, the Congress, and the President. To the dismay of many a chief executive or congressman the bureaucracy can often defy their wishes, as well as the interests of the general public.

The second selection confirms this last fact. Written by associates of Ralph Nader, it describes how the Federal Trade Commission has become a power responsible to almost no one. The first reading, by Herbert Simon, Donald Smithburg, and Victor Thompson, describes why modern society requires the development of bureaucracy.

WHAT IS PUBLIC ADMINISTRATION?

HERBERT A. SIMON / DONALD W. SMITHBURG / VICTOR A. THOMPSON

The Growth of Administration

When the fifty-five men met in Philadelphia to write the Constitution, the United States consisted of about four million people living on the eastern seaboard, most of them east of the Allegheny Mountains. The great proportion of the population were farmers and most of them were relatively self-subsistent. They made their own shoes and clothes, grew their own food, built their own houses, distilled their own whiskey. The need for government was slight, and what cooperative activity was necessary could be accomplished with a minimum of organization. To build a road, the neighbors turned out and, with only rudimentary organization, managed to grade the surface and erect needed bridges. A county poorhouse provided for the few aged persons who had no families to take care of them. To control transgressors, an amateur constable aided by volunteers raised the "hue and cry" and captured the culprit or chased him from the community.

Modern foibles like running water, paved roads, labor unions, large corporations, sewage systems, telephones, electric

---

From *Public Administration*, by Herbert A. Simon, Donald W. Smithburg, and Victor A. Thompson. Copyright 1950 by Herbert A. Simon, Donald W. Smithburg, and Victor A. Thompson. Reprinted by permission of Alfred A. Knopf, Inc., pp. 12–15.

lights, airplanes, automobiles, movie theatres, and atom bombs, all of which require some public supervision of their use, were unheard of. In that earlier kind of simple social structure government was limited in cost, specialization, and number of employees.

The growth of population, the very growth in size of the United States, and, particularly, advances in technology have changed the picture. Many things that could have been handled in Revolutionary times without public authority must now be handled by governments. Many problems that could then be solved by the spontaneous cooperation of neighbors now require the highly organized cooperation of professional specialists.

REASONS FOR THE GROWTH

Critics of government often try to explain the extent of modern government as a conspiracy between un-American individuals and politicians of the opposing political party. Special interest groups continually warn that more governmental interference will lead to socialism or worse. Such warnings are often coupled with an idyllic portrait of life in earlier and more sensible periods in our history when the activities of governments were held to a minimum. While citing the ills of modern civilization, the orators fail to mention the difficulties attendant on primitive life. The expense of maintaining a public health service is bemoaned, the agonies of yellow fever and diphtheria forgotten. The regulation of the telephone is berated, the advantages of phone service at reasonable rates ignored. The gasoline tax is taken as an abhorrent example of the burden of government, the advantages of paved highways taken for granted.

. . .

Sociologists have compared the growth of governmental activities to the rate of industrial invention and traced the demands for governmental action to the impact of various technological advances.[1] An obvious example of this process is the invention of the automobile. The automobile has required a great many governmental innovations. We now have a Federal Roads Administration; in every state there are highway commissions; at the local level there are both county and city road and street departments. A system of Federal grants-in-aid to states and state grants to localities for road administration has appeared—with the consequent employment of new administrative personnel. New techniques of regulating traffic have been devised with an army of policemen to enforce them. Licenses have had to be issued—both for the vehicles and the drivers. Fast transport has increased the scope of interstate commerce and the problems of handling it. New problems of balancing the interests of the automobile and the railroad have appeared and have required increases and adjustments in governmental activities. The general problem of law enforcement is changing, with increasing emphasis on state and federal law enforcement officers because of the ability of criminals to cover long distances in a short time. Roadhouses and autocamps have sprung up, throwing increased demands on enforcement officials. The automobiles are costly, and the common practice of financing them by borrowing has necessitated new regulations covering installment selling. Almost no phase of American life has escaped the impact of this technological innovation, and in a great many phases the impact has led to an increase in governmental personnel.

In addition to technological change as such, the tremendous diversity and specialization of modern life has also led to increased governmental activity. People are no longer self-subsistent. A period of depression or a period of inflation dramatizes the degree to which the man in Portland, Maine,

---

[1] Cf., William F. Ogburn, *Social Change* (New York: The Viking Press, 1922); National Resources Planning Board, *Technological Trends and National Policy* (Washington: Government Printing Office, 1937).

and the man in Portland, Oregon, are dependent on each other for their collective well-being. Increasingly, the government is the agency that must cope with this problem of interdependence. Nor do voluntary aid societies organized by a single community, no matter how well meaning, aid materially in solving problems that are nation-wide. The experiences of local communities in their unsuccessful efforts to meet the depression of the 1930's and the inflation and housing shortage of the 1940's illustrate the futility of this approach to solving community problems. An economy organized on a nation-wide basis requires nation-wide governmental activity.

THE NADER REPORT ON THE FEDERAL TRADE COMMISSION

EDWARD F. COX / ROBERT FELLMETH / JOHN SCHULZ

Before this student task force report on the Federal Trade Commission was issued in January, 1969, Commissioner Philip Elman of the FTC used to complain that one of his agency's biggest problems was that no one was interested in it. This lack of interest developed over the decades from the Commission's wooden, somnolent concept of its statutory mission. On paper, the FTC was the principal consumer-protection agency of the Federal government. As such, the Commission could have been an exciting and creative fomenter of consumer democracy. In reality, the "little old lady on Pennsylvania Avenue" was a self-parody of bureaucracy, fat with cronyism, torpid through an inbreeding unusual even for Washington, manipulated by the agents of commercial predators, impervious to governmental and citizen monitoring.

Throughout its history the Commission has excelled in avoiding monitoring—or, as it is often called, "oversight." A Hoover Commission report, a law review study, a secret Civil Service Commission report—all failed to have any significant impact in the post-1950 period. With political antennae of considerable sensitivity, successive FTC chairmen have placated the Congress by servicing requests of its key

---

"The Nader Report" on the Federal Trade Commission, by Edward F. Cox, Robert C. Fellmeth, and John E. Schulz. Copyright © 1969 by Edward F. Cox, Robert C. Fellmeth, and John E. Schulz. Reprinted by permission of the Richard W. Baron Publishing Co., Inc., pp. vii–xiv, 3–9.

committee chairmen, providing them with exclusive information for public release and attention, and cajoling the better of them through a variety of delaying techniques admirable only for their ingenuity.

These political skills reached their most intense application under the chairmanship of Paul Rand Dixon, whose eight-year tenure was scheduled to end in September, 1969. Having spent his career at the FTC, beginning in the 1930's, with an interval in the late 1950's as general counsel to the Senate Antitrust Subcommittee, Chairman Dixon has comforted and charged key senators and congressmen even to the extent of opening in 1968 an FTC office in Oak Ridge, Tennessee, headed by a friend of Representative Joe Evins, who is chairman of the House Appropriations Subcommittee, which votes funds for the Commission. He faithfully dunned agency officials for contributions to the Democratic party, listened attentively to signals or calls from the White House, and assiduously cultivated powerful trade interests by disseminating the myths that most large businesses are honest and law-abiding, that the problem is the few unscrupulous hucksters who give industry and commerce a bad image. In the meantime, he held a tight rein on other FTC Commissioners and the agency—tighter than any other chairman of a Federal regulatory agency. Not only were powers highly centralized in the chairmanship, but Chairman Dixon also refined the art of usurpation of residual powers and authorities. For example, he unilaterally appointed all the top officials of the Commission—some sixty in all—without consultation or sharing his decision with the other four Commissioners. These Commissioners were allowed to participate in naming only the top seven Commission officials—after Chairman Dixon had nominated them.

As the tide of consumer dissatisfaction rose in the 1960's, the FTC droned on, seemingly oblivious to the billions of dollars siphoned from poor and middle-class consumer alike by deceptive practices hiding shoddy and harmful products and fraudulent services. The Commission's vast information-procurement powers were little used. Hearings were rarely conducted, and never were the transcripts printed. Empirical studies of grass-roots business practices, especially in the urban slums, were nonexistent until 1968. Moreover, the Commission's enforcement policies were ridiculous. It did not have and did not actively seek from Congress powers of temporary injunction or criminal penalty. It almost ignored the enforcement tools that it did have. The strongest of these is the cease and desist order, which merely chastises a culprit company after it has pocketed millions with impunity. And before the Commission invokes even this mild sanction, it is willing to accept profuse assurances of voluntary compliance. This process creates delay and encourages the offender's attorneys to create further delays. Cases of unadulterated thievery have stretched on and on before being resolved, while the offender reaped profits never to be returned and devised new schemes not covered by the cease and desist orders.

Recently, the J. B. Williams Company has been under a cease and desist order for deceptive advertising of Geritol. Twice the FTC has warned the company that it was violating the order. For some reason, the Commission's lawyers were reluctant to forward the case to the Justice Department for prosecution. That reason was largely the powerful Washington law firm of Covington & Burling, in which Thomas Austern is a senior partner. Austern's associates would provide the Commission with arguments and with suggested language, and would plead for further consideration of their client's case. Covington & Burling and its client have little to lose by these delays (even after being cited for violations of the order) and much to gain—continuing sales to people misled into believing that Geritol can make them healthier.

Chairman Dixon's agency has avoided many enforcement problems by avoiding the process of detection. Massive frauds, for example, in home improvements, magazine sales, credit, and sales-promotion games go unnoticed. Only under public criticism and the occasional prodding of Senator Warren Magnuson's Senate Commerce Committee has the FTC acted against some of these. But the Commission is so constituted—because of its high-level cronyism and inadequate personnel and recruitment policies—that these efforts could not get past the symbolic, public-relations stage.

The degree to which documented deceptions are permitted to continue without Commission action is most serious. For years, the FTC has done nothing with its knowledge of the widespread sale of *used* Volkswagens *as new* by nonfranchised dealers. For almost two years it did nothing about Firestone's advertising that its wide-oval tires could stop "25% quicker," despite Commission rules about just such ads. In June, 1969, the FTC issued a press release stating that after a thirty-day period, it would challenge deceptive tire advertisements. But for years it has had the authority and obligation to move against such deceptions. Why was it necessary to issue a release to tell the industry that it would shortly start enforcing the law? Because the Commission was systematically not enforcing the law—a practice that has become its trademark. The FTC has routinely allowed grossly deceptive advertising campaigns to run their course unmolested; and has then been able to declare the matter moot when questioned about inaction.

In the rare instances when the Commission does try to act forcefully against strong economic-political interests—such as with its cigarette-advertising proposals in 1964–65—it finds itself without a consumer constituency and is promptly overwhelmed by the industry concerned. Thus, a Federal agency that should have a strong grass-roots constituency is deprived of this democratic support in large part as a result of its past ineptness and lassitude.

This was the FTC that greeted the students when they began work in the summer of 1968. The surface clues were telling enough—leisurely morning and afternoon coffee breaks, during which elevators to the cafeteria are so jammed that the Commissioners have to use the stairs to get around the building; long lunch periods to permit time for shopping; extended reading of the afternoon newspapers prior to early departure for home as a routine for more than a few FTC lawyers. A 1,300-man agency, including some 500 lawyers, with an annual budget in the neighborhood of $17 million should have little fat and water in its operations, especially considering the challenges this particular agency should meet.

The word that a group of law students was studying the Commission's consumer-protection performance spread rapidly throughout the hierarchy. The Commission employees who were interviewed were almost always polite, but not very informative. Nonetheless, little by little the students began to piece together patterns of behavior that added up to colossal default, demoralizing of younger staff members, and rampant sinecurism for those who remained. By what was lacking, the students came to understand that a reformed Commission could achieve constructive objectives, and from this realization came an optimism that outlasted their dismay. By their persistent questioning and interaction, they formed an indelible understanding of the kind of professional citizenship that would be required for a steadfast, public-interest Commission. In short, unless there can be external professional advocates for consumer interests, even the most fundamental changes in the personnel and procedures of the Commission cannot produce the needed results. A countervailing force in the private sector against the special interests and lobbyists is a vital condition if a regulatory agency is to perform its task well.

By the end of the summer, Chairman Dixon had shown that he did not appreciate the continued presence of the students. Although they took up an infinitesimal portion of the staff's time (and stimulated the staff's thinking), he employed this pretext to direct his subordinates to grant no more interviews and to refer all requests to the office of the Chairman. He added that any further requests for information would have to be rendered in writing to that office, thus severely restricting and delaying access to the agency. Fortunately, an exchange of letters I had with the Chairman led him to reconsider his position. But his hostility was evident when the students returned to Washington in November, 1968, to testify before the Commission during hearings on improving its consumer-protection activities. Two months later, when this report was issued, he reacted with more heat than light in a public statement denouncing the students' report and the students themselves, and avoiding the main issues they raised.

It was Chairman Dixon's behavior that taught the students about the importance of individual characteristics in bureaucratic environments. They had learned about structure, procedures, pressure groups, and other depersonalized dynamics in their university and law-school courses. But the social and legal studies in the universities do not grapple with the personal dynamics of bureaucratic-system leaders. This is not the case with Washington's lobbyist-lawyers and others who distinguish between form and substance. When they wish to detain or obtain Commission action, they bring their knowledge of the commissioners' preferences, concerns, weaknesses, and alliances into highly strategic and effective play. They take the same approach to officials down the agency hierarchy. Aware as they are of their procedural and legal tools, these lawyers value more the personal and political leverage that operates unrecorded and subvisibly within and without the agency's infrastructure. Procedural and other legal tools are tactics of last resort, to be deployed only after the conflict descends to the formal, relatively open, administrative process. It is then that cumbersome procedures can be used to delay and produce the attrition that results in more advantageous concessions by agency officials. As one corporate lawyer once told me, "The last thing I want for my client is administrative due process." For irregularities in formal procedure offer technical opportunities for such corporate counsels to appeal to the courts to overrule the agency's decision—a prospect that further discourages an agency with limited resources.

The release of the students' report coincided with the change of Presidential administrations. With a different political party in the White House, political factors would undoubtedly result in the replacement of Paul Rand Dixon as Chairman. The only apparent response to the students' report and the resultant commentary by the Nixon Administration was the appointment of a committee comprising 16 lawyers and economists, under the auspices of the American Bar Association, to investigate and recommend improvements for the FTC. This report was scheduled for completion by the end of the year.

In the meantime, the FTC did step up some of its initiatory activities in consumer protection that the students covered in this report. (The report does not deal with the antitrust responsibilities of the Commission.) A TV advertising inquiry was set under way; a hearing on the advertising of automotive prices was scheduled for September, 1969, on highly controversial abuses; and several Commissioners were urging the Chairman, with some success, to be less secretive in the agency's information policies. Congress also took an interest in the FTC. Senator Abraham A. Ribicoff held hearings in March, 1969, at which the students presented extensive testimony. Senator Edward M. Kennedy began preparing an inquiry as chairman of the Senate Subcommittee on Administrative Practice and Procedure. Reports from FTC Commissioners highly critical of their own agency were forwarded to that Subcommittee.

It may be that the students have set up a model for young citizen inquiry into the operations of government agencies and the pressure-group hothouses in which they exist. The students seemed to learn a great deal about the regulatory process that could not be learned at law school. Returning to the campus, they found their perceptions deeper, their skills for analysis refined, and their stimulation of fellow students and faculty members encouraging. From their conversations, it appeared that their view of the legal profession's horizons were broadened, and they could see the potential of developing career roles for full-time public-interest lawyers.

During the summer of 1969, more law students would be on their way to Washington to study more agencies—this time with the participation of medical and engineering students. In short time, this scrutiny should extend to state and local governments and other significant institutions. I believe that we may be seeing a social innovation that will produce just and lasting benefits for the country as these young people generate new values and create new roles for their professions.

RALPH NADER

June 4, 1969
Washington, D.C.

At the start of June, 1968, seven volunteers who were to be dubbed "Nader's Raiders" by the Washington press corps straggled into the capital from several campuses. Each in his own way had become acquainted with Ralph Nader and his work on behalf of the consumer. One had participated in a seminar Nader had conducted at Princeton University. Some had heard him speak at their law schools and approached him afterward or wrote to explain their desire to work with him. Others had never met him personally, but believed that the usual run of summer jobs for law students (like interning for one of the "top ten" firms in New York) would be less relevant, even though more lucrative, than whatever employment Mr. Nader might be able to provide in Washington.

As students at Harvard, Yale, and Princeton, we had nothing of the reformer in our backgrounds. One of our number was the great-grandson of President William Howard Taft.

Another had taught for five years at the exclusive Groton School.

None of us had had extensive exposure to the realities of the Washington bureaucracy.

It was a long step for us in many ways, not least in the physical sense, going from the rich and varied, sometimes comical, architecture of our campuses to the stultifying "civic" architecture of Washington. If there is anything in the theory that the external esthetics of a building reflects its internal essence, then the architect of the Federal Trade Commission building had a genius for sensing the mediocre. The structure sits upon a triangular block at the junction of Pennsylvania and Constitution Avenues, inelegantly set down between the National Archives and the National Gallery of Art. The choice offices occupied by the Commissioners in the rounded "prow" of the building offer a view of Capitol Hill, which serves as a continual reminder to the FTC of the limits to its role as an "independent regulatory commission." The building's granite base, limestone superstructure, and tile roof echo an unimaginative pattern of continuous horizontal lines.

Inside, the building is similarly undistinguished. On each floor long corridors walled in green marble form an uninterrupted triangle. The offices on one side of the corridor look out onto the avenues; the offices on the other side enjoy an excellent view of a triangular concrete courtyard. There is virtue only in the simple-mindedness of the plan—compared with the intricate corridors of the Pentagon or the Rayburn House Office Building, where one can wander lost and confused for hours.

We knew something of what we would find inside the FTC building. It provides office space for the five Commissioners and some 319 attorneys, with secretarial and clerical help. The Commission has 155 other attorneys at field offices in Atlanta, Boston, Chicago, Cleveland, Kansas City, Los Angeles, New Orleans, New York, San Francisco, Seattle, and Falls

Church, Virginia, and in the suboffices at Houston and Oak Ridge, Tennessee. The work of these lawyers falls into one of six major bureaus—Field Operations, Restraint of Trade, Economics, Deceptive Practices, Industry Guidance, and Textiles and Furs. (We were to deal mainly with the last three because their work most directly affects the consumer.) Except for the bureau chiefs, the FTC staff hierarchy—including the Chairman, his assistant, one of the Commissioners, the Executive Director, the General Counsel, the Program Review Officer, the Comptroller, and the Director of the Office of Administration—occupies the top or fifth floor of offices.

This bureaucracy traces its history back more than half a century. It was in 1914—the year also of the Clayton Antitrust Act—that the FTC was created to regulate "unfair methods of competition." This was a time when rugged individualism still held a high place in American political thought. The credo *caveat emptor*—let the buyer beware—was sacred in the Congress and the courts.

But the Depression revised—even radicalized—America's social thinking. At the highest levels there was dismay over the widespread and dangerous deceptions suffered by consumers. In 1938—the year also when the present FTC building was finished—the Wheeler-Lea Act amended the original statute, giving it some "teeth." It specified that "deceptive acts and practices" were illegal, and it gave the Commission new enforcement powers to deal with violations. Since then, a whole battery of specialized laws—the Flammable Fabrics Act of 1953, the Fair Packaging and Labeling Act of 1966, and others—have made clear the intention of the Congress: It is the FTC's role to bear a primary responsibility for protecting the consumer.

Now, thirty years later, according to all available information, the Commission was not fulfilling that role. Our first task upon arriving in Washington was to examine that information in the light of real experience. We brought with us a college-bred naïveté, which led us to assume that the

FTC—public-spirited an agency as it was supposed to be—would open itself to a rigorous scrutiny.

Instead, we ran into a bulwark of bureaucratic defenses and evasions. Even simple documents became elusive. One of the first things we needed was a personnel chart, showing the number of FTC employes and their job classifications. At first the Director of Personnel denied that any organization chart existed. When we learned that the agency's budget-control records contained the necessary information, he protested that these were not public documents, because they contained the salaries of all personnel. Our arguments that the salary information could be easily expunged were ignored. Only when we submitted a written request—as a preliminary action to a court suit under the Freedom of Information Act—were the records released. We were careful to specify "without salaries" in our request. Yet the Commission did not even bother to delete that "sensitive" data.

We expected that we could learn much from interviews, hoping for an honest give-and-take. Our hopes for such conversations with FTC upper-staff members were disappointed at the outset. Attempts at frank dialogues degenerated into simultaneous monologues—the interviewers pressing for facts, the interviewees responding with generalizations. In his first interview, one of our project members asked an assistant bureau chief for the approximate number of attorneys in his bureau. The official replied that the request would not be considered unless placed in writing. He would consent to speak only on the legal history of his bureau and not about its present operations. Moreover, he refused to speak at all until another attorney had arrived to witness what turned out to be an inconsequential conversation.

We soon found in all our interviews this same insistence on having two attorneys from the Commission present at all times. Although it is tempting to explain this as a need for group reinforcement of individual security, a more basic reason existed. Apparently, any staff attorney that we interviewed alone became suspect in the eyes of his colleagues and superiors.

A veteran FTC reporter explained to us that a tacit yet institutionalized fear—radiating outward from the Chairman's office—pervaded the entire staff. Younger attorneys no longer with the Commission corroborated this with stories of harassment by superiors for real or imagined transgressions of the FTC's oath of secrecy. One such unfortunate had been seen talking to one of us in the halls of the FTC. His division chief warned him to be careful because "the FTC was back on its heels under criticism." As a result he canceled a prospective interview—and not long thereafter found employment outside the agency.

Despite such pressures, some of the younger attorneys were willing to give frank interviews, but only under controlled circumstances and usually outside the Commission. Invariably, they prefaced even the mildest critical statements with warnings of future denials if the source were identified. Still, this is how we got some highly valuable material.

As we began to learn how to obtain useful information, Chairman Paul Rand Dixon imposed an illegal and unprecedented "lockout," forbidding all staff members to communicate with us. In Mr. Dixon's own words (in a letter to Ralph Nader, dated September 13, 1968):

> *On August 15, I expressed to Mr. Schulz and Mr. Cox my feeling that by then they had had ample opportunity to complete their interviews with our personnel, and informed them that after August 23 they would no longer have unlimited access to staff members. . . . At about the same time I had our staff orally instructed to this same effect . . . I see no reason for rescission of the action I have taken and, considering all the circumstances, I do not believe it will operate to impede the completion of any legitimate study of the Commission or its activities.*

Since any member of the public may talk to government officials as long as the official himself agrees, Chairman Dixon had only the power of institutionalized fear—now supported by a verbal threat—to enforce his edict.

A few of the younger attorneys still consented to be interviewed, but most, including all the bureau chiefs and the acting General Counsel declined to talk. Their secretaries invariably came back with the reply that an interview with any member of the staff had to be "cleared first with Chairman Dixon."

Fear is an effective organizational glue when all else fails. We would have liked to find that, instead of fear, the Federal Trade Commission had a strong set of motivational goals to claim the allegiance of its staff. Clearly, protection of the consumer and vigorous enforcement of antitrust laws are goals to inspire the young lawyers of a socially conscious generation. Although these are the goals outlined for the agency by law, our probings revealed that the FTC had lapsed into a lethargy that would have been uncovered long ago if it were not for the Byzantine defenses that disguise its everyday activities.

Our collective naïveté proved to be our strength: the more we were hampered in finding what we wanted to know, the more we persisted. When we were called to testify in the spring of 1969 before the Senate Subcommittee on Executive Reorganization, Senator Abraham A. Ribicoff of Connecticut remarked:

> *Bureaucracy being what it is, I am fascinated by your ability to get in so deep, and get so much information. I am sure that you gentlemen are the envy of the large number of reporters here.*

THE URBAN ENVIRONMENT

Along with industrialization and technological development there have been great shifts of population from the rural sectors to the urban centers. As is the case with most of the by-products of what we label as "progress," both positive and negative consequences arise. On the one hand, the contemporary metropolis affords cultural opportunities never before conceived of, as well as an atmosphere conducive to social mobility. At the same time, however, this anonymity can lead to the atomization of the individual and the alienation of groups.

New problems must be faced when dealing with the urban environment that encompass the entire panorama of social, economic, and political life. By the same token the concept of mass society raises thorny questions that contemporary democratic theorists cannot avoid. The complexity and interdependence of city life spawn new kinds of bureaucratic and technocratic elites and new types of frustrations for groups, both organized and not, and individual citizens. If America, in this and the ensuing decades, hopes to create a viable system, it must come to grips immediately with the innumerable pressing problems and dilemmas, both tangible and abstract, of its urban environments. Virtually every question in government is involved in one way or another with the city: crime, pollution, transportation, finance, education, health, policy-making, race relations, housing, family structure, and so on.

Wallace S. Sayre and Herbert Kaufman's classic study of New York City provides an excellent review of city government, while Robert C. Weaver, former Secretary of Housing and Urban Development, raises the types of questions that must be faced and faced now.

THE STAKES
AND PRIZES OF
THE CITY'S POLITICS

WALLACE S. SAYRE / HERBERT KAUFMAN

GOVERNMENT AND THE CITY

Government is the city's central agency of change and conservation. It is the city's prime rule-maker, the omnipresent supervisor. Its officials are always important actors in the negotiations, the bargaining, and the numerous settlements which comprise the decisions by which the city lives. Equally important, the government is often the innovator and the provider of indispensable facilities and services for the city and its people.

Many of its piers that serve world shipping, for example, were built by the city. During the nineteenth century a large number were sold to private interests—shipping companies and railroads—but this led to difficulties in accommodating all the vessels seeking to enter the port, and the city subsequently bought back as many piers as it could, to manage them on a coordinated basis. Because the railroads were reluctant to relinquish the advantages of their own facilities, the Port of New York Authority was eventually created by New York State and New Jersey in 1921 to help these companies develop joint operations so as to reduce the number of piers they would need and thus to free the piers for ships. The Port Authority's program was not successful in this re-

---

Excerpted from *Governing New York City*, by Wallace S. Sayre and Herbert Kaufman, © 1960 by Russell Sage Foundation, Publishers, New York, pp. 32-36, 39-40.

gard, but it later did acquire a grain terminal in Brooklyn and a section of the Brooklyn waterfront and renovated these, as well as instituting a large-scale port-promotion program, while the city began to improve its own waterfront properties under the pressure of competition from other Atlantic seaports. Water-borne commerce in the port owes a great deal to governmental action.

The same is true of air-borne commerce. Floyd Bennett Field was constructed by the city in 1931, its first response to air traffic at a time when the airplane was still an experimental and uncertain vehicle. In 1939 air-minded Mayor La Guardia was responsible for the completion of the airport later to bear his name, and in 1941 he initiated work on the mammoth air terminal in the Idlewild district of Queens. (Ultimately, Floyd Bennett Field was purchased by the Navy, and the other two air fields were leased to the Port of New York Authority for development and operation.) It was inevitable that the new medium of transportation should converge on New York, but New York's leadership in air commerce could not have asserted itself had there not been imaginative and resourceful government officials to encourage it and to take the necessary action.

Governmental accomplishments in the realm of ground transportation in New York City are even more dramatic. There are 6,000 miles of streets, virtually all publicly built, illuminated, and maintained. Thousands of traffic lights and other traffic engineering devices keep the colossal stream of traffic moving. Ten major vehicular bridges connect Manhattan and The Bronx; one joins Manhattan, The Bronx, and Queens; another runs from The Bronx to Queens directly; four bridges and two vehicular tunnels span the waters between Manhattan and Long Island (Brooklyn and Queens); there are three Hudson River crossings between Manhattan and New Jersey, and three between Staten Island and New Jersey; and there are many lesser bridges and tunnels scattered elsewhere through the city. The original subways were built by the city, although they were initially leased to private companies for operation; today, all the subways—241 route miles of them—as well as a large number of bus lines are city owned and operated. The Port of New York Authority built and runs a truck terminal and a union bus terminal in Manhattan. A network of limited-access parkways and highways, free of grade crossings and traffic lights, speeds express motor traffic into, out of, and through New York. Without all these, the city's commerce would have strangled itself, and population and commerce could not have grown to their present dimensions.

It takes more than commerce and transportation to sustain the city's population and a large portion of these other things is provided by public agencies. It takes two billion gallons of pure water a day, removal of four million tons of refuse, thousands of miles of sewers and huge sewage disposal plants, regulation and inspection of food and food handlers and processors, disease control to prevent epidemics, air pollution control to prevent the poisoning of the atmosphere, and a fire-fighting organization capable of handling every kind of blaze from small home fires to immense conflagrations in tenements, skyscrapers, industrial structures, and the waterfront. The basic physical and biological requirements of urban life are either provided or guaranteed by government.

So are some of the fundamental social conditions. People would flee the city if they could not educate their children here, and at a cost within reason. The city provides free education from kindergarten through college. For recreation the city furnishes one of the most extensive municipal park systems in the world, hundreds of playgrounds and ball fields and golf courses and even archery ranges, and eight beaches with a total of 17 miles of saltwater surf. The city subsidizes or supports (at least in part) the principal museums, three zoos, botanical gardens, and the aquarium, and maintains an extensive free public library system. It strives to set a floor under living standards for everyone by providing health,

TABLE 1. LARGEST CITIES OF THE WORLD, 1957 [a]

City[b]	Population
New York	7,795,471
Tokyo	7,161,513
Shanghai	6,204,417
Moscow	4,847,000
Buenos Aires	3,673,575
Chicago	3,620,962
London	3,273,000
Bombay	3,211,000
Sao Paulo	3,149,504

[a] *The New York Times*, using a different definition of the term "city" and its own estimates of current populations, reports Tokyo and London as larger than New York. The *Times* list of the seven largest cities in the world includes, in order of size, Tokyo, London, New York, Shanghai, Moscow, Mexico City, and Peiping. See the issue of September 20, 1959, section 4. The figures in the table above are the official UN statistics.

[b] City proper only.

SOURCE: *United Nations Demographic Yearbook, 1957*. Statistical Office of the United Nations in collaboration with the Department of Economic and Social Affairs, pp. 152-160.

hospital, and welfare services for those in need. It protects its residential areas by land-use regulation (which also serves to guide the growth and development of the city). It regulates a great many types of business, either to assure satisfaction of at least minimum standards of quality or to prohibit the kind of destructive competition that might deprive the people of some needed goods and services altogether. Over 84,000 families live in public housing, and urban redevelopment, slum clearance, and enforcement of housing codes have been applied to the fight against urban blight. City agencies combat prejudice and discrimination against minority groups; wage a continuing struggle against juvenile delinquency; furnish protection against crime and disorder. All these things combined help make the city habitable, satisfying, and even reasonably comfortable. And they therefore help it hold together its prime source of greatness: its people.

TABLE 2. LARGEST REPORTED METROPOLITAN REGIONS OF THE WORLD, 1957 [a]

Metropolitan areas [b]	Population
New York	14,066,000
Tokyo	8,471,637
London	8,270,430
Paris	6,436,296
Chicago	4,920,816

[a] *The New York Times*, employing its own definitions of metropolitan areas, or adopting definitions of planning groups, reports Tokyo as the largest metropolitan area in the world with a population of 20 million, and London as third with a population of 10.4 million. See the issue of September 20, 1959, section 4. The figures in the table above are the official UN statistics.

[b] Core city and environs.

SOURCE: *United Nations Demographic Yearbook, 1957*. Statistical Office of the United Nations in collaboration with the Department of Economic and Social Affairs, pp. 152–160.

GOVERNMENT AND POLITICS IN THE CITY

Much depends on the decisions and actions of governmental organs and agencies in the city; some group or groups always have a stake in the outcome of a particular governmental action or decision. Because the city is diverse and constantly changing, rarely do all interests coincide; unanimous approval or disapproval or total indifference with respect to a decision almost never occurs. In the quest for the stakes imbedded in what governmental officials and employees decide and do, competition is the usual state of affairs. Government and politics thus have many attributes of a contest.

The interactions of all those engaged in government and politics have a fascination of their own. There is drama and tension in the conflicts and clashes, the alliances and coalitions, the negotiations and accommodations, the bargains, the surrenders, the victories and defeats comprehended in the outward manifestations of public policy. In the end, however, the most fascinating, and perhaps the most amazing, aspect of this complex of phenomena is that it works. The stakes involved are extraordinarily high; the incentives to acquire them are consequently unusually strong; the opportunities, the risks, and the contestants are numerous; the magnitude of the stresses and strains on the political system is correspondingly great. Yet the system does work. Rarely has the capacity of men of many backgrounds, many statuses, many outlooks, many interests, to live together in peace and mutual respect been put to a severer test. Rarely have men responded as successfully as have the people and the politicians of New York City in devising their political institutions and practices.

The Stakes and Prizes of the City's Politics

Nearly everyone in the city takes some part in the city's political and governmental system. Taking part in "politics"— that is, engaging in deliberate efforts to determine who gets public office (whether elective or appointive) and to influence what public officials and employees do—is an almost universal vocation among New Yorkers. Not all participate to the same extent or with the same intensity, and many of them are unaware that they are participating in politics at all, except as voters on Election Day. But in fact they are engaging in the city's political process in many other ways— as leaders or members of "civic" groups, neighborhood associations, professional associations, economic interest groups, ethnic and racial and religious associations, and not infrequently as individuals seeking directly to influence governmental action in specific instances.

The more continuous, extensive, and intensive participation in the city's governmental and political process is delegated, so to speak, by the citizens of the city to several main categories of actors in the political contest, who are rarely permitted to forget that their role is representative and temporary, subject to change and redefinition. The general electorate retains its rights as critic and customer. Thus the five main categories of leading participants in the city's politics—the party leaders, the city's public officials, the city bureaucracies, the nongovernmental groups and the communication media, and the officials and bureaucracies of the state and national governments, all of whom will be discussed more fully in later chapters—are constantly aware not only of their competitive relationships with each other, but also of their needs for a popular base of support. The principal actors are incessantly seeking to explain and justify their actions to a wider audience, as a way of maintaining their base and recruiting allies. Few citizens remain for long unsolicited or uninvited to participate.

The city presents a rich variety of goals, stakes, rewards, and prizes—all offered by and serving as strong incentives for participation in its political and governmental system. Agreement upon the true nature of the stakes and prizes the participants *seek* is difficult, bound up as the seeking is in the inscrutable and complex motivations of human beings and the strategic vocabularies in which goals are stated by the participants, but it is possible to identify the types of rewards they *get* through political action. Participation in the political and governmental process of the city yields ideological and other "intangible" rewards, public office or employment, economic rewards, and desired governmental services. Whatever their stated objectives and whatever their perceptions and motives, those who take part in the city's political contest receive their observable rewards—or the hope and promise thereof—in these media of exchange.

FUTURE DEVELOPMENT OF THE URBAN COMPLEX

ROBERT C. WEAVER

Just as problems of race harass many central cities and knock at the doors of the smaller communities that surround them, land and its utilization and development are basic concerns of the suburbs. The central cities, too, have land problems; but, as has been suggested above, these relate primarily to re-use rather than initial use. The entire urban complex is threatened by traffic congestion, and a balanced system of adequate highways and mass transit is an indispensable element for efficient development of major urbanized regions. At the same time more rational development of the suburban areas would minimize transportation needs and utility line extensions. And, too, the development of satellite communities affording employment opportunities, and educational—as well as recreational and commercial—facilities, would serve the same purpose.

> *The questions before us have been suggested above. They include:*
> *Will scatterization continue?*
> *Will we saddle a new generation of Americans with having to make lengthy journeys to and from work only to arrive at the end of the day in a culturally sterile community devoid of shops, theaters, libraries, and parks within easy access?*

"Future Development of the Urban Complex," copyright © 1964 by Robert C. Weaver from the book *The Urban Complex*, by Robert C. Weaver. Reprinted by permission of Doubleday and Company, Inc., pp. 278–282.

> *Will we go on developing new subdivisions at random—uncoordinated to any area planning—and dependent upon septic tanks and wells which are destined to be replaced, thereby occasioning unnecessary expense?*
>
> *Will we act to provide basic facilities, such as sewerage and water systems, of sufficient size and capacity to satisfy existing and anticipated needs and to facilitate optimum efficiency in operation?*

Before attempting to discuss the issues suggested by these questions, reference must be made again to the nature of our governmental structure. The locale where most of the problems of land planning and development are concentrated is generally outside the jurisdiction of city government. This locale is the area lying in the county, in a small township, or in an unincorporated village. Thus, in the case of many subdivisions, there will be a viable urban-orientated government only after most of the basic planning and development determinations have been made.

Because of these circumstances, two results seem self-apparent. First, unless the state government establishes programs and procedures for meeting these issues, the Federal Government will assume primary responsibility in this field or else it will remain neglected. Second, in the absence of adequate local controls and inducements, efforts to achieve better land uses must flow through indirect mechanisms, primarily federal inducements to the private developer.

Our concern must be to discourage, to the maximum extent possible, the mistakes of the past, such as the destruction of scenic attributes, while encouraging positive actions that will provide a better physical environment for the homes of tomorrow. Better utilization of sites will allow utilities to be provided more economically. In the process, larger and more meaningful open spaces could be provided. If clustering of houses, utilization of town houses, and multi-family units are incorporated in the large subdivisions of the future, it will be possible to provide sites at lower costs to home-buyers.

The new community concept, involving thousands of dwelling units and varying mixes of industrial and commercial facilities, has even greater potentialities. As this is written, some seventy-five such large-scale developments are in various stages of execution and planning in the Nation. Because of their size and scope, the new communities afford a setting for advanced site and architectural design at the same time that they facilitate maximum economies in basic facilities, such as water and sewerage systems. In addition they utilize land more remote from population concentrations, and consequently less expensive than that which is closer to urban centers.

These large new communities can and should provide site employment and diversified shopping, as well as comprehensive educational, recreational, and cultural facilities. In addition, they present an opportunity for planners to reappraise man's varied needs and devise new modes of satisfying them.

New communities have many unrealized potentialities. They could, and should, be, but, to date give little promise of being, the setting in which truly democratic communities are developed. This means that they should demonstrate how families and individuals of a wide variety of incomes and ethnic attributes can live together. In addition, they should be laboratories where we can develop performance standards for building codes, more realistic and efficient zoning, and experiments in utilization of new materials and construction methods. In the new environment which they create, it should be possible to experiment with new approaches to housing for low- and moderate-income households and develop exciting and novel arrangements for communication and transportation.

Most important, however, is the opportunity that new communities afford to demonstrate to the American people that a better life is possible. This involves all that has been suggested above as well as the creation of aesthetically attractive and pleasing areas of residence. It also implies increasing opportunities to work in the community where one lives, to find recreational and cultural outlets there, and to enjoy to the maximum degree the beauties of nature which reside in the countryside of this Nation.

In all of these matters, the new community enjoys a unique advantage. It is unencumbered by existing social or economic vested interests or by a physical pattern which restricts creative departures from the *status quo*. So far, however, there is only one of the seventy-five new communities in planning or execution which seems to be moving in this direction. Some others are attempting to realize better site planning and a full component of community services and facilities, but the vast majority appear destined to become country-club communities for upper-income families.

The future potential for the urban complex is great. Our tools for achieving this potential are imperfect and still in the process of development. But a nation which is affluent, which is willing to face up to social problems, and which is excited by its possibilities has a real future.

Urban renewal is demonstrating that for many elements in our population the central cities can be attractive. These central cities are becoming economically more healthy, aesthetically more appealing, and culturally more vital. There is no need to despair of them; nor are they threatened by the possibility of better subdivisions and of new communities in the outlying areas. Indeed, the new communities will strengthen the central cities if they face up to the social issues and become truly democratic institutions with a racial and class mix, if they develop new and better approaches to low-income housing, and if they establish novel and more satisfying modes of meeting man's many needs.[1]

---

[1] President Johnson's housing and community development proposals would accelerate and encourage this process by providing financial assistance to new communities while requiring that they house multi-income groups, conform to area plans, and accomplish effective utilization of land.

We have been shown that the residential environment in all parts of the urban complex can be improved. The task ahead is to raise our sights and create the excitement and the expectation which inspire new approaches and successful breakthroughs. The American consumer is exposed to constantly improved products, which affect his tastes. He rapidly demands more and more as he is conditioned to expect more. When, therefore, we are able to provide him with wider choices and new horizons of expectation, he will exert pressure for continuing experimentation and improvement.

In the years ahead, therefore, the housing industry, in all its branches, and government, at all its levels, should strive to whet the appetite of the American people for better housing and community development.

Today, as we stand at the threshold of a new population explosion, involving another major expansion of suburbia, there is a unique opportunity for action. It is vital that the American people be attuned to this possibility; and it is incumbent upon those who value our culture to press for results. Never before has there been such a fortuitous combination of economic resources, technical knowledge, and urban concentration. What we do with these resources will fashion the urban complex in our times and for years ahead.